MENTAL HEALTH
A Guide to the Law in Scotland

MENTAL HEALTH
A Guide to the Law in Scotland

John Blackie
Senior lecturer in law
in the University of Edinburgh

Hilary Patrick
Solicitor, England and Wales

with

Alistair Brownlie
Solicitor in the Supreme
Courts of Scotland

Alan Paterson
Professor of law
in the University of Strathclyde

Butterworths
Scottish Legal Education Trust

Edinburgh   1990

United Kingdom	Butterworth & Co (Publishers) Ltd, 88 Kingsway, LONDON WC2B 6AB and 4 Hill Street, EDINBURGH EH2 3JZ
Australia	Butterworths Pty Ltd, SYDNEY, MELBOURNE, BRISBANE, ADELAIDE, PERTH, CANBERRA and HOBART
Canada	Butterworths Canada Ltd, TORONTO and VANCOUVER
Ireland	Butterworth (Ireland) Ltd, DUBLIN
Malaysia	Malayan Law Journal Sdn Bhd, KUALA LUMPUR
New Zealand	Butterworths of New Zealand Ltd, WELLINGTON and AUCKLAND
Puerto Rico	Equity de Puerto Rico, Inc, HATO REY
Singapore	Malayan Law Journal Pte, Ltd, SINGAPORE
USA	Butterworth Legal Publishers, AUSTIN, Texas; BOSTON, Massachusetts; CLEARWATER, Florida (D & S Publishers); ORFORD, New Hampshire (Equity Publishing); ST PAUL, Minnesota; and SEATTLE, Washington

All rights reserved. No part of this publication may be reproduced in any material form (including photocopying or storing it in any medium by electronic means and whether or not transiently or incidentally to some other use of this publication) without the written permission of the copyright owner except in accordance with the provisions of the Copyright, Designs and Patents Act 1988 or under the terms of a licence issued by the Copyright Licensing Agency Ltd, 33–34 Alfred Place, London, England WC1E 7DP. Applications for the copyright owner's written permission to reproduce any part of this publication should be addressed to the publisher.

Warning: The doing of an unauthorised act in relation to a copyright work may result in both a civil claim for damages and criminal prosecution.

© Scottish Legal Education Trust 1990

A CIP Catalogue record for this book is available from the British Library.

ISBN 0 406 16777 X

Printed and bound by Thomson Litho Ltd, East Kilbride, Scotland

Preface

This book has been written to help all who have any involvement with people suffering from mental illness or mental handicap to understand how Scots law deals with the various issues raised. We have attempted to write it in language which not only lawyers but anyone, doctors, nurses, social workers and relatives and patients themselves, can understand.

However, the law itself is extremely complex and we have not oversimplified at the expense of accuracy. This is not necessarily, therefore, a book which newcomers to the subject should read from start to finish in one sitting; it might be best to dip into it from time to time to look up particular problems.

The major statute dealing with mental health law is the Mental Health (Scotland) Act 1984 and the book attempts to guide readers through its complexities in some detail, looking at the detailed rules governing the admission of patients to hospital and the possibility of helping patients in the community through guardianship.

Patients' rights in hospital are also given considerable coverage, as important sources of dispute, and we look at the role of the Mental Welfare Commission as a major source of assistance for patients and their families.

We deal in outline with what happens if a mentally disordered person comes before the criminal courts; the rules are extremely complicated and in most cases a person will need legal help and representation before the courts.

In many cases a patient or his or her relatives will need to obtain legal advice and we also advise on choosing a solicitor and on legal aid.

Because of space constrictions we have not been able to cover two important topics: education rights and ways of making financial provision to secure the future of mentally handicapped children. On both these topics we recommend Adrian Ward's excellent book, 'Scots Law and the Mentally Handicapped', published by the Scottish Society for the Mentally Handicapped.

To avoid interrupting the text, we have made extensive use of footnotes, which are at the end of each paragraph for ease of use. Those who wish to study the law in more detail should refer to the statutes and to the relevant case law which is set out in Appendix 3.

The law is, we hope, correctly stated as at December 1989.

This is, so far as we are aware, the first book on the subject in Scotland. There are English books on their Mental Health Acts, but there are significant differences between the two systems and English books should be read with caution.

Readers should note that terms in the text which appear in bold script are defined in detail in the glossary. (See page ix.) Bold script will be used on the first occasion a term appears in a chapter; thereafter, for ease of reading, ordinary script will be used.

We are very grateful for the many people who assisted in the preparation of this book. Isabel Anderson, who is now a partner in an Edinburgh legal practice, carried out and wrote up her extensive research work in the initial stages. This provided the essential starting off point, without which the book would never have come into being. Ruth Adler, Wilson Finnie and John Wright read the manuscript at various stages. We are grateful to them but are ourselves responsible for any errors that remain. Valuable assistance was also given by Peter Robson of the University of Strathclyde, Marion Foy, Chris Himsworth of the University of Edinburgh and Martha Brownlie, who gave extensive secretarial assistance.

We gratefully acknowledge financial support given by the Mental Health Foundation in the early stages of preparation.

Finally, we are especially grateful to Maclay Murray & Spens, Solicitors, whose sponsorship has enabled us to make the book available to many people who might not otherwise have been able to buy it. This has allowed us to comply with the objects of the Trust, to make the law available to the person in the street.

John Blackie
Hilary Patrick
Alistair Brownlie
Alan Paterson
Scottish Legal Education Trust

January 1990

Contents

Preface v
Glossary ix

Chapter 1 Mental health

1.1 Introduction 1
1.2 Mental disorder 1
1.3 Community care and hospitals 5

Chapter 2 Compulsory admission to hospital

2.1 Introduction 7
2.2 Emergency admissions 7
2.3 Short-term detention 9
2.4 Detention by nurses 12
2.5 Application to a sheriff for compulsory admission 13
2.6 Reviewing the patient's case 23
2.7 Discharge of the patient 26
2.8 Leaving the hospital 27
2.9 Place of safety orders 28
2.10 Elderly persons or people suffering from 'grave chronic disease' 30
2.11 Transfer of patients within the United Kingdom 31

Chapter 3 Care in the community

3.1 Guardianship 32
3.2 Compulsory medical treatment for patients living in the community 43
3.3 Marriage and divorce 45
3.4 Financial and property matters 46
3.5 Education, training and aftercare 58
3.6 Housing rights of mentally disordered people 61

Chapter 4 Care in hospital

4.1 Introduction 66
4.2 Restrictions on a patient's way of life 67
4.3 Control of patients' activities 72
4.4 Consent to treatment 76
4.5 Money and property 87
4.6 The right to play a part in public life—the right to vote 91

Chapter 5   The criminal courts and mentally disordered people

5.1   Mental disorder and the criminal courts   93
5.2   The State Hospital   104

Chapter 6   Protection of patients' interests and the Mental Welfare Commission for Scotland

6.1   Constitutional and general functions   106
6.2   The Commission's powers and duties   107
6.3   Complaints   110

Chapter 7   Consulting a solicitor

Appendices

Appendix 1   Mental Health (Scotland) Act 1984   117
Appendix 2   Mental Health (Specified Treatments, Guardianship Duties etc) (Scotland) Regulations 1984   193
Mental Health (Prescribed Forms) (Scotland) Regulations 1984   195
Authors' suggested forms of discharge   214
Appendix 3   Case notes   217
Appendix 4   Helpful addresses   223
Appendix 5   Further reading   226

Table of Statutes   231

Table of Orders, Rules and Regulations   237

Table of Cases   239

Index   241

Glossary

Where an entry in this glossary uses a word covered elsewhere in it, that word is printed in bold type.

Accountant of court — the official whose department oversees the work of a **curator bonis**.

advice and assistance — a scheme which enables solicitors to provide advice and assistance, oral or written, to a person whose income and savings fall within certain limits. (See chapter 7.)

aliment — payments made by a parent for the maintenance of a child.

children's hearing — a tribunal which deals with cases of children who are in need of care and protection.

Citizens Advice Bureaux — centres located in about sixty or so towns throughout Scotland which provide members of the public, free of charge, general information and advice.

Court of Session — the most important civil (that is, non-criminal) court in Scotland. It is located in Parliament Square, Edinburgh, and may hear new cases or petitions or appeals from decisions taken by lower civil courts.

curator — short term meaning the same as curator bonis.

curator ad litem — a person appointed by a court to look after the interests of someone in a court case where the person is not capable of looking after his or her own interests.

curator bonis — a person appointed to look after another person's affairs where that person is unable for mental health reasons to do this for him or herself. (See para 3.4.3.)

district council — the lowest tier of local government, responsible for cleansing, housing etc.

grounds for continued detention — the grounds on which a person who is detained in hospital may remain liable to detention following a review of his or her case. See para 2.6.2 for how they vary from the **statutory grounds of admission**.

guardianship — a means of providing care and protection for mentally disturbed people whilst allowing them to live within the community. (See chapter 3.)

guardianship order — a court order appointing a guardian.

health board — the body responsible for National Health Service hospitals in a given geographical area. There are fifteen different health boards in Scotland. (See under 'Health Services' in the telephone directory.)

hospital managers — the staff employed by a **health board** or the members of a committee appointed by a health board to run a hospital. In the case of the **State Hospital**, the managers are the State Hospital Management Committee, a body set up by the **Secretary of State**. In the case of a private hospital, the managers are the people running the hospital.

initial writ — the formal document used to start legal action in the **sheriff court**.

islands council — the tier of local authority in the Northern and Western Isles responsible for social care, including many aspects of the care of mentally ill or mentally handicaped people.

ix

legal aid — when the assistance of a solicitor and, if necessary, an advocate, in Scottish court proceedings is funded in whole or in part through the **Scottish Legal Aid Board**.

managers of the hospital — see **hospital managers**.

medical grounds — the medical conditions which must apply for a person to be admitted into **guardianship**. (See para 3.1.3.)

mental disorder — this term is defined in **the Act**. It means mental illness or mental handicap however caused or manifested. (See chapter 1.)

mental health officer — the social worker(s) appointed by the **regional or islands council** to be responsible for mental health matters for that local authority.

Mental Welfare Commission — a body of people appointed by the **Secretary of State for Scotland** to protect people with a **mental disorder** and to safeguard their interests. (See chapter 6).

nearest relative — this phrase is defined in **the Act**. It means the person whom the Act treats as the closest member of a patient's family and who is able to take certain decisions on the patient's behalf. (See para 2.5.1.)

petition — a formal document used to obtain the permission of a court for something to be done, eg for a **curator bonis** to be appointed.

place of safety — a place to which a mentally disturbed person may be taken if it is considered that he or she is at risk. It could be a hospital or a residential home or any other suitable place, if the occupier is willing to look after the patient temporarily. (See para 2.9.1.)

power of attorney — a document giving someone the power to act on another's behalf.

regional council — a tier of the local authority responsible for social care, including many aspects of the care of mentally ill and mentally handicapped people.

remand — where a court returns an accused person to prison to await a report or some other procedure.

responsible medical officer — the doctor on the staff of a hospital who is authorised by the **hospital managers** to be responsible for a particular patient or a particular class of patients. (See para 2.6.1.) In the case of **guardianship** he or she is appointed by the **regional or islands council**.

restriction directions — restrictions on a patient's discharge from hospital. (See para 5.1.16.)

restriction order — an order by the court restricting a patient's discharge. (See para 5.1.11.)

Scottish Home and Health Department — See **Secretary of State for Scotland**.

Scottish Legal Aid Board — the independent agency through which **legal aid** and legal advice and assistance may be given to a person with a case to raise or defend in the Scottish courts, or on a matter of Scots law on which they require help.

Secretary of State — short form for **Secretary of State for Scotland**.

Secretary of State for Scotland — the senior government minister responsible for Scottish domestic affairs. Amongst his responsibilities is health, including mental health. The **Scottish Home and Health Department**, which is part of the Scottish Office in Edinburgh, is generally the relevant department to contact. The address is St Andrew's House, Edinburgh EH1. (031–556 8400)

served — a term meaning that a **summons** or **initial writ** has been sent or delivered to someone.

sheriff — the judge who deals with cases in the **sheriff court**.

sheriff clerk — the member of the staff of the **sheriff court** who deals with the day-to-day administration of cases in the court.

sheriff court — the local court in Scotland. Sittings of these courts occur in each **district and islands council** area throughout Scotland.

social work department — the department of the **regional or islands council** which has responsibility for social care, including many aspects of the care of mentally ill or mentally handicapped people.

Glossary

State Hospital — the hospital at Carstairs for patients with a **mental disorder** who are deemed to need treatment under conditions of special security. (See chapter 5.)

statutory grounds for admission — the grounds on which a person can be compulsory admitted to hospital. (See para 2.5.3.)

summons — the formal document used to start legal action in the **Court of Session**.

the Act — the Mental Health (Scotland) Act 1984. The main statute dealing with mental health law in Scotland (obtainable from HMSO and some libraries).

the 1960 Act — the Mental Health (Scotland) Act 1960. The principal statute dealing with mental health law in Scotland before 12 July 1984, when it was replaced by **the Act**.

the 1983 Act — the Mental Health (Amendment) (Scotland) Act 1983. A statute introducing a number of provisions which were consolidated in **the Act**.

the Treatment and Guardianship Regulations — The Mental Health (Specified Treatment, Guardianship Duties etc) (Scotland) Regulations 1984, Statutory Instrument 1984/1492.

the Prescribed Forms Regulations — The Mental Health (Prescribed Forms) (Scotland) Regulations 1984, Statutory Instrument 1984/1495.

tutor dative — a person appointed by the **Court of Session** to take decisions relating to a person when the person is not mentally capable of taking such decisions himself or herself.

ward — a person whose money and property is administered by a **curator bonis**.

welfare grounds — the welfare conditions which must be satisfied before a person can be admitted into **guardianship**. (See para 3.1.3.)

1 Mental health

1.1 INTRODUCTION

This book looks at the way the law tries to protect the interests of people who are mentally ill or mentally handicapped. A person may have to be admitted to hospital and this is dealt with in chapter 2. More likely, he or she will continue to live at home or with relatives, and the ways in which the law can be used to meet his or her needs are looked at in chapter 3. Chapter 4 looks at patients' rights in hospital, while chapter 5 examines the ways in which the criminal courts deal with mentally disordered people who come before them.

In chapter 6 we examine the role of the **Mental Welfare Commission**, the independent body charged with representing the interests of mentally disordered people throughout Scotland. In that chapter we also deal with complaints procedures. Chapter 7 advises on obtaining help from a solicitor and the possibility of obtaining legal aid or assistance to help pay the solicitor's costs.

In this first chapter we look at the various terms the law uses to describe and categorise mental conditions. A person's mental condition is relevant to the way the law affects him or her. There is no one test. Instead different tests are used depending on the context. For one situation, for example, the test might be whether a person is suffering from a 'mental disorder'; for another it might be whether he or she is 'capable of managing his or her own affairs'. In each case the relevant test must be applied.

The chapter does not try to analyse or describe the various types of mental illness or mental handicap. That would be beyond the authors' powers and can more properly be dealt with by the professionals in the field. (See Booklist (Appendix 5) for some suggested reading.) What it tries to do is to see how the law attempts to set up different categories of disorder for its own purposes.

In the second part of the chapter we give a brief description of community care and hospitals in Scotland.

1.2 MENTAL DISORDER

The term, 'mental disorder', is a very important concept in the application of the Mental Health (Scotland) Act 1984 (**the Act**). This is the main statute dealing with mental health in Scotland. Mental disorder is a necessary requirement before a patient can be compulsorily detained in hospital (see Chapter 2) (or sent to hospital by a criminal court (see paras 5.1:1 to 5.1:18)). It is also a necessary requirement before a patient can be made subject to a guardianship order (see Chapter 3). There are special provisions dealing with consent to treatment for it (see Chapter 4). It is an essential idea in defining the scope of the duties of the Mental Welfare Commission (see Chapter 6). People suffering from a mental disorder are entitled to aftercare services on discharge from hospital (see para 3.5:6).

Despite the importance of the idea, however, there is some difficulty in stating categorically what it covers. The term is defined in the Act, as meaning 'mental illness or mental handicap however caused or manifested'[1].

1 Mental Health (Scotland) Act 1984, s 1(2). The term is sometimes used in legal books in other contexts as a generic one rather than a technical one (eg Renton and Brown *Criminal Procedure According to the Laws of Scotland* (5th edn, ed Gordon) ch 20: Mental Disorder in Relation to Criminal Procedure).

1.2:1 Mental illness

There is no definition given in the Act of the term 'mental illness', and the term has never been defined by a court. It probably means what would be accepted by a competent body of psychiatrists as a mental illness[1]. In one English case it was suggested that a 'mental illness' is what an ordinary person would recognise as such[2].

Amongst mental illnesses would be included

- Degenerative disorders such as dementia
- Schizophrenia
- Depressions
- Paranoia

The Act also refers specifically to one particular type of 'mental disorder'. This is what is generally termed 'psychopathic disorder'. The Act does not use this term (unlike the English equivalent)[3] but it does recognise the condition by referring to 'a persistent [mental disorder] manifested only by abnormally aggressive or seriously irresponsible behaviour...'[4]. This term is used only in connection with compulsory admission to hospital (see para 2.5:3).

There are some borderline cases of difficulty

- Conditions that are not clearly recognised as illnesses. Some limit on how far these conditions can be seen as mental disorder is established by the Act. The Act states that a person's 'promiscuity or other immoral conduct, sexual deviancy or dependence on alcohol or drugs' does not *of itself* cause him or her to be regarded as suffering from a 'mental disorder' as defined in the Act[5]. But where there is an associated mental illness there may be mental disorder because of that[6].

- Conditions that are recognised as illnesses, but it is not clear where the line is to be drawn between the clearly physical aspects of the illness and the mental aspects.

Just because a condition has a physical origin that does not mean it is not a mental illness. The Act refers to 'mental disorder however caused or manifested'[7]. An example would be a severe case of Parkinson's disease. It is likely that a court would treat such a case as mental disorder for the purpose of the Act only if it were seen as falling into a clearly recognised category of mental, as opposed to physical illness.

Mental disorder

1 This seems to have been the approach taken in the English case, *R v Mental Health Act Commission, ex p W*, (1988) Times 27 May (Divisional Court) (but it was not necessary to decide the matter). A full discussion of the policy issues relating to this approach and other approaches in the light of the slightly different wording of the Mental Health Act 1983 can be found in Hogget *Mental Health Law* (2nd edn) pp 38 – 56.
2 *W v L* [1974] QB 711.
3 Mental Health Act 1983, s 1(2).
4 Mental Health (Scotland) Act 1984, s 17(1)(a)(i).
5 Ibid, s 1(3).
6 *R v Mental Health Act Commission, ex p W* (above): 'In practice, however, it seems likely that the sexual problem will be inextricably linked with the mental disorder, so that the treatment for the one is treatment for the other' per Stuart-Smith LJ (*obiter*) (Lexis Transcript).
7 Mental Health (Scotland) Act 1984, s 1(2).

1.2:2 Mental handicap

People with learning difficulties or special needs, and those who work with them do not use the term 'mental handicap'. The term is misleading and unhelpful because it does not recognise that each person has different needs and should be seen as an individual. However, the term is used in the Act, and this means that it cannot be avoided in considering a number of legal questions. The term is not defined in the Act. But a court would probably approach the matter by relying on a number of criteria, including the medical evidence of psychiatrists[1].

If a person is regarded as having a mental handicap within the Act he or she

- can be committed to hospital under an emergency or short term order if he or she is a danger to him or herself or to other people (see paras 2.2 and 2.3)
- can be placed in guardianship (see chapter 3)
- comes within the remit of care of the Mental Welfare Commission, whether or not he or she is in hospital or under guardianship (see chapter 6).

However, a mentally handicapped person cannot be committed to hospital in the long term unless he or she is suffering from what the Act calls 'mental impairment' or 'severe mental impairment'. These are conditions associated with 'abnormally aggressive or seriously irresponsible conduct on the part of the person concerned'. For further details see para 2.5:3.

The term 'mental impairment' also has a special meaning in the legislation dealing with exemption from paying the community charge ('poll tax') (see para 3.4:9).

The Act protects mentally handicapped women against unlawful sexual intercourse[2] (see para 4.3:4), but for this section of the Act the term 'mental handicap' is not used and instead for a woman to be protected under the section she must be 'suffering from a state of arrested or incomplete development of mind which includes significant impairment of intelligence and social functioning'.

1 Psychiatrists use two tests in tandem, the IQ test and so-called adaptive behaviour tests which try to establish a person's social functioning—his or her ability to cope with day-to-day matters.
   There are borderline cases. One person might have a low IQ but be able to manage well on a day-to-day basis, whilst another person with a higher IQ might not be able to cope so well with the business of life. In such situations the courts would have to weigh up the medical evidence and perhaps also, as in the case of mental illness (see para 1.2:1), take into account whether the person in the street would consider that the patient had a mental handicap.

2 Mental Health (Scotland) Act 1984, s 106.

1.2:3 Disability

This concept is relevant to state benefits and to social work department assistance under the Chronically Sick and Disabled Persons Act 1970.

Many state benefits are targeted at disabled people. Usually the question is: 'is the person disabled through sickness?'. A mental condition counts (see para 3.4:6).

There is also a special term, 'grave chronic disease' which is relevant to committal to hospital under the National Assistance Act 1948 (see para 2.10).

1.2:4 Insanity

Although it is no longer medical practice to describe a person as 'insane' the term still has a meaning for lawyers. If a person is regarded as insane he or she cannot do certain things in a way that is legally valid. In particular someone who is in the legal sense insane cannot:

- be tried in a criminal court (see para 5.1:3)
- commit a crime (see para 5.1:5)
- get married (see para 3.3)
- make a contract
- vote (see para 4.6).

Insanity has a specialised and limited meaning as far as the law is concerned. In criminal law what is emphasised is 'an absolute alienation of reason' (see para 5.1:4). In other areas of law, such as whether a person can be bound by a contract he or she has made, the question is whether the person is capable of understanding the nature and effects of what is being done (see para 3.4:2).

1.2:5 Diminished responsibility

This state of mind is relevant in homicide cases. It reduces the crime from murder to the lesser crime of culpable homicide[1]. It is a state that is less than insanity (see para 5.1:6).

1 In England, manslaughter.

1.2:6 Incapacity to manage financial affairs etc

If a person is unable to manage his or her financial affairs someone else may be appointed to do the job. That person is then known as a **curator bonis** (or **curator** for short) (see para 3.4:2).

Both physical and mental conditions can be taken into account in deciding whether a curator should be appointed.

1.3 COMMUNITY CARE AND HOSPITALS

1.3:1 Care in the community

There has been a move in recent times away from hospital treatment to treatment in the community. The aim is to close down large institutions for the treatment of mental disorder and replace them with small, more flexible units[1]. This can work only if a large amount of resources is directed into local initiatives[2].

The overwhelming majority of patients suffering from mental disorder are already cared for on a voluntary basis in the community, usually in their own homes or those of near relatives. Voluntary treatment may also be undertaken in one of the fifty or so hospitals in Scotland with the facilities to care for mentally disordered patients.

The law is at pains to point out that there should be nothing to prevent people arranging to have themselves admitted to hospital voluntarily for treatment[3]. In this respect mentally disordered patients are no different from physically unwell patients who seek and receive treatment for their condition.

In fact, over 90 per cent of the 26,000 or so mentally disordered patients admitted for treatment each year to Scottish hospitals are admitted voluntarily[4] and are, in theory, free to leave at any time[5].

1 The background to this change is detailed in *Mental Health in Focus*: Report on the Mental Health Services for Adults in Scotland by the Working Group set up by the Mental Disorder Programme Planning Group of the Advisory Council on Social Work and the Scottish Health Service Planning Council, Scottish Home and Health Department. (Published by HMSO 1985). See also *Annual Report of the Mental Welfare Commission for Scotland 1985*, chapter 10).
2 *Community Care: Agenda for Action (the Griffiths Report) (1988)*.
3 See Mental Health (Scotland) Act 1984, s 17(2).
4 Scottish Mental Health In-Patient Statistics 1982, Table 4.
5 In practice when a voluntary patient wishes to leave against the doctor's advice he or she may be compulsorily detained if this is appropriate (see chapter 2).

1.3:2 Compulsory treatment

Compulsory treatment can be undertaken in the community by means of a guardianship order, or in hospital following a court order. After admission the majority of mentally disordered patients, voluntary and compulsory, are discharged within a period of four weeks[1].

After the passing of the Mental Health (Scotland) Act 1960 treatment on a voluntary basis became more common[2]. Following the coming into force of the Mental Health (Amendment) (Scotland) Act 1983 the Mental Welfare Commission in its Annual Reports for 1985 and 1986 noted a substantial rise in emergency and short-term compulsory detentions and has undertaken to monitor this closely[3].

Even the use of compulsory measures of care within the community—guardianship orders—has markedly declined in recent years. (In January 1989 only sixty-one patients in Scotland were subject to guardianship orders[4].) Nevertheless the Mental Welfare Commission has detected new and potentially worrying trends in the use of guardianship applications by some social workers. The Commission therefore considers that it would be appropriate for a special study of guardianship to be instituted in the near future[5].

1 Scottish Mental Health In-Patient Statistics 1982, Tables A, B and C.
2 Scottish Mental Health In-Patient Statistics 1982, Table 4.
3 *Annual Report of the Mental Welfare Commission for Scotland 1984* para 12.12.
4 See footnote 1 to para 1.3:1 and the *Annual Report of the Mental Welfare Commission for Scotland 1988*, para 13.26.
5 See *Annual Report of the Mental Welfare Commission for Scotland 1985* and paras 8.1 to 8.14 of the *Annual Report of the Mental Welfare Commission for Scotland 1987*.

1.3:3 Hospitals

The vast majority of people who are treated in hospital are treated under the National Health Service. Nearly all patients admitted compulsorily are admitted to National Health Service hospitals. Of the hospitals for the treatment of mentally disordered people in Scotland a majority (the psychiatric hospitals) have beds only for mentally ill patients, a substantial minority have beds only for mentally handicapped patients and the remainder have beds for both types of patients. It is possible for a patient to be admitted to a private hospital provided that hospital is registered in compliance with the provisions of the Act.

The Act contains strict rules governing the registration of private hospitals and their inspection by the Mental Welfare Commission and the Secretary of State[1].

In addition to the National Health Service and private hospitals there is also a State Hospital at Carstairs Junction. This hospital provides treatment under conditions of special security (see chapter 5).

The Secretary of State produced a draft code of practice[2] in June 1988 to assist doctors, staff of hospitals and **mental health officers**. The code will give guidance about detention and discharge of hospital patients and about medical treatment. After receiving comments, the code will be put before Parliament, which may suggest alterations. After it is approved it will be published by the Scottish Home and Health Department.

1 Mental Health (Scotland) Act 1984, ss 12–16.
2 Under ibid, s 119.

2 Compulsory admission to hospital

2.1 INTRODUCTION

The Mental Health (Scotland) Act 1984 sets out the various ways in which a person can be compulsorily admitted to hospital. These are dealt with in this chapter, which covers emergency admission to hospital; short-term detention following an emergency admission; detention by nurses; admission at the request of a relative or **mental health officer**; and place of safety orders.

There are various ways in which a person may be compulsorily admitted to or detained in a mental hospital:

- a doctor may arrange for an emergency admission for up to seventy-two hours
- following an emergency admission a person may be further detained under the short-term detention procedure for up to twenty-eight days
- he or she may be compulsorily detained in hospital by a nurse for up to two hours
- a person's **nearest relative** or a mental health officer may apply to the **sheriff** for the person to be admitted for a longer period
- a mental health officer or medical commissioner of the **Mental Welfare Commission** may remove a person to a **place of safety**
- a person may be admitted following criminal proceedings (see chapter 5)

2.2 EMERGENCY ADMISSIONS

Under the **1960 Act** a person could be detained in a mental hospital for up to seven days under the emergency procedure. When the seven day period was up the procedure could (at least in theory) be repeated indefinitely. This was changed by the **1983 Act**, and the present law does not allow successive detentions under the emergency procedure.

The procedure is intended to apply in emergencies, where a person needs to be admitted to hospital without delay and there is no time for an application to be made to the sheriff.

Conditions to be met with

A doctor may arrange an emergency admission if he or she can state that

- because of the patient's mental disorder it is urgently necessary for the health or safety of the patient *or* for the protection of others that the patient should be admitted to hospital; *and*

- undesirable delay would be involved in making an application to the **sheriff**[1]

The emergency admission forms must be signed by a fully registered doctor. The doctor does not have to be specially qualified in the treatment of mental disorder. The doctor must have personally examined the patient on the day he or she signs the emergency admission forms[2].

If this is practicable, the doctor should get the consent of a relative or mental health officer. If it is not practicable for either of these to be asked for their consent, the doctor must explain why[3]. If the relatives refuse their consent, the doctor may then ask the mental health officer for his or her consent. Only if both refuse consent will the detention not go ahead.

Length of detention

A patient may be detained for up to seventy-two hours. The patient must be taken to hospital within three days of the emergency recommendation having been made[4].

People to be notified

When the patient is admitted to hospital, the **hospital managers** must, if possible, notify

- the patient's nearest relative
- a 'responsible person' living with the patient, and
- the Mental Welfare Commission[5].

(Before the 1983 Act the hospital did not have to notify the Mental Welfare Commission of any emergency admissions. Now the Mental Welfare Commission may monitor the number of patients being admitted under the emergency procedure and may get involved in their cases if necessary.)

No further detention after the seventy-two hours are up

The doctors cannot keep a patient in hospital after the seventy-two hours are up by making a new emergency recommendation[6]. But this does not mean that the patient will definitely leave hospital, as other procedures may be used.

Appeal against an emergency admission

There is no right of appeal for a patient admitted under the emergency procedures. Any person concerned that a patient appears to have been wrongly detained under this procedure should urgently contact the Mental Welfare Commission which has the power to look into any case, examine the patient and discharge him or her if necessary (see chapter 6)[7].

Patient already in hospital

An emergency recommendation may be made even where the patient is already in hospital[8]. So a patient who admits himself or herself voluntarily may later be detained compulsorily under the emergency procedure. All the requirements set out above would apply in this case. The only difference is that the hospital managers do not need to advise any person living with the patient before he or she went into hospital[9].

Alternatives when the seventy-two hours are up

- As mentioned above, there can be no further detention under the emergency admission procedure.

- The patient may be discharged. (He or she may even be discharged before the seventy-two hours are up if the doctor making the emergency recommendation thinks this appropriate.)

- The patient may be further detained under the short-term detention procedure (see para 2.3).

- The patient may be detained by a nurse for up to two hours (see para 2.4).

- The patient may agree to remain in hospital as a voluntary patient.

1 Mental Health (Scotland) Act 1984, s 24.
2 Ibid, s 24(4).
3 Ibid, s 24(2), but see para 124 of Annual Report of the Mental Welfare Commission 1986, which indicates the failure of a considerable percentage of doctors to comply with the provisions of the Act. See also paras 13.2 to 13.7 of the 1988 *Annual Report*.
4 Mental Health (Scotland) Act 1984, s 24(3).
5 Ibid, s 24(5).
6 Ibid, s 24(6).
7 In its *Annual Report* for 1988 (para 7.2), the Mental Welfare Commission states that it would not be practical for it to act to discharge a patient within the seventy-two hour period. However, it would be able to monitor the patient's case for the future, and this information might help it to identify any worrying trends.
8 Ibid, s 25(1).
9 Ibid, s 24(5).

2.3 SHORT-TERM DETENTION

After the seventy-two hour emergency admission, a patient may be detained for a further period of twenty-eight days by means of the short-term detention procedure[1].

Steps to be followed

- A report on the patient's condition must be sent to the managers of the hospital where the patient is detained[2].

- The report must be prepared by a doctor who has personally examined the patient. The doctor should have been approved by the **health board** as having special experience in the diagnosis or treatment of mental disorder[3].

- The report must state that the doctor believes that the patient is suffering from a mental disorder of a type which requires him or her to be detained in hospital for at least a short time[4]. The doctor should also state that detention in hospital is necessary in the interests of the patient's own health or safety or to protect other people[5].

- If this is practicable, the nearest relative of the patient or the mental health officer should be asked for their consent[6]. If not, the report must explain why it was not practicable to obtain their consent. If the relative refuses consent, the doctor may apply to the mental health officer, and only if both refuse does the detention not take place[7].

- The doctor must state whether or not he or she is related to the patient and whether or not he or she has any financial interest in having the patient admitted to hospital[8].

Length of detention

If these conditions are complied with, the patient may be kept in hospital for up to twenty-eight days. This detention will take place immediately after the end of the seventy-two hour emergency admission[9].

Limited application of this procedure

The twenty-eight day short-term detention can be used only in the case of patients admitted under emergency recommendations, ie it must always be preceded by the seventy-two hour emergency detention[10].

People to be informed

The hospital managers must notify

- the Mental Welfare Commission[11]
- the patient's nearest relative (unless the nearest relative has already consented to the patient being detained in hospital)[12].
- the **regional or islands council** (unless a mental health officer appointed by such council has already consented to the patient's continued detention)[13].

These people must be notified within seven days of the patient's detention[14].

The duties of the social work department

When the regional or islands council is informed of a patient's detention, it must arrange for a mental health officer to interview the patient. The mental health officer should then as soon as possible prepare a report on the patient's social circumstances. This should be sent to the doctor in charge of the patient's case and to the Mental Welfare Commission within three weeks of the patient's detention[15].

The aim is that the social work department can make full information about the patient available to the doctors. The report should include as much detail as possible and give details of the home background of the patient and the amount of family support there is. These factors can have a considerable influence on whether or not a patient will be discharged.

Appeal against short-term detention

A patient may appeal to the sheriff for his or her discharge[16] (see para 2.6:3).

Alternatives when the twenty-eight days are up

- The only way in which a patient can be further detained in hospital is by an application being made to the sheriff for him or her to be compulsorily detained for up to six months (see para 2.5).

Short-term detention

- There is no question of the patient being detained for a further twenty-eight days under the short-term detention procedure *nor* for a further seventy-two hours under the emergency admission provisions[17].
- The patient may be discharged. (The patient may be discharged before the twenty-eight days are up if the doctor responsible believes that he or she no longer needs to be compulsorily detained.)
- The patient may agree to remain in hospital as a voluntary patient.

Safeguards for the patient

- Before a patient may be detained there must be a report on his or her condition prepared by a qualified psychiatrist.
- The Mental Welfare Commission is advised of the patient's detention and may monitor the case. In certain circumstances it may actually get the patient discharged (see chapter 6).
- A social work report will be available to the doctors in charge of the case so that they can see whether there is family support. This might help to get the patient discharged.
- The patient can appeal to the sheriff for discharge from hospital (see para 2.6:3 for the procedure on appeal). Judicial review might also be available (see para 2.5:4).
- After the twenty-eight days are up the patient must be discharged unless an application is made to the sheriff for compulsory detention.

The procedure in obtaining an order from the sheriff for compulsory admission takes some while to complete (see below). If a patient is to be detained after the end of the twenty-eight day short-term detention period the application to the sheriff must in practice be made well before the expiry of the period so that the whole procedure is completed by that time. It has been held by the courts that if this is not done there is no power to continue to detain the patient, even if a severe deterioration in the patient's condition means he or she is likely to be a danger to himself or herself or others[18].

1 Mental Health (Scotland) Act 1984, s 26.
2 Ibid, s 26(1)(a).
3 Ibid, s 26(2)(a), s 20(1)(b).
4 Ibid, s 26(2)(a)(i).
5 Ibid, s 26(2)(a)(ii).
6 Ibid, s 26(1)(b).
7 Ibid, s 26(2)(b).
8 Ibid, s 26(2)(c).
9 Ibid, s 26(3).
10 Ibid, s 26(1).
11 Ibid, s 26(4)(a).
12 Ibid, s 26(4)(b).
13 Ibid, s 26(4)(c).
14 Ibid, s 26(4).
15 Ibid, s 26(5). Of reports delivered in 1988, 20 per cent were not delivered on time (see para 13.3 of the *Annual Report of the Mental Welfare Commission 1988*). The Commission requires an explanation of why the report is delivered late.
16 Ibid, s 26(6).
17 Ibid, s 26(7).
18 See the important case of *B v F* 1987 SLT 681 in Appendix 3.

2.4 DETENTION BY NURSES

A nurse may detain a patient in hospital for up to two hours if the following conditions are met[1]:

- The nurse must be a nurse registered in Part 3 or Part 5 of the professional register[2].
- The patient must already be in hospital — the procedure cannot be used to admit a patient.
- The nurse must believe that the patient is suffering from mental disorder to such a degree that it is necessary for his or her health or safety *or* for the protection of other persons that he or she be immediately restrained from leaving hospital[3].
- The nurse is unable to find a doctor to examine the patient and thus an emergency recommendation for seventy-two hour detention cannot be made[4].
- The patient must not be detained already under the seventy-two hour or twenty-eight day detention procedure[5].

Alternatives when the two hours are up

If a doctor sees the patient within the two hour period he or she can either order the patient to be discharged *or* make an emergency recommendation. Otherwise the patient will be discharged automatically when the two hours have elapsed.

A patient cannot be detained for another two hours if he or she has not been seen by a doctor by the end of the two hour period[6].

People to be notified

- The nurse must make a report as soon as possible stating, among other things, the time at which the patient was first detained.
- The nurse must deliver the report to the hospital managers as soon as possible[7].
- The hospital managers must send a copy of the report to the Mental Welfare Commission within fourteen days of the date on which they receive it.

It is quite likely that the patient will have been discharged from hospital long before the Mental Welfare Commission receives a copy of the nurse's report, but its right to be kept informed should prevent any abuse of this procedure.

1 Mental Health (Scotland) Act 1984, s 25(2).
2 Ibid, s 25(6), and the Mental Health (Prescription of Class of Nurses) (Scotland) Order 1984, SI 1984/1095.
3 Mental Health (Scotland) Act 1984, s 25(2)(a).
4 Ibid, s 25(2)(b).
5 Although the Act does not state this explicitly, this is the view of the authors of this book, because in such circumstances a seventy-two hour detention, envisaged by the section, would not be possible; see ibid, s 25(2)(b).
6 Ibid, s 25(5).
7 Ibid, s 25(3).

2.5 APPLICATION TO A SHERIFF FOR COMPULSORY ADMISSION

If a person is to be compulsorily admitted to a mental hospital and detained there for longer than thirty-one days, a formal application must be made to the hospital and approved by the sheriff. The application must be made by the person's nearest relative (see para 2.5:1) or by a mental health officer and must be supported by medical evidence.

Although only a small proportion of patients are compulsorily admitted in this way[1] it is of obvious relevance in those few cases where a prolonged stay in hospital may be necessary. It is the only method which can be used to ensure that compulsory treatment of a patient can be effected (see para 3.2).

People able to apply for compulsory admission

Either

- a mental health officer or
- the person's nearest relative

may apply.

A **mental health officer** is an officer of the regional or islands council specifically appointed by it to be responsible for proceedings under the Act[2]. He or she will be a social worker experienced in dealing with mentally disordered people[3].

1 Scottish Mental Health in-Patient Statistics 1982, Table 4.
2 Mental Health (Scotland) Act 1984, s 9.
3 The Secretary of State has directed that all mental health officers must hold a Certificate of Qualification in Social Work (CQSW), or equivalent, have completed a minimum of two years' experience as a social worker, including, normally, work with people suffering from a mental disorder, and have received appropriate training. They should also have shown their ability to apply their knowledge and skills to persons suffering from mental disorder (Social Work Services Group Circular No SW9/1986).

2.5:1 Application by nearest relative

Definition of 'nearest relative'

The term is strictly defined by the Act, which sets out a list of relatives in order of importance[1]. Normally the person highest in the list will be deemed to be a person's nearest relative, but a person may move up the list if they have a particularly close relationship with the patient. Relatives are listed in the following order

- husband or wife
- child (legitimate or illegitimate)
- father or mother
- brother or sister
- grandparent
- grandchild

- uncle or aunt
- nephew or niece

Ordinarily the person highest in the list will be the nearest relative[2] but there are exceptions to this rule[3].

- Any relative on the list who is caring for the patient, or who was caring for him or her immediately before the patient was admitted to hospital, will be preferred to another relative who is not caring for them, even if that relative is higher up the list. (For example, if an old person is being looked after by a niece, she would be the nearest relative even if the old person has nearer relatives alive, such as brothers or sisters).

- If there are two people in the same position on the list the sexes rank equally. Whole brothers and sisters rank higher than half brothers and sisters. An elder relative is preferred to younger relatives in the same category. (So, if a person had a brother of sixty and a sister of sixty-five and they were at the top of the list, the sister would be the nearest relative because she is the elder, *unless* someone else is looking after the person).

- If a person is living apart from his or her spouse, permanently separated either by agreement or by court order, then the spouse is not eligible to be nearest relative. This is also the case if either spouse has deserted the other.

- A person who is 'ordinarily resident' abroad is not eligible (unless the patient is also ordinarily resident abroad)[4].

- A person who is under eighteen years of age cannot be nearest relative (unless he or she is the patient's husband, wife, father or mother)[5].

The law also recognises that certain people might have greater claims to represent the patient even though they are not relatives. It recognises that the common law spouse should be treated as a relative as should the person who has looked after the patient for a considerable period of time. The rules state that:

- The terms 'husband' and 'wife' include a person who is living with the patient as if he or she were the husband or wife of the patient. (Or, if the patient is then in hospital, the person who was living with the patient until the patient went into hospital. The person must have been living with the patient for at least six months)[6].

- A person who normally lives with the patient and with whom the patient has lived for at least five years is treated as the nearest relative if that person is caring for the patient or was before the patient was admitted to hospital. They need not be a relative as listed or a 'husband' or 'wife' as defined above. Such a person will take precedence over blood relatives in the list who have not been caring for the patient[7].

- If a regional or islands council has assumed 'parental rights' in respect of a child under section 17 of the Social Work (Scotland) Act 1968 (or its English equivalent), it will generally be treated as the nearest relative[8].

If there is no nearest relative or if the nearest relative is unwilling to act

In some cases a person may not have a nearest relative within the meaning of the rules. In other cases the person who is the nearest relative may be incapable of acting because of illness, or may be unwilling to act.

Application to a sheriff for compulsory admission

In these circumstances an application may be made to the sheriff for the appointment of some other suitable person to act as nearest relative[9].

Anyone considering making such an application should consider consulting a solicitor. **Legal aid** might be available to meet all or a part of the cost (see chapter 7).

Such an application may be made by

- any relative of the patient (including the nearest relative)
- any other person with whom the patient is living or was living before he or she went into hospital
- a mental health officer.

The application can be made on one of three grounds

- that the patient has no nearest relative within the meaning of the Act *or* it is not reasonably practicable to establish whether there is a nearest relative or who the nearest relative is
- that the nearest relative is incapable of fulfilling the duties of nearest relative because of mental disorder or other illness
- (in cases where the nearest relative applies) that he or she is unwilling or thinks it undesirable to act[10].

Following the application, the sheriff may name a person to act as nearest relative. The person should be named in the application and be a person who, in the opinion of the sheriff, is a proper person to act as nearest relative and who is willing to do so[11].

Preparing the application

The application should

- state which of the grounds mentioned above applies to the case
- name the person the applicant wishes to be appointed nearest relative. (The applicant can name himself or herself). (The mental health officer can name either an individual or the regional or islands council[12].)

Duties of the social work department as nearest relative

If the regional or islands council is appointed nearest relative it takes on all the usual duties of nearest relative. It has the specific duty to arrange for the patient to be visited in hospital. In addition it must take all such other steps as would normally be expected to be taken by a parent whose child is in hospital[13]. (The Act does not specify what these might be.)

Duration of the order

The order appointing someone a nearest relative may be either varied or discharged[14]

- It may be discharged by the sheriff if an application is made by
  - the person appointed nearest relative by the sheriff or
  - the nearest relative of the person

- The order may be varied by the sheriff if an application is made by
  - the person appointed nearest relative by the sheriff or
  - the mental health officer[15].

The sheriff may then substitute the social work department or another person as nearest relative, provided they are proper persons to exercise such functions and are willing to act[16].

If the person appointed as nearest relative dies, the order appointing him or her as nearest relative must be discharged or varied by the sheriff — until this happens nobody has the right to act as nearest relative. Any relative of the patient can apply to have a new order made[17].

The order will cease to have an effect if

- the patient was in hospital at the time the order was made and is later discharged or
- the patient was subject to a **guardianship order** (see chapter 3) at the time the order was made and the guardianship ceases to have effect[18].

A sheriff may be asked to make an order appointing a person as nearest relative before a patient is compulsorily admitted to hospital. This might be the case, for instance, if a friend wanted to be made nearest relative so that he or she could object to an application for compulsory admission made by the mental health officer. In these circumstances the order ceases to have effect after three months if the patient has not during that time become liable to be detained or subject to a guardianship order. However, if the patient is admitted to hospital compulsorily or received into guardianship within the three month period, the order will remain in force until the patient is discharged[18].

1 Mental Health (Scotland) Act 1984, ss 53–55.
2 Ibid, s 53(3).
3 Ibid, s 53(3) and (4).
4 The term 'ordinarily resident' is a technical one. If there were any dispute over the ordinary residence of a patient or nearest relative legal advice would have to be obtained.
5 Mental Health (Scotland) Act 1984, s 53(4).
6 Ibid, s 53(5).
7 Ibid, s 53(6).
8 Ibid, s 54 and see s 55 for the rules where a guardianship order has been made in respect of the child.
9 Ibid, s 56.
10 Ibid, s 56(3).
11 Ibid, s 56(1).
12 Ibid, s 56(2).
13 Ibid, s 10.
14 Ibid, s 57.
15 Ibid, s 57(1).
16 Ibid, s 57(2).
17 Ibid, s 57(3).
18 Ibid, s 57(4).

2.5:2 Application by a mental health officer

If a mental health officer wishes to apply for a person to be compulsorily admitted to hospital he or she must

- inform the person's nearest relative of the application *and* of the nearest relative's right to object to the application[1].
- interview the person within the fourteen days before the date on which the application is submitted to the sheriff for approval[2].

The nearest relative then has the right

- to object to the application and
- to call any witnesses in support of this objection.

(This is a very important right, as it gives the nearest relative the right to bring in medical evidence in support of his or her objections — the sheriff must hear the nearest relative and these witnesses before deciding whether to grant any order[3].)

The nearest relative may request the mental health officer to make an application for admission on his or her behalf. If the nearest relative does make such a request the mental health officer must decide as soon as possible whether to make an application. If the mental health officer decides not to, he or she must notify the nearest relative of the reasons in writing[4].

However, the mental health officer cannot refuse to make an application if requested to do so by one of the doctors who provided the medical recommendations in support of the application[5].

In considering whether or not to make the application the mental health officer is required to consider the wishes expressed by the relatives of the patient and any other relevant circumstances[6].

It should be noted that although mental health officers are appointed by regional or islands councils, a mental health officer can make an application to a sheriff for an area outside that of the regional or islands council for which he or she works.

1 Mental Health (Scotland) Act 1984, s 19(5)(b).
2 Ibid, s 19(5)(a).
3 Ibid, s 21(2)(b).
4 Ibid, s 19(3).
5 Ibid, s 19(6).
6 Ibid, s 19(4).

2.5:3 Conditions for admitting a patient to hospital

Types of mental illness justifying compulsory admission

The following conditions must be complied with

- The person must be suffering from mental disorder which needs treating in hospital — not as an out-patient[1]. The medical treatment needed is defined to include medical or nursing treatment and care or training under medical supervision[2].
- If the person suffers from a disorder whose only symptoms are 'abnormally aggressive or seriously irresponsible' conduct, the doctor must

satisfy the sheriff that medical treatment in hospital would improve this condition or at least stop it getting worse[3].

In dealing with a potentially violent patient the doctor should bear in mind the wide definition of 'medical treatment' in the Act, and consider whether nursing care or training under medical supervision could alleviate or prevent the deterioration of the patient's condition.

- It must be shown that it is necessary *either* for the health and safety of the person *or* for the protection of other people that treatment should be given[4].
- The sheriff must be satisfied that treatment cannot be given unless the person is detained compulsorily.

(The above grounds are from now on referred to as '**the statutory grounds for admission**').

Mentally handicapped people

For the majority of people with a mental handicap, hospital is not necessary or right, and the Act recognises this. Only if the person suffers from what the Act calls 'mental impairment' or 'severe mental impairment' can he or she be compulsorily detained.

'Mental impairment' is defined as meaning arrested or incomplete mental development which has a *significant* effect on a person's intelligence and social abilities. There must be evidence of 'abnormally aggressive or seriously irresponsible' conduct.

'Severe mental impairment' is defined in the same way, except that the effect on the person's intelligence and social abilities is defined as *severe* rather than *significant* (in other words, the test is one of the degree of impairment)[5].

If a person with mental impairment is to be admitted to hospital, the doctors must satisfy the sheriff that treatment (as defined above) would improve his or her condition, or at least stop it getting worse. If a person suffers severe mental impairment he or she can be admitted even if the treatment is not thought likely to make him or her any better[6].

It is for the sheriff to decide whether or not the mental impairment is so severe that a patient should be admitted even though hospital treatment would not necessarily cause his or her condition to improve. In making this decision the sheriff considers primarily the medical reports supplied. In circumstances such as these it is vital for anyone opposing an application to obtain independent medical reports, and probably legal advice as well.

Medical recommendations

Two medical reports must be submitted with the application for admission. Each of them must comply with the following conditions[7]:

- They must be issued on or before the date of the application.
- Each doctor must have personally examined the person; the examinations must not be more than five days apart[8]. The doctors may examine the patient together if neither the patient nor the nearest relative objects.
- At least one medical report must be given by a psychiatrist. The other should, if possible, be given by the person's general practitioner or another doctor who has known the person in the past[9].

Application to a sheriff for compulsory admission

- If the application is for a National Health Service hospital, only one of the reports should be from a doctor who is on the staff of that hospital. If the application is for a private hospital neither report may come from a doctor on its staff[10]. (However if the delay caused by getting two reports from outside the hospital would cause a serious risk to the health and safety of the patient or to any other persons these restrictions are waived[11].)

- The Act provides that, when arrangements are being made for the detention of a patient, the people making those arrangements should 'have regard' to the religious persuasion of the patient. The patient's religious beliefs would not be paramount in determining into which hospital he or she should go, but would be one factor to be taken into account[12].

- The doctor signing the report must say whether he or she
  - is related to the patient or
  - has any financial interest in having the patient admitted to hospital[13].

The rules prescribe special forms for the application to the sheriff — see Appendix 2, pp 195–199.

1 Mental Health (Scotland) Act 1984, s 17(1)(a).
2 Ibid, s 125.
3 Ibid, s 17(1)(a)(i). See para 4.13 of the *Annual Report of the Mental Welfare Commission 1987*.
4 Ibid, s 17(1)(b).
5 Ibid, s 1(2).
6 Ibid, s 17(1).
7 Ibid, s 20.
8 Ibid, s 20(1)(a).
9 Ibid, s 20(1)(b).
10 Ibid, s 20(1)(c).
11 Ibid, s 20(2)(a). For detailed rules on part-time doctors and consultants, see s 20(2)(b), (c).
12 Ibid, s 112.
13 Ibid, s 20(1)(d).

2.5:4 The role of the sheriff

Timing of application

The application must be submitted to the sheriff within seven days of the last medical report[1].

Neither the nearest relative nor the mental health officer may make an application unless they have personally seen the patient within the fourteen days before they apply to the sheriff[2].

Addressing the application

The application is made to the **sheriff court** for the district where the person is living. If the person is in hospital at the time of the application, it is made to the sheriff for the area which covers the hospital. This is done by completing the special form (see pp 196–197) and submitting it to the **sheriff clerk**.

The sheriff's duties

- The sheriff can call witnesses and may make whatever further inquiries are thought necessary. He or she must give the patient (or the patient's representative) an opportunity to be heard[3].

- If the nearest relative objects to the application, he or she must be given the opportunity to be heard by the sheriff and to call any witnesses needed.

(This could obviously be very important if a mental health officer is applying for admission and relatives object. Relatives should note that if a relative questions the medical reports submitted by the doctors, he or she must obtain independent medical reports. Any relative wishing to object should consider obtaining legal advice on how best to do this. Legal aid may be available to meet all or part of the costs. See chapter 7.)

- If the application is being made by a mental health officer asked to do so by one of the doctors giving a report (see para 2.5:2) and the mental health officer does not think the application should be granted, the sheriff must give him or her an opportunity to voice objections[4].

- The sheriff must hear the evidence of the applicant and his or her witnesses before rejecting any application[5].

- The sheriff may decide to have the hearing in private; he or she *must* do so if either the patient or the applicant so requests. The hearing may take place in hospital if the sheriff so directs[6].

- The sheriff clerk must send a copy of the application and notice of the hearing to the patient. If, however, two medical certificates are produced stating that it would be prejudicial to the patient's health or treatment for him or her to receive notice of the hearing personally, the sheriff may order that a **curator ad litem** should be appointed to receive the notice on the patient's behalf[7].

The hearing

The Act provides that in any application for admission (or later, for appeal) if the sheriff considers that it would be prejudicial to the patient's health or treatment for him or her to have to attend court, the sheriff may exclude the patient (but not any representative of the patient) from the court proceedings[8].

There are three possibilities

- the patient may attend the hearing. He or she need not attend if unwilling to do so.

- the patient may appoint a representative to attend on his or her behalf.

  A short letter appointing the representative, signed by the patient, is all that is necessary, as the rules do not specify any particular form for the appointment. If the patient is already in hospital, he or she may tell the responsible medical officer whom he or she wishes to appoint.

  The representative appointed by the patient cannot be excluded from the court proceedings.

- if the sheriff considers that the patient should be excluded from the proceedings and the patient has not nominated a representative, the sheriff may nominate a curator ad litem to represent the patient[9].

Anyone who is concerned about the effect of court proceedings on a patient, therefore, should feel free to raise this matter with the sheriff. It is the duty of the responsible medical officer to advise the sheriff if he or she considers that it would prejudice the patient's health or treatment if the patient had to attend personally[10].

Finally, having heard all the evidence and having made any other enquiries which he or she considers necessary, the sheriff must decide whether or not to approve the application to commit the patient. If the sheriff approves, the person will be admitted to hospital; if the sheriff rejects the application the person will, of course, be free to go.

Appeal

Once the sheriff has made his or her decision it is not possible to appeal from it to a higher court[11]. It may, however, be possible to have the decision reviewed by the procedure known as 'judicial review'.

Judicial review

Judicial review is a procedure whereby administrative decisions taken by persons acting within the framework of a statute or statutory regulations etc can be challenged. The grounds for challenge may be that the decisions were wrong because those taking the decisions did not comply with their legal obligations when making the decision. For example, if a mistake as to the law was made, or if the decision was taken in a 'manifestly unreasonable' way or if the procedure was carried out in a way contrary to 'natural justice' as the law understands this, then the decision might be subject to review by the courts[12].

The kind of decisions which might be challenged in this way are: a doctor's decision to admit a patient[13], a sheriff's approval of an application for short-term detention or a sheriff's refusal to accept an appeal to him or her[14].

The appeal is to the 'supervisory jurisdiction' of the Outer House of the Court of Session under a new procedure laid down in 1985[15] and the court has wide powers to set aside or implement any decision made, to order payment of damages[16] and to make interim orders.

Although the new procedure is intended to simplify and speed up the hearing of applications for judicial review, this is an extremely complex area of law and legal advice would be necessary if a sheriff or doctor's decision were to be challenged in this way[17].

In particular it is very important to realise that the grounds for challenging a decision are not that the decision does not represent the best way of dealing with a particular case but that in some way the basis on which the decision was made was outside the procedures laid down by the relevant legislation. In this way judicial review differs from an appeal, where a reconsideration of the facts may take place.

1 Mental Health (Scotland) Act 1984, s 21(1) (as amended by the Law Reform (Miscellaneous Provisions) (Scotland) Act 1985, s 51).
2 Mental Health (Scotland) Act 1984, s 19(2), (5).
3 Ibid, s 21(2)(a), s 113.
4 Ibid, s 21(2)(c).
5 Ibid, s 21(3).
6 Ibid, s 21(4) and Act of Sederunt (Mental Health (Scotland) Act 1984) 1986, SI 1986/545, para 2(2).

7 Act of Sederunt, para 5(1).
 8 Ibid, para 5(2).
 9 Mental Health (Scotland) Act 1984, s 113(2). In this case the rules do not specify that two medical certificates are required, and the sheriff will probably rely on the certificate of the responsible medical officer and evidence from the mental health officer.
10 Act of Sederunt, para 4(2).
11 *F v Management Committee and Managers, Ravenscraig Hospital* 1989 SLT 49.
12 See the case of *Renfrew District Council v McGourlick* 1987 SLT 538 where Lord McCluskey said that 'where the decision is arbitrary in the sense either that the sheriff has gone outside the jurisdiction by asking himself the wrong question, or by not observing the procedural rules prescribed by the statute or by asking the right question but failing to note that he lacks the necessary information to enable a sustainable answer to be given . . . then . . . the purported ruling . . . of the sheriff is a nullity . . . and is reducible' [ie it may be set aside].
13 See *B v F* (Appendix 3) and the English case of *R v Hallstrom, ex p W* [1985] 3 All ER 775.
14 See *F v Management Committee and Managers, Ravenscraig Hospital* 1989 SLT 49 (Appendix 3) and *T v Secretary of State for Scotland* 1987 SCLR 65.
15 Act of Sederunt (Rules of Court Amendment No 2) (Judicial Review) 1985, SI 1985/500.
16 There is some protection in the Act for doctors against claims made against them whilst they are carrying out their duties under the Act. Section 122 of the Act provides that a person shall not be liable to any civil or criminal proceedings in respect of acts which he or she purports to do under the Act or the regulations made under it unless bad faith or lack of reasonable care can be shown.

   There would be no protection if a doctor was acting outside the powers and duties given by the Act. See *B v F* 1987 SLT 681 (report of the case when in the Inner House) where it was held that the section offered no protection to doctors who 'knew perfectly well that they had no right to detain the patient . . .'. (For the facts of this case, see Appendix 3).
17 A very detailed and thorough discussion of the law is in the 'Administrative Law' title in Volume 1 of *The Laws of Scotland: Stair Memorial Encyclopaedia*. A clear explanation for the layperson is in 'A Guide to Judicial Review in Scotland' by Tom Mullen, published by Shelter and available from them at 65 Cockburn Street, Edinburgh EH1 1BU.

   For an interesting discussion of some of the issues (to be read with care as it deals with English law) see the article by M J Gunn at page 290 of the 1986 Journal of Social Welfare Law, 'Judicial Review of Hospital Admissions and Treatment in the Community under the Mental Health Act 1983'.

2.5:5 Admission of the patient to hospital

Admission

If the sheriff approves an application the patient may be taken to hospital. If the patient is already in hospital, he or she is no longer entitled to leave. He or she may be kept there for a period of up to six months, but should the patient's condition improve, he or she should be discharged before the six months have expired[1]. It is also possible for the six month period to be extended on review (see para 2.6:2).

The patient should be admitted within seven days of the sheriff's approval being granted[2]. The hospital to which the patient is admitted will be the one named in the application. (It is clearly important before an application for admission is made that the applicant checks whether the hospital has a place available; it is entitled to refuse to admit the patient if there are no places.)

Notifications by the hospital

Within seven days of the patient's admission the hospital must notify

- the Mental Welfare Commission[3]

- the social work department for the area in which the hospital is situated (if the application for admission was by a nearest relative)[4].

Each must be supplied with a copy of the application and of the medical recommendations.

Rectifying mistakes

Sometimes the admitting hospital will discover, after the patient has been admitted, that something in the application or the medical recommendation is incorrect. If the error is found within fourteen days of the patient being admitted, the documents can be amended[5]. The sheriff must approve this and they must be amended within twenty-one days of the patient's admission. The amendment must be made by the person who signed the document[6].

If it appears to the hospital managers that one of the medical recommendations is insufficient to justify the patient being kept in hospital, they must notify the applicant and the sheriff. This must be done within twenty-one days of the patient's admission.

A new medical recommendation may then be obtained. It should be sent to the hospital managers and the sheriff. If the sheriff is then satisfied that this is sufficient to justify the detention of the patient and that the **statutory grounds of admission** still apply, the sheriff's original approval will stand[7].

1 Mental Health (Scotland) Act 1984, s 30(1).
2 Ibid, s 22(1).
3 Ibid, s 22(2)(a).
4 Ibid, s 22(2)(b).
5 Ibid, s 23.
6 Ibid, s 23(1).
7 Ibid, s 23(2).

2.6 REVIEWING THE PATIENT'S CASE

2.6:1 The responsible medical officer

Every patient who is compulsorily admitted to hospital is allocated a **responsible medical officer** by the hospital managers. The responsible medical officer is a doctor on the staff of the hospital who has responsibility either for a particular category of patients or for a particular patient[1].

1 Mental Health (Scotland) Act 1984, s 59(1)(a).

2.6:2 The procedures for review

Review within the first month

Within twenty-one days of the patient being admitted to hospital the social work department must arrange to interview the patient. The mental health officer must then prepare a report on the patient's social circumstances and send it to the responsible medical officer and the Mental Welfare Commission.

Between twenty-one and twenty-eight days of the patient's being admitted the responsible medical officer must

- either examine the patient personally or obtain a report from another doctor; and

- consult any other people who seem to the responsible medical officer to be principally concerned with the patient's treatment. (This might include nurses, for example[1].)

The responsible medical officer must then decide whether or not the patient should continue to be detained in hospital. If he or she finds *either*

- that the patient is not suffering from mental disorder of a type which requires the patient to be liable to be detained in hospital for medical treatment *or*
- that it is not necessary for the health or safety of the patient or for the protection of others that the patient should receive such treatment

then the responsible medical officer must order the patient's discharge[2]. (These grounds are henceforth referred to as '**the grounds for continued detention**'[3].)

If the patient is not discharged, the responsible medical officer must notify[4]

- the Mental Welfare Commission
- the patient's nearest relative
- the regional or islands council
- the hospital managers.

Review at four to six months

Between four and six months after the patient has been detained the responsible medical officer must review the case again, on the same basis as above[5].

If the **statutory grounds for admission** do not apply to the patient, then the patient must be discharged.

If they do apply, the responsible medical officer must notify the hospital managers and the Mental Welfare Commission. The authority to detain the patient is then renewed for a further six months, without the need to go back to the sheriff for an extention[6].

Review after the first renewal of the period of detention

After the first renewal of the authority to detain for six months, renewals can be made on the same basis as above for periods of twelve months at a time.

The review takes place within two months of the end of the period of detention. Such renewals can, in theory, continue indefinitely — without the sheriff ever being informed[7].

1 Mental Health (Scotland) Act 1984, s 22(4)(a).
2 Ibid, s 22(4)(b).
3 It is important to note that the **grounds for continued detention** differ subtly from the **statutory grounds for admission**. They do not include the requirement that the responsible medical officer satisfy himself or herself that, in the case of a psychopathic patient, hospitalisation is improving his or her situation or at least preventing it getting worse. Thus, although a patient cannot be admitted unless the doctors believe the outcome to be likely, he or she can continue to be detained if they prove to have been mistaken. The patient would, in theory at least, have to wait until the four to six month review of his or her case when the test is again the statutory grounds for admission.
4 Mental Health (Scotland) Act 1984, s 22(4)(c).
5 Ibid, s 30(3).

6 Ibid, s 30(2)(b).
7 Ibid, s 30(4).

2.6:3 Safeguards for the patient

To prevent the patient being detained indefinitely by successive renewals in this way, the patient has the right

- to appeal to the sheriff against the renewal[1]
- to have his or her case reviewed by either the responsible medical officer, the Mental Welfare Commission, the managers of the hospital or by his or her nearest relative, any of whom may order the patient's discharge.

Any of these courses of action could bring about the patient's discharge. In exceptional cases, judicial review could also be available. See para 2.5:4 and *A R v Secretary of State for Scotland* in case notes.

Appeal to the sheriff

Whenever the authority to detain the patient is renewed the patient may appeal to the sheriff against this.

(But note that there is no right of appeal against the sheriff's initial order that the patient be detained. It is only once the responsible medical officer tries to renew this that the patient obtains the right of appeal.)

The patient will be told of the right to appeal at the time the authority is renewed. When the responsible medical officer informs the hospital managers that he or she will be requesting a renewal of the authority to detain the patient, it is the hospital managers' job to notify the patient and the nearest relative *and* to inform the patient that he or she has the right to appeal to the sheriff[2].

The patient should consider seeking legal advice if he or she intends to appeal. If the patient is not competent to instruct a solicitor, his or her relatives may do so on the patient's behalf. A lawyer would be able to advise on what independent medical reports should be obtained and would be able to help with presentation of the patient's case. See chapter 7.

It is very important that the patient should get independent medical opinions in support of his or her case, as the hospital will generally supply the sheriff with its own medical evidence in support of its claim that the detention should continue. The rules provide that the patient may request a doctor to visit and examine him or her in private[3]. The doctor has the right to inspect the hospital records relating to the detention or treatment of the patient[4].

The sheriff is obliged in any appeal under the Act to give the patient a right to be heard, either in person, or through a representative, *unless* he or she considers it would be prejudicial to the patient's health (see para 2.5:4).

After the sheriff has heard all the evidence and read all the medical reports he or she will have to decide whether the **grounds for continued detention** apply. If the sheriff decides that they do not apply he or she must order the patient's discharge. Otherwise the authority will be renewed[5]. It has been held that the grounds for continued detention only exist if it is actually and not just potentially necessary for the patient to have in-patient treatment[6]. A belief that a patient might not take medication in the future is not enough to show this. But if the effects of medication require observation in hospital that would be enough[7].

1 Mental Health (Scotland) Act 1984, s 30(6).
2 Ibid, s 110(1).
3 Ibid, s 35(3).
4 Ibid, s 35(4).
5 Ibid, s 33(4).
6 *AB and CB v E* 1987 SCLR 419.
7 1987 SCLR 419 at 428 per Sheriff Younger.

2.7 DISCHARGE OF THE PATIENT

Discharge by the responsible medical officer

If at any time the responsible medical officer is of the opinion that the **grounds for continued detention** do not apply in a particular patient's case, then he or she is under a statutory duty to order the patient's release[1]. In other words, despite the fact that the authority to detain the patient is renewed for a fixed period[2], if the patient's condition improves during that period he or she should be discharged. The responsible medical officer is under an obligation, therefore, constantly to keep the patient's condition under review.

Discharge by the Mental Welfare Commission

Any person concerned about the compulsory detention of a person under the Act can notify the Mental Welfare Commission. It has the power to investigate the case and to order the patient's discharge if the grounds for continued detention no longer apply[3]. (For further details on the Mental Welfare Commission see chapter 6.)

Discharge by the hospital managers

An alternative to contacting the Mental Welfare Commission is to contact the managers of the hospital. They also have the power to discharge the patient by requiring the responsible medical officer to review the patient's case[4]. The consent of the responsible medical officer must be obtained to the discharge. If he or she does not consent, the responsible medical officer must supply the hospital managers with a certificate stating that in his or her opinion the **statutory grounds for admission** apply in the patient's case[5].

A discharge by the hospital managers takes effect within seven days of the day on which it was made.

Discharge by the nearest relative

The nearest relative can also get the patient's case reviewed. What happens is that he or she delivers to the hospital a form requesting the discharge of the patient and the hospital managers then have to get the responsible medical officer to review the case. The rules do not specify what wording should be used in the form of discharge. A suggested form is set out at page 215.

The nearest relative should complete the form and deliver it to the hospital managers. The form should be dated at least seven days before it is intended that the discharge should become effective.

If within this seven day period the responsible medical officer issues a report to the hospital managers that the **statutory grounds for admission** apply to the patient, then the nearest relative's order is of no effect and the patient will not be discharged[5]. If no such report is provided, the patient will be discharged on the date set out in the nearest relative's order.

If the responsible medical officer prevents a discharge by the nearest relative in this way, the nearest relative cannot make another attempt to discharge the patient until six months from the date of the responsible medical officer's report[6]. But the nearest relative still has the right to appeal to the sheriff for the patient's discharge. The hospital managers must notify the nearest relative of this right and he or she must appeal within twenty-eight days of having been notified[7].

There is no right for a nearest relative to discharge a patient compulsorily detained in the **State Hospital** at Carstairs[8].

1 Mental Health (Scotland) Act 1984, s 33(3)(a).
2 Ibid, s 30(2).
3 Ibid, s 33(3)(b).
4 Ibid, s 33(6).
5 Ibid, s 34(1)(a).
6 Ibid, s 34(1)(b).
7 Ibid, s 34(2).
8 Ibid, s 34(3).

2.8 LEAVING THE HOSPITAL

2.8:1 Leave of absence

The responsible medical officer may give a patient leave of absence from the hospital instead of a complete discharge[1]. This means that the patient can leave the hospital and live elsewhere but may be brought back in if the responsible medical officer considers this necessary in the interests of the health or safety of the patient *or* for the protection of other people[2].

Leave of absence can be granted for up to six months. It may then be extended for further periods of not more than six months without the patient being required to return to the hospital first. Leave of absence may also be granted for a specific reason, such as attending a funeral[3].

See para 3.2 for medical treatment of patients on leave of absence.

The Mental Welfare Commission must be notified by the responsible medical officer whenever leave of absence is granted. It must also be told whenever leave of absence is extended by more than twenty-eight days at a time[4].

(Leave of absence might be appropriate where a patient has been resident in hospital for a prolonged period. The responsible medical officer can safeguard the patient's interests by arranging to have him or her live with a suitable person and can regularly review the situation. The patient can also be required to attend hospital at regular intervals for medication, for example.)

1 Mental Health (Scotland) Act 1984, s 27(1).
2 Ibid, s 27(5).

3 Ibid, s 27(2).
4 Ibid, s 27(4).

2.8:2 Transfer to another hospital or into guardianship

The hospital managers may transfer a patient

- to another hospital (including the State Hospital at Carstairs) or
- into the guardianship of another person or of the social work department (see chapter 3)[1].

Before making such a transfer the hospital managers must

- obtain the consent of the hospital to which the patient is being transferred[2] or
- get the consent of the social work department to taking the patient into guardianship *or* its approval to the named person chosen as guardian[3].

The managers of the new hospital or the new local authority concerned must inform both the Mental Welfare Commission and the patient's nearest relative of any such transfer within seven days. (It is to be hoped that they will have been consulted, and, indeed, they may have requested the transfer.) If the patient is transferred to the State Hospital, he or she has the right to appeal against this within twenty-eight days (see para 5.2).

1 Mental Health (Scotland) Act 1984, s 29(1).
2 Ibid, s 29(1)(a).
3 Ibid, s 29(1)(b), (c).

2.8:3 Patients absent without leave

If any patient who is liable to be compulsorily detained leaves hospital without consent or fails to return to hospital after leave of absence he or she may be taken into custody by the police and then returned to the hospital. Any mental health officer, officer on the staff of the hospital, police officer or person authorised in writing by the hospital managers can arrrange for the patient to be so taken and returned to the hospital[1].

These powers are also available if a patient refuses to go to hospital following an order for admission by the sheriff[2].

There is a proviso. If a patient remains at liberty for twenty-eight days the hospital is no longer entitled to take him or her compulsorily and the patient will remain free — presumably until a new order for admission is made[3].

1 Mental Health (Scotland) Act 1984, s 121.
2 Ibid, s 28(1).
3 Ibid, s 28(3).

2.9 PLACE OF SAFETY ORDERS

2.9:1 The power to enter private premises

If a mental health officer or a medical commissioner of the Mental Welfare Commission believes that a person suffering from a mental disorder is living somewhere where he or she

Place of safety orders

- has been ill-treated or neglected, or

- is not being kept under control, or

- is living alone and uncared for and is unable to care for him or herself

they may enter and inspect the place. They must provide evidence that they have the authority to inspect the place and must request permission to enter[1].

If permission is refused a warrant may be obtained from a justice of the peace or a sheriff. This will authorise a police officer to enter the house with a doctor (using force if necessary to gain entry). They will then have the power, if necessary, to remove the mentally disordered person and take him or her to a 'place of safety' (see below) while they consider what steps should be taken for his or her future care[2].

The person may be kept in the place of safety for up to seventy-two hours[3].

A **'place of safety'** means a hospital or a residential home for people suffering from mental disorder. It could also include any other suitable place, if the occupier is willing to look after the patient temporarily. A police station should not be used other than in an emergency, when nowhere else is available[4].

This emergency power could be used where a neighbour or some other concerned person has fears for the safety or health of a mentally disordered person. They should contact the police, the social work department or the Mental Welfare Commission without delay.

1 Mental Health (Scotland) Act 1984, s 117(1).
2 Ibid, s 117(2).
3 Ibid, s 117(4).
4 Ibid, s 117(7)(b).

2.9:2 Removal from public places

If a police officer finds someone in a public place whom he or she considers to be:

- mentally disordered, and

- in immediate need of care and control

the police officer may remove such a person to a place of safety (see above)[1]. This can be done

- *either* for the person's own protection

- *or* for the protection of other people.

The person may be kept in the place of safety for up to seventy-two hours so that he or she may be examined by a doctor and arrangements may be made for his or her future care.

Wherever possible the police officer should notify the person's nearest relative and any responsible person who lives with the person[2].

1 Mental Health (Scotland) Act 1984, s 118(1).
2 Ibid, s 118(3).

2.10 ELDERLY PERSONS OR PEOPLE SUFFERING FROM 'GRAVE CHRONIC DISEASE'

Whilst it would appear to be preferable that cases of people suffering from a mental disorder should be dealt with under the Mental Health (Scotland) Act, there remains a power for local authorities to commit to hospital people suffering from 'grave chronic disease' (which could include very serious mental disorder) or who are 'aged or infirm and... living in insanitary conditions'.

The National Assistance Act 1948 provides that if a 'designated medical officer' (ie, usually a medical officer of health specialising in community medicine) certifies in writing to the regional or islands council that

- it is in such person's interest or
- it is necessary to prevent injury to the health of, or serious nuisance to, other people

that the person be committed to hospital, the social work department or the medical officer of health may apply to the sheriff court for an order that the person be committed to hospital or another suitable place[1].

An order may be made for an initial period of up to three months and may then be renewed for another period of up to three months.

There is a right of appeal against any order made. An appeal can be made once six weeks have elapsed from the date of making of the order or the renewal of the order.

Seven days' notice of the application must generally be given[2]. However if there is an emergency the person can be removed immediately if the medical officer of health and another doctor certify that in their opinion it is necessary, in the person's own interests, that he or she be removed without delay[3].

Such an emergency order lasts for three weeks and there is no appeal against it[3]. The initial order may then be extended for three months. The person detained will probably have the right to appeal against the renewal, although the wording of the legislation is somewhat ambiguous[4].

The Mental Welfare Commission has no specified supervisory role in connection with patients detained under this act but it does have a general supervisory role in connection with all patients who appear to be suffering from a mental disorder (see para 6.1). It could, therefore, be contacted if there was any problem with such a patient's detention and it would, if necessary, report on the patient's behalf to the appropriate authorities.

1 National Assistance Act 1948, s 47 (as amended by the National Assistance (Amendment) Act 1951, s 1).
2 National Assistance (Amendment) Act 1951, s 1.
3 National Assistance Act 1948, s 47(6).
4 See ibid, s 47(4), (6) (as amended); there is no right of appeal against an emergency order but it probably does not extend to a renewal of an emergency order, which is made under s 47(4) of the 1948 Act and is not, therefore, covered by the prohibition in s 47(6).

2.11 TRANSFER OF PATIENTS WITHIN THE UNITED KINGDOM

There are detailed rules giving the Secretary of State the power to transfer patients between Scotland, England, Wales, Northern Ireland and the Channel Islands. These are set out at sections 77–89 of the Mental Health (Scotland) Act 1984. These sections also contain provisions allowing the Secretary of State, in certain circumstances, to deport mentally disordered persons who are not British citizens or Commonwealth citizens with the right to live in the United Kingdom.

3 Care in the community

This chapter deals with guardianship; compulsory medical treatment in the community; marriage and divorce; financial and property matters; and the duty of local authorities to provide education, training, and aftercare for mentally disordered people living within their areas. The final section looks at the housing rights of people with a mental disorder.

3.1 GUARDIANSHIP

3.1:1 Introduction

This section deals with applications for reception into **guardianship** under the Mental Health (Scotland) Act 1984.

Since the Mental Health (Scotland) Act 1960 came into force, the number of mentally disordered patients becoming the subject of formal guardianship orders has greatly decreased. Today this procedure applies to less than a hundred people.

Traditionally, guardianship applications have been used more often in the case of people who are mentally handicapped than for people who are mentally ill, although there has been a growing use of the procedure by **social work departments** to protect elderly people suffering from dementia by ensuring their admission into residential care, which they are unwilling or unable to accept voluntarily.

One of the major criticisms of the present system of guardianship is that the limited powers given to the guardian mean that he or she is unable to deal effectively on the patient's behalf. As will be seen later, the guardian cannot consent to medical treatment on the patient's behalf, nor insist that the patient take his or her prescribed drugs, nor deal with the patient's property or financial affairs.

In some cases both a guardian and a curator will have to be appointed.

Guardianship is sometimes used by social work departments as a means of insisting that elderly patients suffering from dementia enter into residential accommodation. However, guardianship would not be the appropriate remedy if hospital admission was necessary.

It has been suggested that some doctors, unwilling to use the 'draconian' remedy of compulsory admission to hospital for elderly dementia patients, instead turn a blind eye to the patient's inability to consent, and admit the patient to hospital 'voluntarily'.

If, however, the patient has no real understanding of what is happening he or she is unable at law to give consent to removal or to treatment and would, therefore, be in a worse position than a patient compulsorily detained under **the Act**. For such a patient the statutory review and appeal procedures afford some protection; for the 'voluntary' patient whose consent is absent, no protection exists.

Any person concerned about the possible wrongful detention of an elderly person should report the matter to the **Mental Welfare Commission** (see chapter 6). For doctors to detain as a voluntary patient a person who is unable to give consent is unlawful, and could give rise to a claim for wrongful detention and for assault (if medical treatment is given), (see para 4.4:2). Compulsory measures of some kind (with the legal safeguards they provide) have to be used in the case of patients who are legally incapable of consent.

Because of the limitation of guardianship there have been calls for a radical restructuring of the system, the aim being to create one body which could deal with all issues concerning patients who do not require compulsory admission to hospital but require some protective supervision.

In a recent report (see booklist) Scottish Action on Dementia calls for the establishment of Mental Health Panels (to be similar to Children's Panels) to deal with all questions relating to the well-being of a mentally disordered person[1]. The Scottish Law Commission is currently looking into the whole area of how decisions should be taken on behalf of persons unable to take them.

1 See *Dementia and the Law: the Challenge Ahead*—available from Scottish Action on Dementia (Appendix 4). For a detailed look at some of the issues raised in guardianship, see chapter 9 of the 1986 Annual Report of the Mental Welfare Commission for Scotland and Scottish Action on Dementia report on Guardianship—see booklist.

3.1:2 The nature of guardianship

Guardianship is a means of providing care and protection for mentally disturbed people while allowing them to live within the community. The guardian, which will usually be the local social work department, is given certain supervisory powers over the patient, the aim being to protect him or her from neglect or the risk of exploitation.

3.1:3 Conditions which must apply

For a person to be admitted into guardianship he or she must be

- at least sixteen years old[1]. (There is no such age limit in the case of patients compulsorily admitted to hospital.)
- suffering from a **mental disorder** of a nature or degree which justifies his or her admission into hospital[2] (the 'medical grounds').

The **sheriff** must also be satisfied that it is in the interests of the welfare of the patient that he or she be admitted into hospital[2] (the 'welfare grounds').

It will be seen that there are two separate tests. Is the patient suffering from the type of disorder which could justify a guardianship order, and would it be in the patient's interests for an order to be made? The doctors must convince the sheriff that the first applies, while the **mental health officer** will have to satisfy him or her that the welfare grounds apply[3].

1 Mental Health (Scotland) Act 1984, s 37(1).
2 Ibid, s 36.

3 A useful practical test was outlined by a consultant psychiatrist in the Scottish Action on Dementia report on Guardianship (see booklist) at page 10: (1) Will the patient recognise the guardian and understand the guardian's powers? (2) Will the guardian be able to exercise his [or her] powers? (3) Does the guardian have access to the appropriate services? (4) Can others act as 'informal' guardians? (5) Is it a 'hammer to crack a nut'?

3.1:4 Application to the sheriff

An application for a person to be taken into guardianship must be made to the sheriff in the prescribed form laid down by **the Act** (see Appendix 2, pages 207, 208)[1].

The application form may request that any one of the following be appointed as guardian:

- the local social work department
- any other person chosen or approved by the social work department as suitable to act[2]. (This could be a relative of the patient or another suitable person).

The person making the application may request that he or she be appointed guardian.

The Act provides that, when making arrangements for the reception into guardianship of a patient, the people making the arrangements should 'have regard' to the religious persuasion of the patient. The religious beliefs of the patient would not be the overriding factor which would determine the decision on who should be guardian, but would be one factor to be taken into account[3].

1 Mental Health (Scotland) Act 1984, s 37(1).
2 Ibid, s 37(2).
3 Ibid, s 112.

3.1:5 Medical recommendations

The guardianship application must be accompanied by two medical recommendations. Each report must be in the form prescribed by law[1] and must

- state the type of mental disorder from which the patient is suffering (this could be mental illness or mental handicap, or both). The reports must agree on which form of mental disorder applies.
- state that the medical grounds set out above apply to the patient[2].
- be signed on or before the date of the application
- be given by a doctor who has personally examined the patient. The examinations may take place together if neither the patient nor his or her **nearest relative** objects. Otherwise there must not be more than five days between the two examinations.

    One of the doctors must have special experience, recognised by his or her **health board**, in the treatment or diagnosis of mental disorder. The other should, if possible, be the patient's general practitioner or another doctor who knows the patient[3].
- contain a statement as to whether the doctor is related to the patient or has any financial interest in him or her being taken into guardianship. Neither doctor can be the person making the guardianship application[4].

It is for the doctors, therefore, to use their professional judgment to determine whether the patient is suffering from a mental disorder and, if so, whether this is of a type which would justify the imposition of the limited supervisory powers of guardianship. They must also set out the reasons for their having reached such a judgment.

If a patient or his or her nearest relative does not believe that the medical grounds apply, then it is essential that he or she obtain independent medical reports to put before the sheriff.

He or she should consider obtaining legal advice from a solicitor. Legal aid may be available to help with this (see chapter 7).

1 See page 209.
2 Mental Health (Scotland) Act 1984, s 37(3)(a).
3 Ibid, s 39.
4 Ibid, s 37(3)(b)(ii).

3.1:6 Welfare report

In addition to the medical reports, the mental health officer appointed by the social work department must supply a recommendation in the prescribed form (see page 210) stating

- that it is in the interests of the welfare of the patient that he or she be received into guardianship
- whether or not the social worker is related to the patient
- whether or not the social worker has any financial interest in having the patient received into guardianship[1]

The social worker, like the doctors, has to use his or her professional judgment to determine whether it is in the patient's interests that he or she be admitted into guardianship. He or she must state the grounds for this belief. Again, if either the patient or his or her nearest relative does not think that these grounds do apply, then they should, if at all possible, find independent witnesses prepared to give evidence. It may be advisable to obtain legal advice from a solicitor.

1 Mental Health (Scotland) Act 1984, s 37(3)(b).

3.1:7 Persons able to make guardianship application

The application is addressed to the social work department for the area where the patient lives and may be made by

- the nearest relative of the patient (see para 2.5:1) or
- a mental health officer[1]

The applicant must have seen the patient within fourteen days of making the application.

If the nearest relative prefers, he or she may request the mental health officer to look into the patient's case. The mental health officer is then under a duty to look into the case as quickly as possible and if he or she decides not to apply for guardianship, to give the nearest relative a letter setting out his or her reasons for this[2].

It may be that the relatives of a patient bring a case to the mental health officer's attention, or he or she may become involved in some other way. In any event the relatives must be kept informed and their views heard. The law says that the mental health officer must

- (so far as reasonably practicable) inform the nearest relative if it is proposed to make a guardianship application and advise the relative of his or her right to object to this[3] and

- bear in mind any views expressed by the relatives of the patient (not just the nearest relative) on the course of action which they would prefer[4].

Finally, though, when the mental health officer has taken all these matters into account, if he or she is of the opinion that an application ought to be made and should be made by him or her, then the law places the mental health officer under a duty to do so[4].

1 Mental Health (Scotland) Act 1984, s 38(1).
2 Ibid, s 38(3).
3 Ibid, s 38(5)(b).
4 Ibid, s 38(4).

3.1:8 Approval by the sheriff

The application should be submitted to the sheriff whose court covers the area where either the patient lives or is in hospital. The application must be delivered to the sheriff within seven days of the patient's last medical examination and must contain a statement that the guardian is willing to act[1].

As in the case of compulsory admission to hospital, the sheriff is under a duty to hear the evidence of both the parties making the application and of those opposing it. Both sides also have the right to call witnesses. The patient has the right to be heard, either in person (unless some reason to the contrary has been established) or through his or her representative.

The sheriff is entitled to stop the patient receiving notice of the proceedings or appearing in person in any guardianship proceedings if he or she considers this would be prejudicial to the patient's health or treatment. (The rules are the same as on compulsory admission to hospital: see para 2.5:4 above)[2].

Any individual wishing to bring or oppose a guardianship application should seriously consider taking legal advice. Legal aid may be available to assist. See chapter 7.

Both the patient and the applicant have a right to request that the proceedings be held in private, and the sheriff may also decide that a private hearing would be advisable[3].

The sheriff may make further inquiries or call other witnesses before reaching a decision. If he or she finally approves the application, the application can then be forwarded to the local social work department.

1 Mental Health (Scotland) Act 1984, s 40(1) (as amended by the Law Reform (Miscellaneous Provisions) (Scotland) Act 1985, s 51).

2 Mental Health (Scotland) Act 1984, ss 40(2), (3), 113 and see Act of Sederunt (Mental Health (Scotland) Act 1984) 1986, SI 1986/545.
3 Mental Health (Scotland) Act 1984, s 40(4).

3.1:9 Errors in application

The rules on amending any errors later found to exist in the application are broadly the same as the rules applying to compulsory admission to hospital (see para 2.5:5). It would be for the social work department to act to amend a guardianship application, however, whilst the **hospital managers** deal with errors on compulsory admission to hospital.

3.1:10 The procedures after admission

If the sheriff approves an application, the social work department must notify the Mental Welfare Commission within seven days of the patient being received into guardianship. The Commission must also be supplied with a copy of the application and the medical and mental health officer's recommendations[1].

After the sheriff grants his or her approval, the application must be forwarded to the social work department within seven days[2]. The guardianship order lasts for a period of up to six months unless it is renewed[3]. The rules relating to renewal are described later in this section. After the first six months, the order may be renewed for a further six months and thereafter for successive periods of one year[4].

1 Mental Health (Scotland) Act 1984, s 41(1).
2 Ibid, s 41(2).
3 Ibid, s 47(1).
4 Ibid, s 47(2).

3.1:11 Renewal of the authority

Between four and six months of the patient being received into guardianship, the **responsible medical officer** must either examine the patient or obtain a report from another doctor on the patient's condition. If the responsible medical officer is the patient's general practitioner he or she may decide to refer the patient to a specialist for an opinion. This examination is intended to establish whether the medical grounds for guardianship still apply, ie whether the patient is still suffering from mental disorder of a nature or degree which warrants the continuation of guardianship. If the doctor considers that the grounds still apply he or she must forward a report to the mental health officer[1].

The mental health officer, on receiving the report of the responsible medical officer, must consider whether the welfare grounds for guardianship still apply, ie whether it is still necessary in the interests of the welfare of the patient that the guardianship order should stand. If he or she considers that it is in the interests of the patient's welfare, the mental health officer must supply the social work department and the Mental Welfare Commission with a report to that effect. He or she must also forward to the Commission the reports already received from the responsible medical officer[2].

When the social work department receives the papers, authority for the guardianship order is renewed from the expiry of the previous period for a further period of six months. If during the next six month period this procedure is repeated, the authority is renewed for one year. The order may be renewed annually thereafter[3].

When the authority is renewed the social work department must inform the patient's nearest relative and the guardian[4]. The social work department also has a general duty to ensure that as far as possible, the patient understands the effects of the provisions under which he or she is being detained and the right of appeal which is available. A copy of any written information given to the patient must be supplied to the patient's nearest relative[5]. These last two provisions are particularly important because the patient has a right to appeal to the sheriff for his or her discharge once during each period in which authority for guardianship has been renewed[6].

1 Mental Health (Scotland) Act 1984, s 47(3)(a).
2 Ibid, s 47(3)(b).
3 Ibid, s 47(4).
4 Ibid, s 47(5).
5 Ibid, s 110.
6 Ibid, s 47(6). See para 3.1:15 for appeals.

3.1:12 Powers and duties of the guardian

The Act is not very precise about the general nature of a guardian's duties. Regulations[1] made under the Act give certain powers to the guardian and certain duties, mainly to keep various people informed, but nowhere is it spelt out in detail what exactly a guardian has to do for the patient in his or her care.

The remit of the guardian must be inferred, therefore, from the powers and duties which are spelt out in detail—thus the duty to keep people informed of the patient's progress and the power to decide where the patient may live, imply that the guardian has a duty to keep him or herself similarly informed and to consider where the patient should live.

There is power in the Act for the **Secretary of State** to make regulations to impose additional duties on guardians and to regulate guardians' exercise of their powers, and this would clearly be necessary if there appeared to be any confusion as to what these powers and duties were[2].

In the case of the social work department there is an overall duty to exercise a 'general supervision' over each patient subject to guardianship[3] and in cases where the guardian is not the social work department the relationship between the individual guardian and the social work department can give rise to some confusion. Whilst the Regulations give the social work department the right of general supervision of all patients subject to guardianship orders, and impose on individual guardians the duty to keep the local authority informed of certain matters, the Act is quite clear that the powers which it gives to guardians are given to them to the exclusion of anyone else—there is no right for the local authority to interfere in the individual guardian's exercise of these powers[4].

Some social work departments may believe that they have a general right to give instructions to the individual guardian on how he or she should make decisions (and this is, in fact, the view taken by the **Scottish Home and**

Health Department's Guide to the Act[5]) but this does not appear to be borne out by a careful study of the wording of the statute. Whilst it is in the interests of all parties, therefore, that the guardian and the social work department do co-operate, the bounds of responsibility should be made quite clear.

Powers of the guardian

The guardian assumes certain controls over the patient once the guardianship application is approved. The guardian can

- decide where the patient should live
- make the patient attend for medical treatment, work, education or training
- insist that certain people, such as doctors and the mental health officer, have access to the patient[6]. But the guardian cannot consent to actual treatment on a patient's behalf. For further information on consent to treatment, see paras 3.2 and 4.4.

What the guardian cannot do

- The guardian does not have any power to use or dispose of the patient's property or to carry out any financial transactions on the patient's behalf[7]. If this is required someone will have to become appointed the **'curator bonis'** of the patient. For further information, see para 3.4:3[8].
- The guardian is not permitted to administer corporal punishment to the patient. Moreover the use of corporal punishment by a guardian is a statutory criminal offence, which must be reported by the court to the Mental Welfare Commission[9].

Duties of the guardian towards the social work department

If the guardian is an individual, not the social work department, he or she must

- supply the social work department with such reports or information about the patient as it may require[10]
- advise the social work department in advance in writing of any permanent change of address proposed by the patient or the guardian[11]
- notify the social work department in writing of the name and address of the patient's general practitioner and any change of general practitioner[12]
- notify the social work department, as soon as practicable[13] if the patient dies
- notify the social work department as soon as practicable if the patient is absent from his or her required place of residence without leave; or if the patient then returns or is brought back[14].

1 The Mental Health (Specified Treatments, Guardianship Duties etc) (Scotland) Regulations 1984, SI 1984/1494, reg 4 (The Treatment and Guardianship Regulations).
2 Mental Health (Scotland) Act 1984, s 43.
3 The Treatment and Guardianship Regulations, reg 4.
4 Mental Health (Scotland) Act 1984, s 41(2).

5 Notes on the Act, paras 224 and 228. The argument turns on what is meant by the power of 'general supervision' given to the social work department. Is it merely the power to oversee the exercise by the guardian of his or her functions or does it also give the right to prescribe regulations and control that exercise? The writers, relying on the dictionary definition of the word, would take the former view. The Scottish Home and Health Department appear to take the latter. The approach in the equivalent English legislation is different. There it is specified that 'it shall be the duty of a private guardian—(c) in exercising the powers and duties conferred or imposed upon him... to *comply with such directions as that authority may give*' (authors' italics): the Mental Health (Hospital, Guardianship and Consent to Treatment) Regulations 1983, SI 1983/893. There is no such duty in the Scottish Regulations. The only remedy the local authority would have if the guardian appeared to it to be unsuitable would be to request the guardian to stand down, and if he or she refused, to apply to the sheriff to have a new guardian appointed. (See Mental Health (Scotland) Act 1984, s 45(1)).
6 Mental Health (Scotland) Act 1984, s 41(2)
7 Ibid, s 41(3)
8 Many people consider this one of the fundamental weaknesses in guardianship as a means of giving practical help to a person who may be confused or unable to deal with his or her household finances. For a discussion of the limitations of guardianship as a means of helping the elderly confused person see the *Report on the Workship on the Rights of the Elderly with Mental Disorder* by Dr W D Boyd of the Mental Welfare Commission (to be published by the World Health Organisation).
9 Mental Health (Scotland) Act 1984, s 41(4)
10 Mental Health (Specified Treatments and Guardianship Duties Etc) (Scotland) Regulations 1984, SI 1984/1494, reg 7(a).
11 Ibid, reg 7(b).
12 Ibid, reg 7(c).
13 Ibid, reg 7(d).
14 Ibid, reg 7(e).

3.1:13 Duties and powers of the social work department

Whether or not the social work department is the guardian, it has a number of duties to persons subject to guardianship who live within its area. It must

- authorise a doctor to be the responsible medical officer[1]. All questions relating to review, renewal, continuation and discharge of a guardianship order are exercised by the responsible medical officer.

- exercise general supervision over every patient subject to guardianship[2]

- arrange for every patient to be visited at least every three months[3]

- notify the Mental Welfare Commission in writing as soon as practicable, if the guardian or the patient changes address permanently[4]

- notify the Mental Welfare Commission in writing as soon as practicable if the patient absents him or herself without leave, returns after a period of absence, dies or if the guardianship order is terminated or discharged[5].

Powers of the social work department

- If the patient absents him or herself without leave from the place where he or she is required to live, it may authorise any officers on its staff (or any other person in writing) to take the patient into custody and return him or her to the guardian. There is a provision that if the patient remains at liberty for twenty-eight days, the guardianship order lapses.

1 Mental Health (Scotland) Act 1984, s 59(1)(b).
2 Mental Health (Specified Treatments and Guardianship Duties etc) (Scotland) Regulations 1984, SI 1984/1494, reg 4.

3 Ibid, reg 5.
4 Ibid, reg 6(1).
5 Ibid, reg 6(2).

3.1:14 Transfer of guardianship

- If the guardian dies or gives notice in writing that he or she no longer wishes to be the guardian, the guardianship vests in the social work department which automatically assumes all the powers which the guardian had[1].
- If the guardian is unable to fulfil his or her duties because of illness or for some other reason the social work department may take over as guardian or approve somebody else to act as guardian on a temporary basis for as long as is necessary[2].

The social work department also has the power to transfer a patient into the guardianship of another person providing both the new and old guardians consent. If the old guardian does not consent then the sheriff must be requested to approve the transfer to the new guardian[3]. The nearest relative and the Mental Welfare Commission must be informed[4].

1 Mental Health (Scotland) Act 1984, s 46(1).
2 Ibid, s 46(2).
3 Ibid, s 45(1).
4 Ibid, s 45(2).

3.1:15 Discharge from guardianship

The patient will not necessarily remain in guardianship for as long as the guardianship order lasts. The patient must be discharged if his or her condition changes or if the relevant medical and welfare grounds cease to apply.

The following people may arrange for the patient to be discharged from guardianship

- the responsible medical officer
- the social work department
- the Mental Welfare Commission
- the nearest relative
- the sheriff.

Discharge by the responsible medical officer

The responsible medical officer may make an order discharging the patient[1]. He or she must make an order if satisfied that the patient is no longer suffering from a mental disorder of a nature or degree which warrants the patient remaining under the guardianship[2], ie that the medical grounds for guardianship no longer apply. In order to discharge this duty, the responsible medical officer must constantly keep the patient's condition under review.

Discharge by the social work department

The social work department has a duty to make an order for discharge where it is satisfied that it is no longer necessary in the interests of the welfare of the patient that he or she should remain under guardianship, ie that the welfare grounds for guardianship no longer apply[3]. In deciding whether a guardianship order should be discharged, the social work department will rely on the opinion of the mental health officer who is dealing with the case.

Discharge by the Mental Welfare Commission

The Commission is entitled to make representations to the social work department about any patient whom it considers is being improperly kept under guardianship[4]. This could result in the patient's case being reviewed and he or she may later be discharged by the social work department itself.

The Mental Welfare Commission also has the power and duty to order the discharge of any patient who is the subject of a guardianship order if it is satisfied that either the medical or welfare grounds for guardianship (see para 3.1:3) have ceased to apply[5]. The Commission may order a patient's discharge at any time[6].

Discharge by the nearest relative

The nearest relative of a patient may order the patient's discharge subject to certain restrictions[7].

- The nearest relative must give at least fourteen days notice in writing to the social work department concerned[8]. If the social work department considers that the welfare grounds for the guardianship no longer apply it may either discharge the patient itself or take no steps to prevent the nearest relative from doing so. If the social work department believes the welfare grounds continue to apply, it must inform the responsible medical officer[9].

- The responsible medical officer must inform the social work department if he or she considers that the medical grounds for the guardianship still apply[10]. The social work department must then inform the nearest relative of its views and the views of the responsible medical officer.

- If both the social work department and the responsible medical officer object to the discharge of the patient, then the patient is not discharged. Moreover, the nearest relative is prohibited from attempting to discharge the patient again within the six months after he or she receives the social work department's report[11]. He or she may, however, appeal to the sheriff within twenty-eight days of hearing from the department[12].

If the nearest relative receives no notification of refusal from the social work department within fourteen days, he or she may then make a written order discharging the patient[13]. Such discharge will take effect immediately[14].

See pages 215 and 216 for suggested forms of application for discharge and for discharge of the patient.

Discharge by the sheriff

The sheriff may order a patient's discharge if

- an appeal has been submitted by the patient after a renewal of the guardianship order[15] or
- an appeal has been submitted by the nearest relative[16].

The sheriff must discharge the patient if he or she is satisfied that

- the patient is not at the time of the hearing of the appeal suffering from mental disorder of a nature or degree which warrants his or her remaining under guardianship, or
- it is not necessary in the interest of the welfare of the patient that he or she should remain under guardianship

ie unless both the medical and welfare grounds for guardianship apply, the sheriff must discharge the patient[17].

Discharge on compulsory admission to hospital

In certain circumstances a patient under guardianship may be compulsorily admitted to hospital. Where an order is made by a sheriff admitting the patient to hospital, the guardianship order automatically comes to an end[18]. The order is not, however, terminated if the patient is admitted to hospital under the emergency or short-term detention procedures.

1 Mental Health (Scotland) Act 1984, s 50(2).
2 Ibid, s 50(3).
3 Ibid, s 50(4).
4 Ibid, s 3(2)(d).
5 Ibid, s 50(3), (4).
5 Ibid, s 50(2).
7 Ibid, s 50(6).
8 Ibid, s 51. The Act does not prescribe any particular form for the discharge notice, simply that it should be in writing. A suggested form is set out on pages 215 and 216.
9 Ibid, s 51(1)(a).
10 Ibid s 51(1)(b).
11 Ibid, s 51(1)(c).
12 Ibid, s 51(2).
13 Ibid, s 51.
14 Ibid, s 51(1).
15 Ibid, s 47(6).
16 Ibid, s 51(2).
17 Ibid, s 50(5).
18 Ibid, s 50(7).

3.2 COMPULSORY MEDICAL TREATMENT FOR PATIENTS LIVING IN THE COMMUNITY

With the advancement of modern drugs, there are certain conditions which can be kept under control, even if they are not cured, by the regular administration of drugs, which may be given daily or by periodical injections.

Provided he or she continues to take the appropriate drugs, a patient suffering, for example, from schizophrenia, may be able to live in the community, returning either to hospital or to his or her general practitioner under the hospital's supervision, for a regular injection. However, should the patient fail to take the prescribed drugs, his or her condition may deteriorate to a state even worse than it was before treatment started.

This has revealed what some doctors have described as an 'unfortunate lacuna' in the Mental Health Acts in England and Scotland[1]. Many patients, understandably, dislike and wish to free themselves of the regular reliance on drugs and will not agree voluntarily to take the drugs which are prescribed for them.

There is no way that compulsory medical treatment can be given to anyone other than a patient compulsorily detained under section 18 of the Act (see para 4.4).

A patient can be compulsorily detained only if his or her mental disorder is such that it is 'appropriate for him [or her] to receive medical treatment in a hospital' and [such treatment] 'cannot be provided unless he [or she] is detained under . . . the Act'[2].

An order can be made under s 18 only if some degree of in-patient treatment is envisaged by the doctors—they cannot obtain an order for a patient whom they wish to treat in the community by compulsory drug treatment[3].

Treatment for the first six months

Once a patient has been admitted under the s 18 procedure, reviews of his or her case are made and the test of what degree of in-patient care is required is different.

The responsible medical officer who examines the patient must order the patient's discharge if he or she is satisfied that the patient is not suffering from a mental disorder which makes it appropriate for him or her to be 'liable to be detained' in a hospital for medical treatment[4].

The distinction between the requirements for admission and for review is that for admission the patient requires to be 'detained' in hospital, whereas on review he or she merely needs to be 'liable to be detained'. A person who is on leave of absence from the hospital, living in the community, is still liable to be detained and is still subject to the provisions of the Act and the requirement to submit to compulsory treatment[5].

The test for the responsible medical officer reviewing a case, therefore, is whether the patient should remain subject to the restrictions of the compulsory admission procedure, possibly whilst living in the community, or whether the patient should be totally discharged.

Renewal of the authority to detain

If the doctors consider that a patient remaining in the community continues to require the compulsory administration of drugs after the initial six month period of detention they will have to apply to have the initial authority renewed (see para 2.6:1). The test is then, again, the **statutory grounds for admission**—ie the responsible medical officer must report and the sheriff must be satisfied that the patient needs treatment in hospital which cannot be provided unless he or she is detained[6]. At least some degree of in-patient care must be envisaged.

Treatment in the community

Psychiatrists have felt that this requirement has made it very difficult for them to treat patients whom they consider unco-operative, who do not strictly need hospital treatment and who could be released into the community if there were some way of compelling them to take their drugs.

It can be said only that the legislation does not envisage the compulsory administration of drugs outside the hospital setting, and whilst care in the community remains less than ideal there is clearly some logic in this approach.

One way to encourage a patient to take his or her drugs whilst living in the community is to use the guardianship procedure. A guardian does not have the power to consent to treatment on the patients' behalf or to force him or her to take drugs, but he or she does have the power to insist that the patient attends for medical treatment and to insist that doctors have access to the patients[7]. Using this procedure the doctors could continue to monitor a patient's case and the patient could remain in the community so long as he or she was willing to continue the relevant drug treatment voluntarily.

1 Diana Brahams 'Treatment of Unco-operative Psychiatric Patients in the Community: Mental Health Act in need of Reform' The Lancet, 12 April 1986, page 863.
2 Mental Health (Scotland) Act 1984, s 17(1).
3 Ibid s 96, and for a full discussion see *AB and CB v E* 1987 SCLR 419.
4 Mental Health (Scotland) Act 1984, s 22(4)(b).
5 Ibid, s 27(5).
6 Ibid, s 30(3).
7 Ibid, s 41(2)(b), (c).

3.3 MARRIAGE AND DIVORCE

3.3:1 Marriage

The fact that someone is suffering from a mental disorder does not necessarily mean marriage is not possible. However, it is not possible for a valid marriage to take place where one of the parties would be regarded by the courts as insane. What is meant is that the person is not capable of understanding what he or she is doing or its effect[1].

1 Marriage (Scotland) Act 1977, s 5(4).

3.3:2 Divorce

Where a mentally disordered person's spouse seeks a divorce

A divorce may be granted on a number of different grounds. Two of these are particularly relevant to mentally disordered people. These are divorce on the ground of unreasonable behaviour[1] and divorce on the ground that the parties have lived apart for five years[2].

It is not a defence to a divorce action on the ground of unreasonable behaviour, that the behaviour relied on arose from mental disorder[3].

If a patient has been in hospital for more than five years then divorce could be obtained by the patient's spouse without the patient's consent.

Even where there is no defence to the divorce being granted, there may be a defence on the financial aspects[4] and matters to do with who is to have the children and the right to see them. In the divorce the spouse may seek **aliment** for children under eighteen. For themselves, they may seek a lump sum payment out of any capital. In appropriate circumstances there can be an order transferring property from one party to the other, for example, the matrimonial home. The court can also require the making of a recurrent financial payment (periodical allowance).

When a patient is sued for divorce he or she will be **'served'** with a **'summons'** if the action is to be in the Court of Session in Edinburgh, or an '**initial writ**' if it is to be in the sheriff court. A solicitor should be contacted immediately so that the patient's interests can be safeguarded. There is a procedure for appointing a person to take on the position as defender where the action is against someone who is mentally disordered. The person is appointed by the court and is known as a **curator ad litem**. **Legal aid** may be available (see chapter 7).

Failure to defend may result in money becoming payable in excess of what the court would have ordered if the defender's case had been presented to it. Failure to defend might result also in the defender being deprived of any right to see the children in circumstances where that could have been avoided. It may also result in a husband being found liable for all the expenses of the action in circumstances where that, too, could have been avoided.

Where a mentally disordered person seeks a divorce

A person's right to get a divorce is not likely to be affected by being mentally disordered. A solicitor should be contacted. Financial aid in the form of 'legal advice and assistance' and 'legal aid' may be available to pay for advice from a solicitor and for expenses connected with the court action (see chapter 7).

3.3:3 Protection from sexual abuse

There are special provisions in the criminal law designed to protect mentally handicapped people. These are dealt with in chapter 4 at para 3.4:4.

1 Divorce (Scotland) Act 1976, s 1(2)(b).
2 Ibid, s 1(2)(e).
3 Ibid, s 1(2)(b).
4 The relevant legislation is the Family Law (Scotland) Act 1985.

3.4 FINANCIAL AND PROPERTY MATTERS

This section deals with managing patients' business and financial affairs; wills and trusts; employment rights; social security benefits and the community charge ('poll tax').

3.4:1 Managing a patient's affairs: introduction

If a mentally disordered person is living in the community, whether under a formal guardianship order or not, various day-to-day financial and business decisions will have to be made by him or her or on his or her behalf, if he or she cannot take such decisions on his or her own.

Who will collect the person's pension? Should he or she enter residential accommodation? Who should manage his or her bank account? How can property of the mentally disordered person be protected when he or she is unable to take care of it?

3.4:2 The distinction between people capable of managing their own affairs and others

The rights of people to deal generally with their own money and property and the rights of other people to deal with it, depend upon whether the person has the physical and mental capacity to manage his or her own affairs or not. Normally this will depend on the seriousness of the mental disorder (*Fraser v Paterson* 1987 SLT 562). Mental incapacity means that the person is not able to understand the transaction he or she is being asked to enter. Physical disabilities may also be relevant.

A clear distinction between people capable of managing their own affairs and people who are not, is to a considerable extent unreal. There have been suggestions that the law should be reformed on a basis that takes this into account[1].

The person capable of managing his or her own property and affairs

There is no legal reason why such a person should not continue to deal with his or her financial and personal property affairs on the same basis as if he or she were not suffering from a mental illness or handicap. It may be, however, that he or she would welcome help. Anyone can give permission for someone to act on his or her own behalf. For ordinary day-to-day expenditures this can be done satisfactorily on an informal basis—for example getting a relative or friend to purchase small items.

In practice a member of the family or a friend will often be allowed to collect a pension. A particular person can be appointed to deal with social security benefits[2].

Powers of attorney. For more important business the best practical solution is for the person to grant a **power of attorney**. This simply means signing a formal document, giving the person named in the document power to act on behalf of the mentally disordered person either in connection with certain specified matters, or generally. The document should preferably be signed in front of two witnesses, and, if the power extends to dealing with a flat, house or land of any sort, it must be[3]. Solicitors have standard forms available.

The person incapable of managing his or her own affairs

Where there is immediate danger of property being lost or damaged anyone can step in and act to save the property, unless in doing so they act so negligently that they make things worse than they would have been if nothing had been done. The person acting is entitled to claim any reasonable expenses incurred[4].

The regional or islands council has a duty to take reasonable steps to try and avoid damage to or loss of property belonging to a hospital patient (and this would include someone on leave of absence from the hospital) who is not able to act or to take the necessary steps to do this[5]. They can enter the person's house without permission in the course of carrying out this responsibility.

It may be that a power of attorney was granted at a time when the person was capable of doing that. Powers of attorney come to an end if the granter becomes incapable of managing his or her own affairs[6]. If there is someone with a power of attorney, that person's powers do not exclude other people, who may be entitled, from acting.

Any person holding a power of attorney for another, should be kept advised of that person's state of health. If the relatives and friends do not feel the person holding the power of attorney is responding appropriately when told of someone's deteriorating mental health, the Mental Welfare Commission should be consulted, and, if necessary, a solicitor too[7].

1 See Workshop Report by Dr W D Boyd, Mental Welfare Commission for Scotland, Workshop on the Rights of the Elderly with Mental Disorder, Edinburgh—19–20 November 1987 (to be published by the World Health Organisation); Scottish Action on Dementia: *Dementia and the Law: The Challenge Ahead* (December 1988).
2 Social Security (Claims and Payments) Regulations 1987, SI 1987/1968, reg 33(1), (3).
3 The Scottish Law Commission has proposed important changes in the law regarding witnesses to signatures. It has prepared a draft bill, the Requirements of Writing (Scotland) Bill.
4 In law the person is known as a *negotiorum gestor*.
5 National Assistance Act 1948, s 49 as amended.
6 This is so whether the document creating the power of attorney states it or not. It is not quite clear in law just exactly when the power of attorney comes to an end. A possible view is that rather than being the moment when the person becomes incapable of managing their own affairs, it is when the person acting under it came to know or ought reasonably to have known of the incapacity. It is not possible in Scotland to have a power of attorney that lasts beyond incapacity. In England it is, under the Enduring Powers of Attorney Act 1985.
7 The Mental Welfare Commission has specifically expressed interest in this in *Does The Patient Come First?—An Account of the Work of the Mental Welfare Commission for Scotland between 1975 and 1980* pp 18–19. Problems have been encountered and there are special difficulties where a mentally disordered person is living in the community and his or her assets are not large enough to justify the appointment of a curator (*Annual Report of the Mental Welfare Commission for Scotland 1987* para 5.16).

3.4:3 Curator bonis

Where a curatory is appropriate

A person known as a **curator bonis** (or **curator** for short) may be appointed by the **sheriff court** or the **Court of Session** to administer the person's property and affairs[1]. It costs more in the Court of Session.

The person whose affairs the curator is appointed to manage is referred to by the law as the **ward**.

Once a curator is appointed there must always be a curator until the ward becomes once again capable of managing his or her own affairs. Curatories cost a significant amount of money to operate. Many people regard them as expensive and over-complex.

It is not necessary to appoint a curator if the person's sole form of finance is state benefits. Someone can be appointed to uplift social security benefits[2].

Where money is limited it may be best to see if informal arrangements can be made[3]. But sometimes that may be impossible, either because some legal formality is involved in doing something (e.g. selling a flat), or because somebody refuses to go along with the arrangement (e.g. a building society might require a curator to be appointed before money is withdrawn from an account).

Applying for a curator

The procedure for the appointment of a curator involves submitting to the court a formal document, called a petition. Two written statements by doctors who have examined the patient have to accompany the petition. The process takes around three months on average to complete[4].

Anybody concerned about the patient, such as a husband or wife, a relative or a friend, can go to the court to get a curator appointed. The regional or islands council can ask the court to appoint a curator if no one else does[5]. So may the Mental Welfare Commission[6].

In practice many curators are solicitors or accountants. A curator is entitled to be paid[7]. But relatives or others involved with the ward may be appointed. If so, they must be in a position to deal efficiently with the ward's affairs—keeping accounts and so on—perhaps with help.

The curator's task

The job of the curator is to manage the ward's affairs with a view to the best that can be done for him or her. The curator has no duty to consider the best interests of the ward's relations or heir to any property. A curator has in a general sense a duty to preserve the estate of the ward[8].

There has been criticism by many working with mentally disordered people that the law overemphasises keeping the ward's estate intact, and so limits the curator's using it in the best way to enhance the day to day life of the ward. Because of this anyone considering making long-term financial support for a mentally disordered person will probably find it is likely to be appropriate to set up a trust (see para 3.4:5).

However, financial support of the ward comes within a curator's powers[9]. The power given in certain circumstances to sell assets belonging to the ward underlines this[10].

Major decisions affecting the ward's property can be taken only with the approval of the Accountant of Court and, in certain cases, of the court which appointed the curator. Some concern has been expressed that it appears that anything beyond payment for routine maintenance might be seen as a major decision. Curators certainly have to get the Accountant of Court's permission to use the ward's capital assets[11]. Recently it has been held by the Court of Session that the Accountant of Court may allow the use of the ward's capital for his or her maintenance even if the result sooner or later would be that it would all be used up[12].

1 Solicitors will find it helpful to consult the papers of the Law Society of Scotland PQLE Curatories Seminar, 7 June 1988 for detailed guidance on both the law and practice of running curatories.
2 See above at para 3.4:2 (footnote 2).
3 Guidance is given in *Information for Families of Person Subject to Curatory*, p 4, issued by the Accountant of Court.
4 In a situation where it is absolutely essential it is possible to get an interim (ie temporary) curator appointed before the process is complete.
5 Mental Health (Scotland) Act 1984, s 92(1). The Act says that the local authority (ie regional or islands council) 'shall petition the court'. There is thus a duty, although it is subject to the authority being satisfied that a curator ought to be appointed (s 92(1)(b)).
6 By contrast to the position with regard to the regional or islands council the Mental Welfare Commission '*may* petition the court'. The primary responsibility where no individual petitions the court, is thus conceived as lying with the regional or islands council.
7 The amount is fixed by the accountant of court and depends on the value of the assets.

8 *Broadfoot's Curator Bonis, Noter,* Court of Session, Inner House, 1989 SLT 566, SCLR 317.
9 Walker *Judicial Factors,* pp 107–108.
10 Trusts (Scotland) Act 1961, s 2 (as amended by Law Reform (Miscellaneous Provisions) (Scotland) Act 1980, s 8). The Mental Welfare Commission does sometimes suggest to curators that more money be spent on a patient (*Annual Report of the Mental Welfare Commission for Scotland 1987* para 5.14).
11 *Annual Report of the Mental Welfare Commission for Scotland 1986,* paras 11.6 to 11.11. The Accountant of Court will generally only permit special expenditures on the basis that there is income that has accumulated.
12 *Broadfoot's Curator Bonis, Noter* (above). A petition has to be made to the court for special powers.

3.4:4 Employment[1]

A person may have been dismissed by an employer because of a mental illness. If dissatisfied with the reasons given for dismissal or the circumstances surrounding it, they may be in a position to challenge the dismissal by applying to an industrial tribunal. If the industrial tribunal thinks the dismissal is unfair, it can award compensation or can recommend reinstatement, normally the former.

Forms can be obtained from **Citizens Advice Bureaux** or the Department of Employment or through a solicitor.

Applications can be made without using a solicitor. However, employment law is complex and constantly changing. There are also strict time limits on making an application to an industrial tribunal. So, expert advice should be obtained, normally from a solicitor. If the patient is a member of a trade union, a union representative could be consulted.

Whether an employer's decision to dismiss on the ground of ill-health will be held to be unfair depends on the circumstances. Each case must be considered on its own facts and particular circumstances and perhaps on the size and nature of the firm. In some cases four to six weeks' absence from work may justify dismissal while in others six months may not.

Employers with twenty or more workers have an obligation to employ registered disabled people. People with mental illness or handicap can register[2].

1 The importance of employment for people with mental illness is emphasised in *Mental Health in Focus,* Report on the Mental Health Services for Adults in Scotland (HMSO, 1985), paras 4.20–4.33.
2 Disabled Persons (Employment) Acts 1944 and 1958. See also Code of Good Practice on the Employment of Disabled People (published by the Manpower Services Commission).

3.4:5 Wills and trusts[1]

It is not possible for a person who would be regarded by the courts as insane, to make a legally valid will. In this context, that means that someone will be regarded as 'insane' if that person is not capable of understanding what he or she is doing by making a will, and the effect of that will[2]. It is not possible for a person who becomes insane to cancel a valid will previously made.

It is not possible for either a person with a power of attorney or a curator bonis to make a will on the patient's behalf.

A patient's mental disorder may not be of such a nature as to amount to insanity in the eyes of the law. In this case a valid will can be made. But it is

Financial and property matters

possible that people who might benefit from challenging a will might be encouraged to do so by the fact that it was signed by an in-patient.

Accordingly, to avoid dispute, if a patient wishes to make a will, it is a good idea to get written statements from two doctors with knowledge of the patient's condition to the effect that the patient is mentally fit to make a will and that the patient understands what he or she is doing. These can then be kept with the will.

Even where a very simple will is intended it is advisable that it be drafted by a solicitor, since there is always a danger that it will be ambiguous.

If the patient suffers from some disability, other than mental disorder, that prevents him or her reading or signing a document, there is a special procedure called 'notarial execution' for the will to be read aloud to the person making it and then signed on that person's behalf by a minister or a lawyer. Unless this procedure is available a will can be valid[3] only if:

- it is signed at the bottom of every page by the person making it and also signed by that person at the end before two witnesses, who also sign there, or
- it is entirely in the handwriting of the person making it and signed at the end. If there is more than one page they must be in some way linked to the last. (This is called a holograph will), or
- the person writing it writes the words 'adopted as holograph' in handwriting at the end and signs immediately below that. (These words mean 'this is to be treated as my handwriting'). Again if there is more than one page they must be in some way linked to the last.

A person suffering from mental disorder of any degree can benefit from another person's will. Such a person can also be the beneficiary of a trust[4], whether it is set up by someone during their life or on death in a will. It may in some circumstances be a good way of providing an income for a mentally disordered person for a relative or a friend to set up a trust for his or her benefit. Anyone thinking of doing this should consult a solicitor.

If a patient is a beneficiary under a will or trust and is not receiving what is due, the Mental Welfare Commission should be advised, and a solicitor consulted in any case of doubt.

1 For a straightforward basic guide to the law of succession see Nichols *In The Event of Death*; Ward, *Scots Law and the Mentally Handicapped*, Chapter 17 (see Booklist).
2 'The question is simply whether he understands what he is about.' (*Sivewright v Sivewright's Trs* 1920 SC (HL) 63 at 64, per Viscount Haldane LC.
3 The Scottish Law Commission has suggested that the law relating to the witnessing of signatures should be changed and has produced a draft bill, the Requirements of Writing (Scotland) Bill.
4 Useful guidance is in *Ward* (see footnote 1), chapters 15 to 17.

3.4:6 Social security benefits available to the patient

Introduction

Mental illness or handicap is likely to have an impact on financial resources. This is obviously the case if the person affected loses a job, or cannot carry on working if self-employed. Mental disorder may also have financial consequences for any family the person may have or others who are closely involved in looking after him or her.

There are accordingly various social security benefits that may be claimed depending on the circumstances. Mental illness can also affect rights to social security benefits already being received. In particular going into hospital for an extended period of time can result in certain benefits being reduced or stopped altogether. There is a DSS leaflet (NI. 9) summarising the position. The local social security office should be informed where someone receiving benefit goes into hospital or comes out of hospital.

Sometimes sufferers are paid for work they do in the context of their treatment.

There are some sixty social security benefits in existence. Broadly speaking in cases of illness, and disability generally, the factors relevant to determining what benefits are available depend on:

- whether the claimant (or sometimes the claimant's husband or wife) has paid enough national insurance contributions. Some benefits are available only if contribution conditions are met
- the seriousness of the disability
- the length of time the disability has lasted
- the claimant's financial resources. Some benefits are available only if existing resources have fallen below a certain level.

Social security benefits and the conditions of entitlement to them are often changed. So it is essential to get up-to-date information. A good starting point is a leaflet produced by the Department of Social Security called 'Which Benefit' (Leaflet FB. 2). It is available from local social security offices and some post offices. It can also be obtained by post from DSS Leaflets Unit, PO Box 21, Stanmore, Middlesex HA7 1AY. The leaflet deals briefly with all of the most common benefits and gives references to other more detailed leaflets dealing with each benefit mentioned. These can be obtained from the same sources.

The following is a brief outline of the principal benefits likely to be relevant in cases of mental disorder:

Statutory sick pay (SSP) (DSS Leaflet NI. 244). This is available only to employees (not self-employed) and is paid by employers.

Many employees are entitled as one of the conditions of their contract of employment to be paid their normal wage for a period of illness. Statutory sick pay is designed to cover the situation where there is no such entitlement. Any payment made as a contractual entitlement is set against statutory sick pay due and vice versa.

The employer must pay statutory sick pay for twenty-eight weeks where an employee is unable to work through illness (including mental illness) in any tax year. If the employee has a recurrent illness there are provisions for separate shorter periods of being off to be treated together so that statutory sick pay is payable for all of them until they add up to a total of twenty-eight weeks.

There is no requirement to have paid a certain amount in national insurance contributions. But employees who do not earn enough to have to pay national insurance contributions are not entitled to statutory sick pay.

Sickness benefit (DSS Leaflet NI.16). This benefit depends on sufficient national insurance contributions having been paid and the claimant being unable to work because of illness (including mental illness). It cannot be paid while statutory sick pay is being paid. The period it is paid for depends on whether statutory sick pay was paid or not. If it was, sickness benefit is paid for twenty weeks after statutory sick pay stops. In other cases it is paid for twenty-eight weeks.

Invalidity benefit (DSS Leaflet NI. 16A). This is available where someone is still unable to work because of illness (including mental illness) after the periods for which statutory sick pay and sickness benefit are paid have come to an end. The benefit can have a maximum of four components:

- basic invalidity pension
- additional invalidity pension
- invalidity allowance
- increases for dependants.

To get basic invalidity pension, sufficient national insurance contributions have to have been paid to have qualified for sickness benefit, even if the claimant has actually been receiving statutory sick pay (for which national insurance contributions do not need to have been paid).

Additional invalidity pension is an extra amount paid on top of the basic invalidity pension. It is available only to people who have been employees (not self-employed). The amount paid depends on the level of earnings as an employee, that the claimant has had since April 1978.

Invalidity allowance is an extra amount paid on top of the basic invalidity pension or on both that and additional invalidity pension. The claimant must be under sixty (if a man) or under fifty-five (if a woman) when the illness began. (The amount paid also varies with age.) If a person gets additional invalidity pension, the allowance is reduced by the amount they receive.

Increases for dependants are payable depending on certain earnings limits.

There are special rules affecting payment of invalidity benefit where someone reaches retirement age. The invalidity pension will usually stop, but any allowance payable may be added to retirement pension.

Severe disablement allowance (DSS Leaflet NI. 252). This is paid to people below retirement age who cannot work but cannot get sickness benefit or invalidity benefit because they do not satisfy the contribution conditions. It takes the place of the benefits known as non-contributory invalidity pension and housewives non-contributory invalidity pension, which were phased out from 1984. It is payable if the claimant was getting one of these benefits; or was less than twenty when incapacity began; or was assessed as being eighty per cent. disabled. A severe mental disorder could amount to this level of disablement on its own. So could a less severe one if there are other physically incapacitating factors.

In all cases special disablement allowance is payable only after the first twenty-eight weeks of being unable to work.

Attendance allowance (DSS Leaflet NI. 205). This is paid in addition to other benefits to people who require a lot of looking after. No contribution conditions have to be satisfied. The person being looked after must be at least two years old, severely disabled, physically or mentally, and have required looking after for at least six months. A medical examination is carried out. There are two rates of benefit: a higher rate to cover attendance day and night and a lower right to cover night or day attendance only.

Mobility allowance. This is an allowance payable to a person, who because of a physical condition, is

- unable to walk
- virtually unable to walk or
- unable to walk because the exertion required would constitute a danger to life or a serious deterioration in the person's health.

It is a very important benefit, because people receiving mobility allowance do not have the amount they receive deducted from other benefits, such as income support, which they receive.

Although the inability to walk must be caused by a physical condition, that does not mean that people with mental disorders would never be eligible. An autistic person might qualify if it could be shown that his or her inability to walk was caused not by 'controlled or hyperactive' movements, but by a form of 'temporary paralysis'. On the other hand, a person suffering from agoraphobia, who was unable to walk outside the house, would not qualify as his or her inability to walk would caused by a mental condition.

Down's Syndrome is regarded as a physical condition for the purpose of the regulations.

For further information see the *Rights Guide to Non-Means Tested Benefits* published by the Child Poverty Action Group or the *Disability Rights Handbook* (see Booklist).

Income Support and Social Fund (DSS Leaflets SB20 and SB16). These sources of support are 'means-tested'. They were a new system of benefits designed to replace supplementary benefit from 11 April 1988.

Income support is paid to bring income up to a certain level. This means that either it is paid to people with no income at all, or it may be paid to someone with a very low income to bring his or her income up to that level. However, there are special rules in this latter case, so we deal with the two cases separately.

Help with housing costs. Different regulations apply to people living in residential homes; people living in hostels; people living in bed and breakfast accommodation and people living in 'supported accommodation'. The rules are very complex and cannot be adequately explained in a book of this size. To make sure that a person is getting the full benefit to which he or she is entitled, advice should be sought from the citizens advice bureau or welfare rights office. For further reading, see the *National Welfare Benefits Handbook* or *Disability Rights Handbook* (see Booklist).

Someone with no income

In deciding whether someone has an income or not, it is the income of the 'family' that is looked at. The family members whose income is taken into account are husbands/wives, unmarried partners living together and children.

Financial and property matters 55

The benefit will not be available if the claimant has savings of more than £6,000. Where his or her savings are between £3,000 and £6,000 a weekly income of £1 per week for every £250 over £3,000 is assumed to exist whether it does or does not in reality.

There is a special flat rate of benefit for people in residential care. Otherwise the benefit is made up of different elements:

- a personal allowance—ie the basic benefit
  This is based on age and family status. So, for example, quite apart from an amount paid for each dependent child there is a different rate paid to parents over eighteen than to other single people of the same age.

- premium payments
  These are additional payments. Broadly they relate to whether the person has dependent children, is over sixty or is disabled. This would include disability caused by mental disorder.

- housing costs
  Rent will be paid by way of housing benefit (DSS Leaflet RR2). People paying mortgage interest get this paid as a further addition to their income support. Up to 80 per cent. of the community charge (poll tax) is paid as a further addition to income support.

People with some income

Generally people who work for twenty-four hours a week or more will not be able to claim, whatever their income. (If they have dependent children they may be in a position to get family credit (see below).) However, disabled people with a reduced earning capacity will be able to claim even if they are working more than twenty-four hours a week. This would include people disabled because of a mental disorder.

In working out whether someone will be treated as having income the income of the 'family' is taken into account and savings over £3,000 can affect the calculation (see above under 'People with No Income'). In any event a certain amount of income is disregarded. This varies from £4 to £15. The amount is currently £15 a week in the case of disabled people.

The amount of benefit paid is what the claimant would have got with no income, less the amount of the income they do have.

Family credit (DSS Leaflet NI. 261). This benefit is paid to people who work more than twenty-four hours per week, have at least one child and have an income (including the income of any partner) after tax that falls below a certain amount. As explained above there can be situations where disabled people who are working are anyhow entitled to income support.

Fares to hospital (DSS Leaflet H.11). In and out-patients (including those being treated for mental illness) of NHS hospitals can be entitled to payment of all or part of the cost of fares to and from hospital.

Patients living in the Highlands or Islands can get paid fares if they have to travel more than thirty miles (or five miles by water), whatever their income.

For other patients the entitlement depends on having a low income. This condition is satisfied if the patient is getting income support or family credit. People not receiving these benefits can still qualify if their income is low enough. Ask at the hospital and take any benefit order book.

3.4:7 Social security benefits available to people other than the patient

The following benefits are particularly likely to be relevant.

Invalid care allowance (DSS Leaflet NI. 212). This is available to people who give up work to look after someone getting attendance allowance (see above).

Fares to hospital (DSS Leaflets H. 11 and AB 11). If it is medically necessary for someone to travel with a patient who is entitled to payment for fares, the person travelling with them can also get paid.

If you require advice about social security benefits contact your local citizens advice bureau, welfare rights office or the Disablement Income Group (Scotland). (See Appendix 4.)

3.4:8 Social Fund (DSS Leaflet SB 16)

Payments to help with exceptional expenses may be made from this source. Of particular importance to mentally ill or mentally handicapped people in the community are grants known as 'community care grants' from this fund. They may be paid to support a person's move back into the community after a period in hospital or residential care and can be paid to ease exceptional pressures on families[1].

Other payments from the social fund will generally take the form of loans. There is a scheme for crisis loans to deal with emergencies or disasters where the loan is necessary to prevent serious damage or serious risk to health or safety. There is also a general scheme of 'budgeting loans'. As social fund payments are generally discretionary and are also cash-limited the DSS suggests a system of priorities for these to its staff considering applications[2]. Amongst the high priorities are essential items of furniture and household equipment. Suggested medium priorities include clothing, redecoration and repaying of debts. An example of a suggested low priority is the cost of removal.

1 Useful guidance and examples are given in Ennals, Spaull and Thompson, *Rights Guide for Home Owners* (7th edn, 1988/89, published by CPAG/SHAC). It is important to note that these are grants, not loans. The Child Poverty Action Group has reported an unwillingness by DSS officials to make information about community care grants available to claimants.
2 The details are in the *Social Fund Manual* used by DSS offices. See Ogus and Barendt *The Law of Social Security* (3rd edn, 1988) p 516.

3.4:9 Independent Living Fund

Payments from this fund are designed to enable severely disabled people to carry on an independent life in the community. Payments may be made for personal and domestic care needed and also for items of equipment if these considerably reduce the cost of caring. The fund is not part of the income

Financial and property matters 57

support system. It is administered by trustees on a discretionary basis. To apply for support from the fund write to: The Independent Living Fund, PO Box 183, Nottingham, NG8 3RD.

3.4:10 Community charge ('poll tax')

Most people who are eighteen or over have to pay the community charge ('poll tax'). People on very low incomes pay 20 per cent. However, some people are exempt altogether. To get an exemption it is necessary to apply to the Community Charges Registration Officer. If exemption is refused there is a right of appeal to the Community Charges Registration Officer to reconsider[1]. After that there is a right to appeal to the **sheriff**.

Long-term[2] patients in hospital[3] (including nursing homes etc where care or treatment is given)[4] are exempt. But only some mentally disordered people living in the community are exempt. For them it is necessary to get a certificate from a doctor that the person is 'severely mentally impaired'[5]. In addition he or she must be getting or entitled to get one of the long-term social security benefits for disabled people[6]. There is a list of these benefits in the community charge ('poll tax') legislation[7].

Just what state will amount to being 'severely mentally impaired' as required in this context hs been changed[8].

The change is retrospective. In this context a person is 'severely mentally impaired' if he or she 'has severe impairment of his intelligence and social functioning which appears to be permanent'[8]. This would include severely mentally handicapped people. It also would include people whose intelligence and social functioning have been severely impaired by other conditions. A clear example is the case of sufferers from the most common form of dementia, Alzheimer's Disease. It was principally as a result of a campaign by people closely involved with Alzheimer's Disease that the definition was changed. But there are many other conditions that would also be covered, for example other forms of dementia, or genetic degenerative conditions, such as Huntingdon's Chorea, or, indeed, conditions arising from a host of different causes, for example vitamin deficiencies, or physical injuries. The cause is not important. The condition does have to 'appear to be permanent'. What this means seems to be that the condition is incurable or otherwise long term, rather than a state that is absolutely continuous without temporary improvements.

Health boards give advice to doctors on what would be covered. But this is only guidance as to how the Health Board sees that law. The law itself is contained only in the legislation[9].

1 Abolition of Domestic Rates etc (Scotland) Act 1987, s 16 (as amended by Local Government Finance Act 1988, Sch 12, para 25). Where exemption is refused on the ground that a person has not been able to get a doctor's certificate that he or she is severely mentally impaired, the appeal could not be sustained. Having the certificate is itself a requirement for exemption. Judicial review (see para 2.5:4) of the doctor's (or doctors') decision would seem the only possible course open.
2 The hospital (or nursing home etc) must be the person's 'sole or main residence': Abolition of Domestic Rates Etc (Scotland) Act 1987, Sch 1A, para 8(1) (added by Local Government Finance Act 1988, Sch 12). This could also be the case with a long-term patient who is on temporary leave of absence.
3 Abolition of Domestic Rates Etc (Scotland) Act 1987, Sch 1A, para 8 deals with National Health Service hospitals.

4 Ibid, para 9 covers private institutions.
5 Ibid, para 4(1)(c). There is a standard form certificate: National Health Service (General Medical and Pharmaceutical Services) (Scotland) Amendment (No 2) Regulations 1988, SI 1988/1454. The doctor's certificate is not binding on the Community Charge Registration Officer. The person must actually be 'severely mentally impaired' as well: Abolition of Domestic Rates etc (Scotland) Act 1987, Sch 1A, para 4(1)(b).
6 Exemption can be obtained for 1989–1990 also on the basis that the severely mentally impaired person is of retirement age (sixty for women, sixty-five for men). Personal Community Charge (Exemption for the Severely Mentally Impaired) (Scotland) Regulations 1989, SI 1989/2234, reg 6.
7 Abolition of Domestic Rates Etc (Scotland) Act 1987, para 4(2); Personal Community Charge (Exemptions) (Scotland) Regulations 1989, SI 1989/63, reg 4 and sch 1; SI 1989/2234, reg 3.
8 Abolition of Domestic Rates etc (Scotland) Act 1987, Sch 1A, para 4(3) (as amended by SI 1989/2234, reg 4).
9 The original advice in NHS Circular No 1988 GEN 25 is now out of date.

3.5 EDUCATION, TRAINING AND AFTERCARE

3.5:1 Introduction

As 'care in the community' becomes the stated aim of the government, we need to examine what legal resources are available to ensure that the needs of patients in the community are met. 'Community care' envisages that as many patients as possible will be removed from the restrictions of institutional life in a hospital to a form of care in the community which could offer a greater diversity of response to their needs.

A necessary consequence of this approach is that there should be adequate provision of services and facilities for mentally ill people in the community. This entails the provision of adequate resources and, indeed, implies some diversification of resources or commitment of extra resources. Without this, community care is not a viable possibility. Critics argue that adequate resources have not yet been put into community care.

Local authorities have legal duties to provide facilities for persons suffering from mental disorder living within their area. These duties are sometimes little known. They are laid down in a variety of statutes. These are outlined below.

Campaigners concerned to achieve a greater diversification of resources into community care, as well as those directly concerned with patients being cared for in the community, should examine the range of statutory duties on local authorities that exist at present and consider whether the statutes could be used to improve services for a particular community.

Legal action directed against a local authority may be an appropriate method of seeking an improvement in the level of services or facilities.

The chances of obtaining an order from a court will depend firstly on the way in which the statute phrases the obigations of the local authority.

In many cases the local authority will have a very wide discretion, for example to provide such facilities 'as it thinks fit' or as 'it considers reasonable'. In other cases there may be a positive duty. This itself may allow for some discretion as to the amount and form of the services and facilities the authority must provide. The degree to which a court would take into account a local authority's discretion in these matters will accordingly vary.

If you consider the facilities in your area for the mentally disordered are not adequate, as part of pressing for them to be better, see a solicitor. Legal action may be a worthwhile course.

3.5:2 Statutory background

The duties of social work departments to provide services and facilities for mentally disordered people are set out in the following statutes

- the Social Work (Scotland) Act 1968, ss 12, 59

- the Chronically Sick and Disabled Persons Act 1970 (as amended by the Chronically Sick and Disabled Persons (Scotland) Act 1972)

- the Disabled Persons (Services, Consultation and Representation) Act 1986. This Act extends the rights of disabled people (including people disabled by a mental disorder) by enabling them to have a greater say in the provision of services and it enlarges the duties of the social work departments to assess disabled people's needs.
  Not all of the 1986 Act has yet come into force, and the government has said that those sections which require financial outlay will be postponed until resources are available. Nevertheless, workers with mentally disordered people should monitor the 1986 Act's progress as it makes important reforms in the present system.

3.5:3 General welfare duties

Each social work department is under a duty

- to make available, on such a scale as it may consider suitable, adequate and appropriate for the area, advice, guidance and assistance for mentally disordered people[1]. The help envisaged includes the provision of facilities and the making of cash grants.

- to provide such residential and other establishments (including day care centres) as may be required to enable them to comply with the above requirement[2].

1 Social Work (Scotland) Act 1968, s 12 (amended by the Disabled Persons (Services, Consultation and Representation) Act 1986, s 12).
2 Social Work (Scotland) Act 1968, s 59 (amended by the Disabled Persons (Services, Consultation and Representation) Act 1986, s 12).

3.5:4 Information

There is a duty on social work departments to provide information on services which they and other organisations provide within their area for mentally disordered people and to take steps to make sure that mentally disordered people receive such information[1].

1 Chronically Sick and Disabled Persons Act 1970, s 1 (as amended by the Chronically Sick and Disabled Persons (Scotland) Act 1972 and the Disabled Persons (Consultation, etc) Act 1986, s 9). For an example of what can be done, see Lothian Regional Council's excellent *Directory of Services for People with a Mental Handicap*.

3.5:5 Practical help

If a social work department believes that a disabled person 'has a need of' any of the following, they must make them available

- practical help in the home
- radio, television, library or other recreational facilities
- lectures, games, outings or other recreational facilities outside the home
- help in taking advantage of educational facilities available
- help with travelling costs to day centres etc provided by the social work department
- help in adapting his or her home to provide greater comfort, security, or convenience
- help with taking holidays, at holiday homes or elsewhere
- help with meals at home or elsewhere
- a telephone[1]

Section 4 of the Disabled Persons (Services, Consultation and Representation) Act 1986, provides that a social work department is under a duty to assess the needs of a disabled person if it receives a request from

- him or her
- his or her 'authorised representative' (as defined in that Act)
- his or her 'carer' (as defined in that Act).

This reform to the law gives a clearer duty to the social work department to act on a request and give disabled people the practical help they may need.

1 Chronically Sick and Disabled Persons Act 1970, s 2 (as amended by the Chronically Sick and Disabled Persons (Scotland) Act 1972).

3.5:6 Aftercare services

The Mental Health (Scotland) Act 1984 provides that it is the duty of the social work department to provide aftercare services for people who have been or who are suffering from mental disorder[1]. The local authority may provide these services on its own or in co-operation with health boards or voluntary organisations as it thinks fit[2].

This is an absolute duty of the social work department. There is no limitation in the Act to the effect that the services should be of such nature or extent as the social work department thinks fit. If, therefore, a person who is mentally disordered does not appear to have adequate aftercare support, the social work department may be in breach of its statutory duty.

1 Mental Health (Scotland) Act 1984, s 8(1).
2 Ibid, s 8(2).

3.5:7 Training and occupation for people with a mental handicap

Whilst section 1 of the Education (Scotland) Act 1980 imposes a duty on education authorities to provide education facilities for mentally handicapped people, the Mental Health (Scotland) Act 1984 goes further. This imposes on the regional or islands council the duty to provide suitable training and occupation for people suffering from mental handicap who are over school age and who are not hospital residents[1]. The local authority can discharge this duty by helping voluntary or other bodies to set up such facilities.

The regional or islands council must also arrange for transport to be available for people wishing to use training facilities[2].

If adequate training facilities are not available in a particular area, the regional or islands council may be in breach of its statutory duty.

1 Mental Health (Scotland) Act 1984, s 11(1).
2 Ibid, s 11(2).

3.6 HOUSING RIGHTS OF MENTALLY DISORDERED PEOPLE

3.6:1 Introduction

This book cannot deal in detail with the various types of housing which may be available for people who have had a mental illness or who are mentally handicapped. There are various bodies, both statutory and voluntary, which provide sheltered housing and supported accommodation, although this is in no way adequate to deal with the numbers of mentally disordered people who could potentially benefit.

Information on what housing may be available in any area, is available from

- the social work department
- the housing department
- the Scottish Association of Mental Health (see Appendix 4), which has a list of voluntary supported accommodation projects for people who have been or are suffering from mental illness
- the Scottish Society for the Mentally Handicapped (see Appendix 4), which has details of local housing projects for mentally handicapped people
- Ark and Key Housing Associations (see Appendix 4) which provide accommodation specifically for mentally handicapped people in the east and west of Scotland respectively.

Each body offering accommodation will have different criteria for accepting applicants. These rules are not the law, but the policy of the body involved. This book cannot cover all the differing admission procedures for the various agencies. Instead it aims to state the law relating to the housing rights of mentally disordered people and the legal obligations of local authorities' housing and social work departments to mentally disordered people.

Advice on housing rights can be obtained from the local Citizens Advice Bureau, welfare rights office or Shelter Housing Aid Centre.

The legal duties of local authorities are dealt with in two sections, the first covering their obligations towards people who require some degree of supported accommodation and the second the rights of people who are able to cope with a greater degree of independence.

3.6:2 The duty to provide supported accommodation

There is only one explicit duty on housing departments to consider the need for supported accommodation for people who are suffering from a mental disorder. This is a provision which says that each housing department in considering housing conditions in its area and the needs of its area for the future should 'have regard to' the special needs of chronically sick and disabled persons[1]. This would extend to people suffering from serious mental disorder.

This is a very general and vague requirement. It does not impose on the housing department any duty to provide supported accommodation in any particular case, but merely to consider the needs of mentally disordered people when making its plans. Only if it could be shown that a housing department had never even considered these needs could any action be taken against it.

More clear-cut obligations to provide supported accommodation are given to social work departments. It is the duty of every social work department to promote social welfare by making available advice and assistance on such scale as may be appropriate in its area[2].

To do this social work departments must make arrangements to provide or secure the provision of such facilities (including residential or other establishments) as they may consider suitable and adequate[3]. In carrying out their duties they may provide residential accommodation themselves, or in conjunction with the housing department, or by assisting a voluntary or other organisation to set up such establishments[4]. There is also a duty on the social work department from time to time to visit people living in such residential accommodation[5].

One problem which may arise is that it is not always clear who is responsible for providing appropriate housing for mentally disordered people in a particular area. Responsibility is divided between the housing department (the district or islands council) and the social work department (the regional or islands council). Who has the prime responsibility?

The legislation is not clear. The only provision which appears to tackle the problem is a section which gives to a housing department, which is dealing with a case of a homeless person, the power to request the social work department to exercise its functions in relation to such case. The social work department must then give such assistance to the housing department as may be reasonable in the circumstances[6].

Any applicant, then, would be advised to apply to both the housing department and the social work department for housing. As will be seen later, if he or she is homeless, ultimately the responsibility for housing him or her would fall to the housing department, under the homelessness provisions.

1 Housing (Scotland) Act 1987, s 1(4).
2 Social Work (Scotland) Act 1968, s 12.
3 Ibid, s 12. Note that these are discretionary powers given to the social work department. Only if it was manifestly unreasonable in exercising them could any legal action be taken against the department.
4 Ibid, s 59.
5 Ibid, s 68.
6 Housing (Scotland) Act 1987, s 38.

3.6:3 People able to cope with some degree of independence

The statutory duties of housing departments are, as might be expected, more clearly set out in the case of people able to cope with some form of independent living. The law gives special protection to disabled people.

There are three main possibilities

- succeeding to a parent's tenancy

- applying for a place on the council's waiting list

- obtaining housing by virtue of being 'homeless'.

Succession to a tenancy

A very important right for a person who is mentally ill or handicapped is his or her right to succeed to his or her parents' tenancy of a property when the parents die. A child of a tenant can succeed to the tenancy if it was his or her principal residence throughout the twelve months before the tenant's death[1]. A similar right exists for a person who is living with a member of his or her family on that person's death. Any 'secure tenancy' can be so inherited. This includes tenancies of council and housing association properties and certain private tenancies.

In such circumstances another relative or friend might be able to come in and share the accommodation and provide the support needed. Moreover the mentally disordered person could also require improvements to be made to the house to make it more suitable for his or her use, in accordance with the provisions of the Chronically Sick and Disabled Persons Act (see para 3.5:5).

Applying for a place on the council's waiting list

Any person, whether mentally ill or mentally handicapped, is free to put his or her name down on the housing department's waiting list. (If there is any difficulty in completing the forms a friend or relative may apply on his or her behalf). Some housing departments are now accepting applications from groups of potential tenants who are able to show that they have a network of support, perhaps from a voluntary group or the social work department. The application is made to the housing department for the area where the applicant is living or where the hospital in which he or she is staying is situated.

Housing departments will often require people to be living or working in the area before they can even put their names on the list. This could be difficult for someone who wishes to obtain housing near a relative or friend in an area where he or she has not lived before.

The law has addressed this problem in two ways. The first is by providing that if a person is sixty or over and wishes to move into an area to be near a younger relative, he or she can be accepted onto the list even though not resident in the area. The second, very useful, provision states that if an applicant has special social or medical reasons for requiring to be housed within the area of a particular housing department, he or she will not have to be resident in that area before being admitted to the list[2].

This means that even if a person has no previous local connections with an area, he or she could be admitted to the list if they could show a good reason why they should be. The fact that there were relatives or friends in that area who could offer support or, for example, that daycare services which the applicant attended were situated in that area, could be such a reason.

Obtaining housing immediately as a homeless person

If a person is in immediate need of housing, his or her main rights are to apply to the housing department for immediate housing under the homelessness rules. These give housing departments, in certain circumstances, a duty to make accommodation available to homeless persons immediately.

The provisions are complicated and dealt with here only in outline. Any person who is homeless should, if possible, obtain advice from his or her local citizens advice bureau, welfare rights office or Shelter housing aid centre before approaching the housing department.

The rules say that if a housing department has reason to believe that a person

- is homeless (or threatened with homelessness) and
- is 'in priority need' and
- is not 'intentionally homeless' and
- has no 'local connection' with any other housing department (which would then be required to house him or her)

then it must make accommodation available for him or her[3].

Such housing will not always be from the general housing stock, but may be particular housing which the housing department have decided to use for housing homeless people, and may be bed and breakfast accommodation. However, when allocating tenancies from the ordinary council waiting list, the housing department, must give 'reasonable preference' to people who are homeless[4]. So in theory, at any rate, a person who receives housing from a housing department under the homelessness laws should have a reasonable chance of being allocated a house from the general housing stock in due course. If this does not happen, advice should be sought.

Homelessness. A person is homeless if he or she has no accommodation available for his or her use.

Priority need. A person is in priority need if he or she is vulnerable as a result of (among other things) mental illness or handicap. (Or if he or she lives, or might reasonably be expected to live, with a person so vulnerable)[5]. If a person who is in priority need is homeless the housing department must make housing available for him or her temporarily while they make inquiries into his or her case[6]. Any person suffering from a mental disorder is, therefore, entitled to at least temporary housing if he or she is homeless.

Intentional homelessness. A person is regarded as intentionally homeless if he or she has done something voluntarily to give up accommodation which was available to him or her. If the housing department finds that a person is intentionally homeless but is in priority need, they have no duty to offer him or her permanent housing but they must give him or her temporary accommodation and advice and assistance as appropriate to help him or her find somewhere else[7].

Local connection. If a person has

- no local connection with the area of a housing department

- a local connection with another housing department's area

- no risk of domestic violence in that other area

the housing department to which he or she has applied may notify the other housing department to that effect and it would be the duty of that other department to house the applicant[8].

In such circumstances the homeless person's only alternative would be to accept such accommodation and put his or her name on the first council's waiting list if there were special reasons for wanting to be housed there (see above).

To sum up, if a mentally disturbed person is homeless, not intentionally homeless and has no local connection with the area of any other housing department, then it is the duty of the housing department to which he or she applies to offer him or her housing.

The rules are complex, however, and there have been many cases in the courts considering what is meant by 'intentional homelessness' and 'local connection', and various other parts of the legislation. It is very important to obtain proper advice, particularly if any problems are experienced with the housing department.

1 Housing (Scotland) Act 1987, s 52.
2 Ibid, s 19(2).
3 Ibid, s 31(2).
4 Ibid, s 20(1)(b).
5 Ibid, s 25(1)(c).
6 Ibid, s 29(2).
7 Ibid, s 31(3).
8 Ibid, s 34.

4 Care in hospital

4.1 INTRODUCTION

This chapter deals with the effect of in-patient treatment on a patient's rights. In some situations these rights are restricted. Broadly speaking the rights we shall discuss cover three areas:

- the way a person leads his or her life
- finances and property
- the right to play a part in public life.

An in-patient's rights may be restricted for various reasons. One prominent reason is that there are situations where treatment cannot effectively take place without some restrictions on the patient's personal rights. Another reason is that there are situations where a patient is not capable of managing his or her personal affairs. As all restrictions on personal rights are a limitation on basic freedom it is important to be clear about the detailed rules that are laid down in the law for determining when rights are restricted.

In many situations, too, there are special procedures that must be followed in dealing with patients in these situations.

The law is to be found not only in legislation relating directly to mental health but also in case law and other legislation.

As personal rights are at issue, the European Convention of Human Rights also has to be borne in mind. However, for someone to seek to take a case against the government on the basis that the law is not in accordance with this Convention, it is necessary to exhaust all remedies available in the Scots Courts first. It should be noted too that **the Act** seeks to safeguard patients' rights and it is not likely that our law is now out of line with the provisions of the Convention[1].

The following matters concerning a patient's way of life are dealt with in this chapter:

- Freedom to leave the hospital
- Visits by relatives and friends
- Relations with children
- Correspondence
- Control of patients' activities
- Freedom to refuse treatment
- Money and property
- The right to vote

1 See the remarks of Lord Justice Lawton on the equivalent English legislation in *R v Oxford Mental Health Tribunal, ex p Secretary of State for the Home Department* [1986] 3 All ER 239.

4.2 RESTRICTIONS ON A PATIENT'S WAY OF LIFE

4.2:1 Freedom to leave the hospital

The important distinction is between patients who are not subject to one of the compulsory measures described in chapters 2 and 4 and patients who are.

Patients not subject to compulsory measures ('voluntary' patients)

These patients have the same rights as patients in a general hospital and may discharge themselves at any time. They can do so even against medical advice. However, the doctor in charge may in such circumstances require such a patient to stay in hospital by using compulsory powers. A nurse may detain the patient for up to two hours (see chapter 2). In cases where patients are required to stay in hospital in these ways the strict procedures applying to compulsory detention (as discussed in chapter 2) have to be followed.

Compulsorily detained patients

Such patients are not free to leave the hospital.

The **managers of the hospital** where the patient is compulsorily detained must take such steps as are practicable[1] to inform the patient verbally and in writing[2] so that the patient understands the effect of his or her detention. This must be done as soon as is practicable[3]. The patient must be told:

- under what provisions he or she is being detained[4]
- the effects of these provisions[4]
- any rights of appeal against detention that there may be[5]
- that representations can be made to the **Mental Welfare Commission**[6] (see chapter 6).

A copy of the information given in writing to the patient must be given by the managers of the hospital to whoever appears to them to be the patient's **nearest relative**[7]. This must be done at the same time as the information is given to the patient or within a reasonable time after that[7].

1 Mental Health (Scotland) Act 1984, s 110(1).
2 Ibid, s 110(3). The Scottish Home and Health Department have given guidance as to the content of this (SHHD Circular No 1984 (GEN) 23, 29 September 1984.
3 Mental Health (Scotland) Act 1984, s 110(1).
4 Ibid, s 110(1)(a).
5 Ibid, s 110(1)(b). Guidance as to the content of this is given by the Scottish Home and Health Department (see footnote 2 above).
6 Ibid, s 110(1)(c).
7 Ibid, s 110(4).

4.2:2 Visits by relatives and friends

Hospital staff are generally keen to encourage visits by relatives or friends. Links are important, especially as the patient will, it is hoped, be returned to the community. Anyone wishing to make a visit should get in touch with the hospital. It may be that it is necessary to arrange a special time to visit. It is particularly important to contact the hospital before visiting a patient who is compulsorily detained.

If the hospital stops anyone from visiting a patient the Mental Welfare Commission should be contacted. It may be able to take steps to arrange the visit.

Many mental hospitals are situated in isolated places. This can result in some expense in travelling to visit a patient. If this expense causes financial hardship the local office of the Department of Social Security should be approached. (See para 3.4:6 for details of financial assistance available.)

Welfare of children in hospital

Parents whose child is in hospital may naturally be very anxious to visit as often as possible. There is no legal right to insist on visiting whenever one wishes, but Scottish Office recommendations have laid down that it is a child's right to keep in touch with his or her parents and hospital visiting arrangements should reflect this[1].

Therefore, unless the child's consultant sees some medical reason why visits should not be made, the hospital should use its best efforts to make visiting as unrestricted as possible for parents. If this does not happen, the parents should contact the National Association for the Welfare of Children in Hospital (see Appendix 4—Helpful names and addresses) for advice.

A child who is likely to be in hospital for a long time or who is in for a short period of 'respite care' should not, if at all possible, be placed in a geriatric ward.

This is because the law says that if a person who is under sixty-five is suffering from a chronic illness or disability and is in hospital for long-term care or for respite care while his or her carer is not available, then the **health board** should use its best endeavours to ensure, so far as practicable, that he or she is not cared for in a part of the hospital which is normally mainly used for patients aged over sixty-five or for patients who are suffering from the effects of premature ageing[2].

If a child patient is placed in such a ward, the nearest relatives should take this up with the Unit Administrator (see Complaints, para 6.2) or the Mental Welfare Commission.

The *Annual Report of the Mental Welfare Commission 1987* notes that there have been cases of children being detained in adult closed psychiatric wards for short periods[3]. While this is not unlawful, it is clearly not a desirable practice. The Commission recommends that if appropriate accommodation cannot be found for child patients, consideration should be given to applying to a **children's hearing** for a place of safety order for the child, so that appropriate arrangements can be made by the social work department.

1 Scottish Home and Health Department recommendations 1968.
2 Chronically Sick and Disabled Persons Act 1970, s 17(1). In 1988 473 patients in Scotland were resident in accommodation which did not comply with s 17(1): *House of Commons Report 1988/89 512.*
3 See *Annual Report of the Mental Welfare Commission 1987*, para 5.21.

4.2:3 Relations with children

The fact that a parent is an in-patient in a mental hospital does not as such affect his or her rights in respect of children. It would, however, be a factor that would be taken into account in considering questions as to who is to have custody of any children in a divorce action or in any other dispute over custody.

A ground for a child being taken into the legal care of a regional or islands council is that a parent or guardian is unable to look after the child[1]. Mental illness as well as physical illness could give rise to this situation. However, it would occur only if there was *no* parent or guardian who could look after the child. A child may be taken into legal care in four different ways:

- The child may be referred to a children's hearing as being at risk, and an order follow that[2].
- The child in an emergency may be removed from the home to a place of safety. (The question is then referred to a children's hearing.)
- The child may also be placed in care voluntarily.
- There is a general power to take into care children who are lost or abandoned[3].

If a child is taken into care the social work department can then pass a resolution to take over the parents' rights[4]—the right to have custody of the child, see to the child's education, general upbringing and so on. One ground on which this can be done is that the parents or guardian are unable to care for the child because of mental illness[5]. The local authority must notify the parent or guardian that they have passed the resolution[6]. The parent or guardian has one month to object to the resolution[7]. If he or she does, the matter will then be considered by a **sheriff**.

If the parent's or guardian's circumstances change, for example the parent ceases to be suffering from a mental disorder, he or she can apply to the sheriff to resume parental rights again.

The taking over of parents' rights by a local authority does not mean that a parent loses his or her right to refuse agreement to the child being adopted. However, one ground on which a parent's consent to having a child adopted may be dispensed with is that the parent is incapable of giving agreement[8]. Some serious forms of mental disorder could have this result.

If there is any possibility of a parent or guardian being in a position where the local authority may assume parental rights, they or those concerned for them would be strongly advised to see a solicitor. Advice can then be got on how best to protect the parent's position. **Legal aid** might be available in such circumstances (see chapter 7).

It should be noted that if a *child* is an in-patient the parents or guardian continue to have the normal rights and duties in respect of the child.

1 Social Work (Scotland) Act 1968, s 15(1)(a). But note the Mental Welfare Commission is encouraging the provision of a suitable facility for providing care to patients with their babies: *Annual Report of the Mental Welfare Commission for Scotland 1988* chapter 11.
2 Ibid, s 37.
3 Ibid, s 15(1)(b).
4 Ibid, s 16(1).
5 Ibid, s 16(2)(b) and s 16(2)(c).

6 Ibid, s 16(5).
7 Ibid, s 16(7).
8 Adoption (Scotland) Act 1978.

4.2:4 Correspondence

Patients may wish to send and receive letters, parcels etc through the post. The word 'correspondence'[1] is used here as a general term to cover all the various types of mail that may arise.

In certain situations the managers of the hospital are entitled to interfere with correspondence sent to or by a patient by keeping the correspondence back or removing things from it. They may open correspondence in order to find out whether it is a case where they can interfere with it[2].

If they do exercise their powers to interfere with correspondence they must record in writing that they have done so[3].

Whether there is any right to interfere with the correspondence sent to patients or correspondence sent by patients depends on the category into which the patient falls. Again there is a distinction between patients not subject to compulsory measures and those who are. There are also special rules for **State Hospital** patients.

Patients not subject to compulsory measures ('voluntary' patients). The correspondence of these patients cannot be interfered with. This is so even if the medical staff consider it to be in their or anyone else's best interests that it should be.

Compulsorily detained patients. Any person who does not want to receive any correspondence from such a patient has a right to request that all communications addressed by the patient to him or her should not be posted[4]. These requests must be made in writing to the managers of the hospital, the **responsible medical officer** or the **Secretary of State**[5]. Following such a request communications may be kept back from the post[6].

There is no power to interfere with correspondence addressed *to* a patient unless the patient is detained in a State Hospital.

State Hospital patients

Correspondence sent by a patient. The managers of the State Hospital have certain powers to withhold correspondence sent by a State Hospital patient in addition to their power where a request has been made to them to do so. There are two further grounds on which they may do this:

- if they consider that the item in question is likely to cause distress to someone (not necessarily the person to whom it is addressed)[6]. They cannot, however, exercise their power on this ground where the correspondence is sent to someone on the staff of the hospital.

- if the item in question is likely to cause danger to someone[7]. In this situation there is no exception in respect of correspondence sent to a member of the staff of the hospital.

They do not have power to interfere with correspondence with the following people and institutions. These are people to whom a patient might want to write to make a complaint or to defend his or her rights. They are[8]:

- A Minister of the Crown or a member of the House of Lords or House of Commons
- The Mental Welfare Commission or any individual member of that body or a lawyer appointed by it to head an enquiry
- The Parliamentary Commissioner for Administration, the Health Service Commissioner for Scotland, or the Commissioner for Local Administration in Scotland
- A judge or clerk of court
- A health board, the Common Services Agency for the Scottish Health Service or a local health council
- A local **regional** or **islands council**
- The managers of the hospital in which the patient is detained
- Any legally qualified person instructed by the patient to act as his or her legal adviser
- The European Commission of Human Rights or the European Court of Human Rights.

Correspondence sent to a patient. The managers of the State Hospital may withhold correspondence addressed to a patient if it is in their opinion necessary to do so in the interest of the safety of the patient or for the protection of other people[9]. This power, however, does not extend to correspondence sent to the patient by any of those people and bodies listed above[10].

The duty to notify. Where correspondence to or from a State Hospital patient is withheld, the managers of the hospital must notify the patient of this in writing within seven days[11]. They must also within this time notify in writing the person to whom it was addressed, where known[11]. In the notifications they must advise the patient and the sender that there is a right to seek a review by the Mental Welfare Commission of the decision to interfere with the correspondence.

Duty to notify the Mental Welfare Commission and review. In all cases where correspondence is interfered with (including those where this is requested by the person to whom it is sent) the managers of the hospital must notify the Mental Welfare Commission in writing within seven days of the name of the patient concerned, the nature of the correspondence which has been withheld and the reasons why the power to interfere has been exercised[12].

The Mental Welfare Commission has no power to review a decision to withhold correspondence in situations where that has been requested by the person to whom it has been addressed.

In cases where the power to withhold correspondence to or from State Hospital patients is exercised on other grounds, they must review the decision if a review is sought by the patient[13].

In cases where correspondence to a patient is at issue, they must also carry out a review if a review is requested by the person to whom the item was addressed[14].

A person requesting a review must do so within six months of receiving the hospital managers' decision[15].

The Mental Welfare Commission in carrying out its review will consider whether interference with the correspondence should have occurred. The managers of the hospital must comply with its decision[16].

1 The relevant sections of the legislation refer to a 'postal packet'. In terms of s 115(9) of the Mental Health (Scotland) Act 1984 this is defined as having the meaning it has in the Post Office Act 1953. Section 87(1) of that Act contains an extensive definition which includes 'every packet or article transmissable by post'.
2 Mental Health (Scotland) Act 1984, s 115(4).
3 Ibid, s 115(5).
4 Ibid, s 115(1)(a).
5 Ibid, s 115(1).
6 Ibid, s 115(1)(b)(i).
7 Ibid, s 115(1)(b)(ii).
8 Ibid, s 115(3).
9 Ibid, s 115(2).
10 Ibid, s 115(3).
11 Ibid, s 115(6).
12 Ibid, s 115(5).
13 Ibid, s 116(1)(a).
14 Ibid, s 116(1)(b).
15 Ibid, s 116(1).
16 Ibid, s 116(2). The *Annual Report of the Mental Welfare Commission for Scotland 1987*, para 1.20, notes that the Commission considered one case in the year covered by the *Report* of an appeal by a State Hospital patient against the hospital's decision to withhold mail.

4.3 CONTROL OF PATIENTS' ACTIVITIES

The hospital staff are entitled to take reasonable steps in controlling the activities of patients in the hospital.

4.3:1 The distinction between control and punishment

A distinction first has to be drawn between things done by hospital staff to *control* patients and things done to *punish* patients. Hospital staff are subject to the normal criminal (and civil) law of assault[1]. Physical punishment is certainly not legal in the case of adults, whatever their mental capacity. Hospital staff will be forbidden by the hospital from using physical punishment in the case of children as well. Any use of it will almost certainly result in dismissal[2].

Physical punishment of a child in hospital would probably be held by the courts to be illegal. The question is not specifically dealt with in the Act[3], but there is a general offence covering ill-treatment or neglect of patients[4]. This can be argued to be broad enough to cover corporal punishment[5]. Moreover, it would probably amount to the crime of assault.

Parents and teachers[6] have a defence to a charge of assault, on the ground that the punishment was reasonable. Even if hospital staff were to be found in law to have such a defence (on the grounds that they are in 'lawful control or charge'[7] of a child patient), it is unlikely that a judge could consider that physical punishment, as opposed to physical methods of control, of a young patient in a mental hospital could be seen as reasonable today.

In the unlikely event of it being held that hospital staff could legally administer corporal punishment to child patients and this being confirmed on

Control of patients' activities 73

appeal, a remedy might be available under the European Convention of Human Rights[8].

1 The Mental Welfare Commission has a concern in this area and in addition to any court proceedings may itself hold a formal enquiry. (See in particular *The Report of the Mental Welfare Commission for Scotland 1984* paras 4.1–4.11).
2 This is likely to be considered 'fair' by an industrial tribunal. See *Retarded Childrens' Aid Society v Day* [1978] 1 WLR 763.
3 Mental Health (Scotland) Act 1984, s 41(4) specifically makes it an offence by **guardians** (see chapter 3).
4 Ibid, s 105.
5 The Children and Young Persons (Scotland) Act 1937, s 12, which deals in similar terms with the offence committed by parents and others who neglect or ill-treat children, specifically reserves the right to administer corporal punishment (s 12(7)). There is no such reservation in s 105 of the Mental Health (Scotland) Act 1984. It has been suggested, however, that the offence is one that requires a course of conduct. (See Archbold *Criminal Pleading Evidence and Practice* (43rd edn, 1988) para 20–204, with reference to the identical wording of the English Mental Health Act 1983). But there is a reported case in England of a single blow being held to constitute the offence (*R v Holmes* [1979] Criminal Law Review 52).
6 Eg *Gray v Hawthorn* 1961 JC 13; *Stewart v Thain* 1981 JC 13.
7 See Gordon *Criminal Law* (2nd edn) paras 29–38.
8 Compare the situation of punishment of children in schools (*Campbell and Cosans v UK* Judgements and Decisions of the European Court of Human Rights, Series A, Vol 48, 25 February 1982). Proceedings under the Convention are taken against the United Kingdom Government on the basis that the law is not in accordance with the obligations of the government under the convention.

4.3:2 Reasonable control

Hospital staff may *control* patients in reasonable ways. What is reasonable depends on the circumstances. Guidance to staff through codes of conduct[1] is relevant but not the only factor to be considered.

In one case a nurse who stood on the arms and legs of a very violent patient was found guilty of assault[2].

There is a special provision in the Act[3] which states that someone is not to be liable if he or she does something that purports to be following the legislation unless what they did was 'in bad faith or without reasonable care'. This has been held by the House of Lords, in considering the equivalent provision in the English legislation, to cover the ordinary work of hospital staff, not just when they are performing special statutory functions[4].

Following this approach in the one reported Scottish case, a sheriff applying this provision found an accused nurse not guilty where the nurse had to deal with aggressive and disruptive mentally handicapped children and young people, and had on various occasions thrown water at some of them and struck (not severely) others of them on the head with one of his knuckles. It was held the nurse had acted with reasonable care. His acts were reasonable control and not punishment[5].

Such actions could still, however, result in dismissal by the hospital[6].

1 Eg Health Circular HC 76(11) referred to in the case in footnote 9.
2 *Norman v Smith* 1983 SCCR 100.
3 Mental Health (Scotland) Act 1984, s 122(1): 'No person shall be liable, whether on the ground of want of jurisdiction or on any other ground, to any civil or criminal proceedings to which he would have been liable apart from this section in respect of any act purporting to be done in pursuance of this Act or any regulations thereunder, unless the act was done in bad faith or without reasonable care.'

4 *Poutney v Griffiths* [1976] AC 314, [1975] 2 All ER 881.
5 *Skinner v Robertson* 1980 SLT (Sh Ct) 43—applying the identical provision in the **1960 Act** (s 107). The Mental Welfare Commission reports a statement to it of the Crown Agent (the head of the administration of the prosecution service) that 'Courts will countenance protection of staff under this section [s 122(1)] only if the force was reasonable and the minimum necessary and was part of the member of staff's responsibility for the care and control of patients' (The *Annual Report of the Mental Welfare Commission for Scotland 1984*, para 4.1).
6 The accused charge nurse who was acquitted in *Skinner v Robertson* (footnote 5) was dismissed. The dismissal was upheld as not being unfair by an industrial tribunal (Decision of Industrial Tribunal (Scotland) in Case No S/424/79. Inverness 16 January 1980).

4.3:3 Seclusion and time out

Two general methods of control have given rise to some comment: 'seclusion' and 'time out'. 'Seclusion' is removing patients during the day on a long-term basis from the company of fellow patients and staff. 'Time out' involves removing patients for a short period of time, typically minutes, from normal activities so that they are not on their own. A clear distinction between the two things is not made by everyone[1]. However, it is preferable to draw the distinction since they have a very different impact on the patient's freedom within the hospital[2].

'Seclusion' if done reasonably to prevent disruption or harm to other patients or to the patient in question is legal. However, the Mental Welfare Commission has reviewed its use and disapproves of the practice[3]. In the unlikely event of its being used it must not be used oppressively. 'Seclusion' is a deprivation of liberty[4]. However, in the case of compulsorily detained patients a patient's liberty is already diminished to some extent. What is important in law is the surrounding circumstances (including the frequency and duration) and the method of 'seclusion' used[5].

In the case of a voluntary patient it would be illegal to use seclusion against the patient's will. If the proposed seclusion was reasonable, and the patient refused to agree to it, the hospital could discharge the patient as it is entitled to determine the conditions on which voluntary patients attend hospital so long as they are reasonable[6]. Alternatively it may be that the patient's state is such that there are grounds for compulsory detention. But a patient cannot be treated as a compulsory patient unless he or she is detained as one (see para 2.5).

'Time out' is less drastic than seclusion. However, by contrast to seclusion it is usually seen as a form of 'treatment'. It is designed to modify a person's behaviour by removal from surroundings which might encourage him or her to think it is all right to go on behaving in a particular way[7]. The definition of 'medical treatment' in the Act seems to cover this form of 'treatment'[8]. In the case of compulsorily detained patients this may be an additional reason why it can be done without consent[9]. (The law relating to consent and treatment is discussed fully later in the chapter at para 4.4.) In the case of voluntary patients the same issues arise as with 'seclusion'.

'Time out' like 'seclusion' can thus be used so long as it is not used oppressively or as punishment. There should be procedures laid down in each hospital that uses 'time out' to ensure that this is so[10].

1 The *Draft Code of Practice* (1988) issued by the Scottish Home and Health Department in terms of s 119 does not make the distinction clearly. It states that 'it is for the clinical team to decide when one or other of these forms of treatment needs to be applied'.

2 See *Annual Report of the Mental Welfare Commission for Scotland 1985*, chapter 7.
3 *Annual Report of the Mental Welfare Commission for Scotland 1988,* chapter 8.
4 It has been suggested that in England it could give rise to a civil claim by the patient simply on this basis. See Hogget, *Mental Health Law* (2nd edn) page 194 for a discussion of the English position.
5 Compare *Mackenzie v Cluny Hill Hydropathic* 1908 SC 200—a case about a hotel manager keeping a guest in a room to force her to apologise to another guest.
6 But if the patient is a potential suicide the hospital may run the risk of being liable for negligence, if, as a result of being required to leave the hospital a suicide or injury from a suicide attempt takes place. (Compare the duty of the police where a vulnerable person has been in their direct custody: *Wilson v Chief Constable of Lothian and Borders Police Force* 1989 SLT 97 (Court of Session—Outer House).
7 'A therapeutic procedure which derives from the application of behavioural analysis and intervention to the treatment of people with mental illness or mental handicap'. (*Annual Report of the Mental Welfare Commission for Scotland 1985*, para 7.2).
8 Mental Health (Scotland) Act 1984, s 125. It 'includes nursing, and also includes care and training under medical supervision'.
9 Ibid, s 103.
10 The Mental Welfare Commission recommends that the procedures laid down in each hospital should ensure the safety and 'methodological appropriateness' of the conditions in which 'time out' takes place. It should be recorded. The hospital should monitor it and the staff should be appropriately trained in its use. (*Annual Report of the Mental Welfare Commission for Scotland 1985*, para 7.25).

4.3:4 Criminal offences

The normal criminal law applies to people who are involved in the care of mentally ill or mentally handicapped people (see eg para 4.4:2). There are also a number of offences laid down in the Act.

Ill-treatment or wilful neglect

This is an offence under the Act[1]. The offence can be committed by hospital staff[2]. It can also be committed by **guardians** (see chapter 3) or anyone else who has 'custody or care' of the patient[3].

Sexual offences

There are two sexual offences laid down in sections 106 and 107 of the Act. They are in addition to the normal sexual offences such as rape.

Essentially what the two offences amount to is that any man having intercourse anywhere with a mentally handicapped[4] woman who is not his wife commits an offence under s 106[5] unless it can be established that he did not know she was mentally handicapped[6]. In addition, if he is a member of the staff of the hospital where the woman is an in-patient, he will have committed the further offence under s 107 of having intercourse (outside marriage) with someone who is suffering from a mental disorder. If she is an out-patient he will have committed the further offence only if the intercourse takes place at the hospital[7].

Any male member of the hospital staff will have committed an offence under s 107 if he has intercourse anywhere with an in-patient who is not his wife and who is suffering from a mental disorder of any kind, unless he did not know she was suffering from mental disorder[8]. If the patient is an out-patient he commits the offence only if the intercourse takes place at the hospital[9].

Section 107 also makes it an offence for a man to have intercourse with a woman suffering from a mental disorder who is subject to his **guardianship** or otherwise in his custody or care under the Act or who is in the care of the local authority or resident in a home provided by the local authority[10].

It is also an offence for an owner, occupier or person managing premises, who induces a mentally handicapped woman to come or be there for intercourse with someone who is not her husband[11]. Again it is a defence that he or she did not know that the woman was mentally handicapped[12].

Patients absent without leave

It is an offence under s 108 of the Act to induce, knowingly assist or knowingly 'harbour' compulsorily detained[13] patients or patients subject to guardianship, who are absent without leave.

Obstructing persons carrying out functions under the Act

This is an offence under s 109. The offence covers obstruction generally. In addition it is specifically stated to cover refusal to allow inspection of premises, visiting, interviewing or examining of patients by such people, refusing to produce documents etc and refusing to leave when asked by someone interviewing or examining in private.

It is an offence under s 104 to make a false statement in any document or form submitted in connection with the Act if there is 'intention to deceive'.

1 Mental Health (Scotland) Act 1984, s 105. (See also para 1.2:2)
2 Ibid, s 105(1)(a). Included are any 'officer on the staff of or otherwise employed in a hospital or nursing home' and managers of a hospital or person carrying on a nursing home.
3 Ibid, s 105(1)(b).
4 Ie a woman suffering from a state of arrested or incomplete development of mind which includes significant impairment of intelligence and social functioning' (ibid, s 106(6)). See also para 1.2:2.
5 The idea is that the protection for under-age girls is extended to mentally handicapped women of any age.
6 Ibid, s 106(2). The test is subjective. A person accused of the offence will not be guilty if it can be shown on the balance of probabilities that he himself did not know and had no reason to suspect that the woman was mentally handicapped. On the other hand he 'cannot shut his eyes to the obvious'. See *R v Hudson* [1966] 1 QB 448 at 449 per Ashworth J.
7 Ibid, s 107(1)(a).
8 Ibid, s 107(2).
9 Ibid, s 107(1)(a).
10 Ibid, s 107(1)(b).
11 Ibid, s 106(1)(c).
12 Ibid, s 106(2), and see note 6 above.
13 Patients who are detained in custody under ibid, s 120 are also included (s 108(1)(b)).

4.4 CONSENT TO TREATMENT

4.4:1 Freedom to refuse treatment

The law relating to consent to treatment is highly complex. It is also controversial. It is very important in practice. It covers all forms of medical intervention, including ordinary medical and surgical treatment, treatment for mental disorder and procedures that are medical but not designed to save life or relieve suffering directly, such as most abortions and sterilisation. As we have seen the question of the control of patients' activities also has a connection with the question of consent to treatment.

There is an important distinction between treatment given to a patient for mental disorder (see para 4.4:3) and other treatment. The basic position is:

- *Treatment for a condition other than mental disorder.* In all cases (including those of compulsorily detained patients), the need to obtain consent is determined by the general law, which is the same as that applicable to patients in a general hospital
- *Treatment for mental disorder of a voluntary patient and certain patients compulsorily detained for short periods of time.* The general law is also applicable
- *Treatment for a mental disorder of other compulsorily detained patients.* There are special rules to be found in the Act[1].

1 Mental Health (Scotland) Act 1984, ss 96–103.

4.4:2 Treatment for a condition other than mental disorder

A distinction can be made between treatment designed to cure or alleviate a condition and other treatment which is designed to avoid disadvantages in a patient's way of life. Prominent examples of this are sterilisation or abortion in cases where pregnancy would not present any abnormal physical dangers. These examples are covered separately below.

All patients are entitled to refuse any particular treatment. Where there is an emergency and the patient is in a position where consent is in practice impossible (eg in a coma), a doctor can proceed with reasonable treatment[1]. In all other cases consent must be obtained before treatment. The patient should not be put in a position where it is felt that there is no entitlement to refuse treatment simply because of being in a mental hospital. If treatment is carried out to which no consent at all has been given and adverse results follow, the patient could sue for damages and a prosecution for assault is technically a possibility.

Children. If the patient is a girl under twelve or a boy under fourteen, the parent's/guardian's consent must be obtained. With a child over these ages and under eighteen it is a question of fact as to whether the child has sufficient maturity and understanding to be able to consent on his or her own behalf[2]. It is appropriate, however, also to discuss the matter with the parents. If a child of such an age does not have such maturity and understanding, it appears to be the law in this context that parents may consent on the child's behalf[3].

Adults incapable of understanding what is proposed as treatment. Where a patient aged eighteen or over is incapable of understanding what is being proposed as treatment, uncontroversial surgical and medical treatment can, it seems, proceed so long as it is reasonable[4].

It is possible to have a person appointed and authorised to consent to treatment on a patient's behalf. The person is appointed by the Court of Session and is known as a **tutor-dative**[5]. For anything other than uncontroversial treatment this procedure is appropriate. Further details of the procedure and other possible procedures for such an appointment is outlined later in this section under 'Sterilisation and Abortion'.

What should be explained. Reasonable steps must be taken to explain the nature and risks of the treatment to the patient (or person acting for them). Should this not be done, a patient could sue for damages in respect of adverse results from the treatment. However, in such a case, if consent in general terms has been given to the treatment, no criminal offence of assault would have been committed.

What risks must be explained is a question of circumstances. A reasonable level of information about possible risks must be given. The law at present is not entirely clear as to what the yardstick for deciding what is reasonable in this connection[6]. It has been said that a reasonable amount of information is what a competent doctor would consider reasonable[7]. In any event information as to substantial risks of grave consequences must be given.

Some commentators have suggested an approach more favourable to the patient so that such information should be given as a prudent patient would consider reasonable[8]. It is unlikely that this test will be followed by the courts now[9]. Even if it were adopted it would not be necessary to inform the patient of a risk where the information itself would pose a serious threat of increased psychological detriment to the patient[10].

But this does not mean that it is not necessary to inform a patient of the potential risks involved in a course of treatment simply because that patient is suffering from a psychiatric condition.

Sterilisation and abortion

Cases have arisen where doctors, parents or social workers have considered it desirable that a mentally handicapped person undergo sterilisation or have an abortion. They may feel that a female patient would not be able to cope emotionally with pregnancy or with bringing up a child and that contraception would not be practicable. These matters have been considered by the courts in England[11].

At present there is some doubt about the appropriate legal procedure in Scotland for considering the patient's rights. A doctor should not proceed without authority from a court. Nor should a doctor proceed even in the case of a child under eighteen on the consent of a parent or guardian[12]. This is because, first, on one view of the law parents do not have a parental right to consent to such treatment on a child's behalf and, secondly, even if they do, it is extremely doubtful that a parent or guardian has the right without a court order to permit treatment that is not designed to cure, alleviate or avoid an illness or injury.

Accordingly in such cases those concerned should apply to a court for an order. There are the following procedures available:

Where the patient is under eighteen and the parents/guardians[13] *agree.* A petition could be made to the Court of Session (Inner House) to ask for a **tutor-dative** to be appointed. That person could be a parent. (Parents are anyhow automatically tutors of their daughters under twelve and sons under fourteen.) The petition should in addition ask for the appointment to carry with it a specific power to consent to the procedure proposed[14]. Although this procedure has been little used in modern times it has the attraction of bringing the matter properly before a court and provides, too, for the decision to be taken by someone with specific authorisation from a court. It may be possible to petition the Court of Session for an order without the appointment of a tutor-dative. There is, however, some doubt as to the form of order that the court could grant[15].

There is perhaps another procedure, available in the sheriff court as well as the Court of Session. This is to seek an order under section 3(1) of the Law Reform (Parent and Child) (Scotland) Act 1986. The application[16] would be to exercise the parental right of approving the medical procedure. It is not clear, however, that this procedure can be used because on one view of the law there is no 'parental right' to consent, and so it is not something to which this procedure relates[17].

Where the patient is under eighteen and the parents/guardians do not agree. Again an application for the appointment of a **tutor-dative** in the Court of Session could be made (or for an order without such an appointment).

If parents are able to make an application under section 3(1) of the Law Reform (Parent and Child) (Scotland) Act (discussed above) then it would appear that an application in this form could also be made by someone other than a parent who has an interest in the patient's welfare[18]. The applicant must be a 'person claiming interest'. There is a decision by a single judge (and therefore not a binding precedent) holding that this restricts such applications to 'parents'[19]. The decision, however, has been extensively criticised by commentators[20] and appears to be incorrect. There is a potential difficulty in the applicant being the doctor who is going to carry out the proposed procedure[21].

Where the patient is under eighteen and the parents/guardians want the procedure but some other interested party considers it undesirable. If the parents/guardians apply to a court for authorisation, the judge or sheriff could order that other interested parties be informed. In any event such parties may apply to the court to be represented and have their views taken into account[22].

Where the patient is eighteen or over. In this situation the only courses of action open would be to apply to the Court of Session for the appointment of a tutor-dative with power to consent to the proposed procedure or possibly for an order without such an appointment. The appointment of a tutor-dative does not depend on the existence of 'parental rights'.

Whatever procedure is appropriate and whatever the age of the patient in question, the court must be satisfied before granting an order that it is in the best interests of the patient. Such treatments are drastic and effectively irreversible. Accordingly a court would require evidence that there were exceptional circumstances making it appropriate. Probably the court would have to be satisfied in cases involving sterilisation that pregnancy was likely and both in cases of sterilisation and in cases of abortion, that it would cause serious damage to the physical or mental health of the patient if the procedure was not carried out[23].

1 *F v West Berkshire Health Authority* [1989] 2 All ER 545, HL, at 548, 551 and 566.
2 For a general discussion see J M Thomson *Family Law in Scotland*, pp 168–172; Scottish Law Commission Consultative Memorandum 65 *Legal Capacity of Minors and Pupils*, paras 2.47–2.54.
3 Scottish Law Commission Consultative Memorandum 65, para 2.45. There is no direct case law authority on this point. See also note 17 below.
4 The authority for this is only *obiter dicta* in *F v West Berkshire Health Authority* (above).
5 See A D Ward 'Revival of Tutors-Dative—Morris Petitioner' 1987 SLT (News) 69–72.
6 The various differences of approach are contained in the leading case, *Sidaway v Board of Governors of the Bethlem Royal Hospital and the Maudsley Hospital* [1985] AC 871.
7 This approach is emphasised by the Court of Appeal in England in *Gold v Harringey Health Authority* [1987] 2 All ER 888.
8 *Sidaway v Board of Governors of the Bethlem Royal Hospital and the Maudsley Hospital* (above) at 883–890 per Lord Scarman.
9 *Gold v Harringey Health Authority* (above).

10 The 'prudent patient' test suggested by Lord Scarman is modified by a concept of 'therapeutic privilege', *Sidaway v Board of Governors of the Bethlem Royal Hospital and the Maudsley Hospital* (above) at 887–890.
11 See *Re B* [1988] AC 199, HL; *Re X* (1987) Times, 4 June (Abortion) (single judge); *T v T* [1988] 1 All ER 613 (Sterilisation) (single judge); *F v West Berkshire Health Authority* (above) (sterilisation) (HL).
12 See J M Thomson: *Sterilisation of Mentally Handicapped Children* 1988 SLT (News) 1 at 3.
13 A regional council that has assumed parental rights under the Social Work (Scotland) Act 1968, s 16 is treated as a parent for this purpose. (For 'assumption of parental rights' see para 4.2:3).
14 See note 5 above.
15 The difficulty is technical. With patients under eighteen the English courts exercise wardship jurisdiction and 'give leave' for the operation to go ahead (*Re B,* above). It has been suggested that the appropriate form in Scotland is 'that the parental consent to the operation is in the best interests of the child' (J M Thomson 'Sterilisation of Mentally Handicapped Children' 1988 SLT (News) 1 at 3). This depends on the legal position being that the parents have a *prima facie* right to consent (which has not so far been definitely established in the case law). Scottish courts may be able to take the course adopted in England for adult patients and declare the operation to be not unlawful. But there is no direct Scots precedent for this (see *F v West Berkshire Health Authority* (above).
16 A parent in this context again includes a regional council that has 'assumed parental rights': Social Work (Scotland) Act 1968, s 16 (see also note 13 above).
17 The wording of the provision is: 'Any person claiming interest may make an application to the court for an order relating to parental rights and the court may make such order relating to parental rights as it thinks fit'. If the basic law is that parents do not have any 'parental rights' to consent to treatment of their children of this age then clearly the procedure under this section is not available. On the other hand if there is in law such a parental right, then such an application would be something 'relating' to that right (see also notes 3 and 15 above).
18 J M Thomson 'Applications for Parental Rights' 1987 SLT (News) 165.
19 *AB v Mrs M* 1987 SCLR 389 per Lord McCluskey.
20 See the commentary to the report by E M C[live] at 392–394; J M Thomson 'Applications for Parental Rights' 1987 SLT (News) 165–166; E E Sutherland (1987) Journal of the Law Society of Scotland 274–275.
21 It is an artificial use of language to say that someone is authorised to consent to something done by his or herself. Put another way such an application might not in truth be one 'relating to parental rights'.
22 By lodging a 'Minute' in the 'Process'.
23 In *Re B* (see footnote 11) the patient in question had a mental age of five or six. She could not understand the link between sexual activity, pregnancy and the birth of a child. Childbirth would be for her a terrifying experience. There would have to be a caesarean delivery if she did become pregnant. Because of behavioural problems she would have special difficulty in recovering from that. (See J M Thomson 'Sterilisation of Mentally Handicapped Children' 1988 SLT (News) 1 at 4 for a discussion of the attitude that the court should take.)

4.4:3 Treatment for mental disorder

Different rules apply to voluntary patients and compulsorily detained patients. However, the position of certain patients who are liable to be detained for relatively short periods is in this context the same as that of voluntary patients. In the case of such patients and voluntary patients the general law relating to consent to treatment is applied, as with ordinary patients in hospital. In the case of other compulsorily detained patients there are special rules contained in the Act.

The *Draft Code of Practice* (1988) by the Scottish Home and Health Department (see para 1.3:3) emphasises that in all cases there should be a 'care plan'[1]. The treatment should be discussed with and explained to the patient[2] and any 'intervention' should be the 'minimum necessary to restore the patient to an optimum level of mental health appropriate to his or her particular circumstances'[3].

Consent to treatment

These general principles are to be applied in the light of the specific legal rules laid down in the Act and elsewhere.

Voluntary patients (and certain patients compulsorily detained for short periods)

The following patients compulsorily detained for short periods are in the same position as voluntary patients:

- Patients detained by virtue of emergency recommendations[4]
- Patients compulsorily detained by nurses of the prescribed class[5]
- Patients in certain circumstances who have been conditionally discharged and who have not been recalled to the hospital[6].

Such patients are entitled to refuse their consent to any particular course of treatment proposed in connection with their mental disorder. The rules relating to the type and amount of information which should be given to them are the same as those outlined above[7].

Compulsorily detained patients

There are complex rules contained in Part X of the Act relating to the requirement of consent to treatment of compulsorily detained patients for mental disorder. The main group of people to whom this applies is people detained under s 18 of the Act (see para 2.5).

'Compulsorily detained'[8] patients also includes patients who are in hospital under a hospital order or interim hospital order following conviction of a crime (see paras 5.1:7 and 5.1:16). Also included are patients remanded to a mental hospital before trial. Unfortunately the position of this group of patients is not clearly spelt out in the relevant legislation[9]. They are, however, referred to as 'detained' in the Criminal Procedure (Scotland) Act 1975[10]. (As a matter of policy it would have been preferable that the provisions should have been modified for this group, as in some situations this can result in such a patient being treated without consent and without a second opinion (see para 4.4:6) even though only one doctor has been of the view that their condition was such as to warrant compulsory detention). The legislation does not specify at precisely what point in time the provisions of the Act regarding consent to treatment begin to apply to this group. It appears to be when the **responsible medical officer** has examined the patient and become satisfied that he or she is in a condition which would have warranted compulsory admission under the Act if a criminal court had not been involved[11]. As a matter of good practice the responsible medical officer should record his or her conclusion in writing before treatment is given to which the consent to treatment provisions in the Act apply[12].

People remanded by a court after conviction for a psychiatric report are not, it seems, for these purposes compulsorily detained patients and must be treated as if they were voluntary patients[13].

1 This care plan should be recorded in the patient's medical notes (para 4.5).
2 SHHD Draft Code of Practice (1988) paras 4.2 to 4.7.
3 Ibid, para 4.7.
4 Mental Health (Scotland) Act 1984, s 96(1)(a).
5 Ibid, s 96(1)(b).
6 Ibid, s 96(1)(c).
7 Ibid, s 96.

8 Mental Health (Scotland) Act 1984, s 125(5) ('Any reference to a patient... detained in... a hospital... under this Act... or under Part VI of this Act shall include reference to a patient who is... detained in a hospital... under the Criminal Procedure (Scotland) Act 1975.').
9 It is clear in the English legislation: Mental Health Act 1983, s 36.
10 Criminal Procedure (Scotland) Act 1975, ss 25, 380.
11 At one point in ibid, ss 25(3) and 330(3) the wording of the section seems to assume that the person became 'detained' at an earlier point as it refers 'when the responsible medical officer has examined the person so detained...'. However, the whole scheme of consent to treatment provisions contemplates people compulsorily detained under the Act and people like them who come by way of the criminal courts.
12 In any event, after his or her examination he or she must make a report to the court: ibid, s 25(3).
13 Ibid, ss 180, 381. In s 381(4)(a) there is a reference to 'detained'. However, given that there is no doctor's report that the person is suffering from a condition that would otherwise have warranted compulsory detention means that they do not come naturally within the scheme of the consent to treatment provisions (see also footnote 11). In England the equivalent people are expressly excluded: Mental Health Act 1983, ss 35, 56.

4.4:4 The three categories of treatment for mental disorder—introduction

What is required in respect of consent depends on the category into which a treatment for mental disorder falls. The general position is that the consent of a compulsorily detained patient is not required for a treatment for his or her mental disorder which is given by or under the direction of the responsible medical officer. But (and this is a vital safeguard) there are certain treatments that may not be given without the consent of the patient *and* a second medical opinion, and certain other treatments that may not be given without the consent of the patient *or* a second opinion[1]. So there are three categories:

- treatment requiring consent *and* a second opinion
- treatment requiring consent *or* a second opinion
- treatment which may be given without consent.

The rules are contained in the Act. The Mental Welfare Commission has issued detailed guidance to psychiatrists on its understanding of these provisions and how they should be operated[2]. For the role of the Commission generally see chapter 6.

1 In any situation of ambiguity under the Act a court would interpret the provision on an assumption that Parliament will not have removed the requirement of the patient's consent unless this is clear (*R v Hallstrom, ex p W (No 2)* [1986] 2 All ER 306 at 314 per McCullogh J. The background (in the light of the equivalent English provisions) is detailed in this case at 312–313.
2 This 'Part X Letter' was revised in June 1986 and is currently (1989) being revised again in the light of the experience of the Mental Welfare Commission, much of which is also detailed in its *Annual Reports* (see in particular chapter 6 of the *Annual Report* for 1987 and chapter 12 of the *Annual Report* for 1988). It may in due course be associated with the *Code of Practice (Annual Report of the Mental Welfare Commission for Scotland 1988*, para 12.4.

4.4:5 Category 1: Treatment requiring consent *and* a second opinion

The scope of this category may in the future be extended by regulations issued by the Secretary of State[1]. At present the treatments covered are:

- surgical operation for destroying brain tissue or its functioning[2]

- surgical implantation of hormones for the purpose of reducing male sexual drive[3]. (Not all treatment for reducing male sexual drive is 'hormone' treatment and not all implantation is 'surgical'. Treatments that are not, do not come under this provision.[4])

The patient's consent must be obtained[5]. In addition a doctor appointed by the Mental Welfare Commission and two non-doctors, appointed by it, must certify in writing that 'the patient is capable of understanding the nature, purpose and likely effect of the treatment in question and has consented to it.' The doctor must not be the patient's responsible medical officer[6].

The doctor must also sign a certificate confirming in writing that 'having regard to the likelihood of the treatment alleviating or preventing deterioration of the patient's condition, the treatment should be given'[7].

Before signing the first of these certificates the doctor and the other two people may (but do not have to) visit and interview the patient in private at any reasonable time[8]. The doctor may (but does not have to) also examine the patient and look at any records relating to the patient's treatment[9].

In connection with preparing the second of these certificates the doctor must consult all those he or she considers principally concerned with the patient's treatment[10]. This involves consulting the responsible medical officer and, depending on the circumstances, other people involved, for example doctors, nursing staff, social workers and psychologists.

A copy of both certificates must be sent to the Mental Welfare Commission within seven days[11].

A report on the treatment and the patient's condition must be made by the responsible medical officer to the Mental Welfare Commission whenever it requires a report to be made[12]. If no report is asked for, it must in any event be made on the next occasion when the responsible medical officer prepares a report with a view to renewing the authority to detain the patient compulsorily[13].

There are two situations where treatment falling into this category can be stopped from proceeding after it has been validly started:

- where the Mental Welfare Commission issues a notice to the responsible medical officer to the effect that the certificates issued are no longer to apply to the treatment after a certain date[14]
- where the patient withdraws consent[15].

In both of these situations, the treatment can continue only if the responsible medical officer considers that stopping it would cause serious suffering to the patient[16], or there now exists a situation where treatment can be given without consent anyway (see Category 3 below). Otherwise the treatment must be stopped.

The only way the treatment can be resumed is through the whole procedure being repeated as if the continuation of the treatment was a new treatment with new certificates being produced. If it has been stopped because the patient has withdrawn consent, it is likely that the patient will not in fact renew the consent that has been withdrawn. If that is the case the treatment, of course, cannot be resumed.

1 Mental Health (Scotland) Act 1984, s 97(1)(b).
2 Ibid, s 97(1)(a).
3 Mental Health (Specified Treatments, Guardianship Duties etc) (Scotland) Regulations 1984, SI 1984/1494, reg 3(1).

4 See *R v Mental Health Act Commission, ex p W* (1988) Times, 27 May.
5 Mental Health (Scotland) Act 1984, s 97(2). Treatments under this section have not occurred since 1984. The Mental Welfare Commission requires in its 'Part X' letter (see note 2 at para 4.4:4 above) that the responsible medical office should consult at the earliest opportunity with one of its full-time medical commissioners. Forms for the certificate are provided by the Mental Welfare Commission.
6 Mental Health (Scotland) Act 1984, s 97(2)(a).
7 Ibid, s 97(2)(b). Forms for the certificate are provided by the Mental Welfare Commission.
8 Ibid, s 97(5)(a). The Mental Welfare Commission in its *Annual Report* for 1987, paras 6.7–6.10 has emphasised the importance of this being taken seriously.
9 Mental Health (Scotland) Act 1984, s 97(5)(b).
10 Ibid, s 97(3).
11 Ibid, s 97(4).
12 Ibid, s 99(1)(b).
13 Ibid, s 99(1)(a).
14 Ibid, s 99(2).
15 Ibid, s 101(1).
16 Ibid, s 102(2).

4.4:5 Category 2: Treatment requiring consent *or* a second opinion

The scope of this category may in the future be extended by regulations issued by the Secretary of State[1]. At present the treatments covered are:

- electro-convulsive therapy (ECT)[2]

- long-term administration of drugs where it is three months or more since drugs were first administered after the patient's detention[3]. This is so even if drugs have not been administered continuously for this period.

Where the patient does consent, the responsible medical officer or a doctor appointed by the Mental Welfare Commission must certify in writing that the patient is 'capable of understanding the nature, purpose and likely effects of the treatment and has consented[4].'

If the patient later withdraws consent, the treatment must be stopped unless the responsible medical officer is of the opinion that stopping the treatment would cause serious suffering to the patient[5].

Otherwise the whole procedure must be repeated as if continuation of the treatment was a new treatment. If the patient continues not to consent then the only way the treatment can then take place is by obtaining a second opinion as follows.

A doctor, appointed by the Mental Welfare Commission, must certify in writing either that

- 'the patient has not consented [to the treatment] but that, having regard to the likelihood of its alleviating or preventing a deterioration of his or her condition, the treatment should be given', or

- 'that the patient is not capable of understanding the nature, purpose and likely effects of [the treatment] but that having regard to the likelihood of its alleviating or preventing a deterioration of his or her condition, the treatment should be given[6]'.

As with certificates for cases falling under Category 1 the doctor signing these certificates must consult people who appear to him or her to be principally concerned with the patient's medical treatment. The doctor giving the certificate cannot be the patient's responsible medical officer[7].

A report must be made by the responsible medical officer to the Mental Welfare Commission whenever it requires a report to be made[8]. If no report is asked for, it must in any event be made on the next occasion when the doctor prepares a report with a view to renewing the authority to detain the patient compulsorily[9].

If the treatment is carried out on the basis of a second opinion, it must stop if the Mental Welfare Commission issues a notice to the responsible medical officer to the effect that the certificate shall no longer apply to the treatment after a certain date[10]. The treatment can then only continue if the responsible medical officer considers that stopping it would cause serious suffering to the patient[11], or there now exists a situation where treatment can be given without consent anyway (see Category 3 below). Otherwise the treatment must be stopped. The only way it can be resumed is through the whole procedure being repeated as if the continuation of the treatment was a new treatment with a new certificate being produced.

A copy of any certificates issued must be sent to the Mental Welfare Commission within seven days[12].

1 Mental Health (Scotland) Act 1984, s 98(1)(a).
2 Mental Health (Specified Treatments, Guardianship Duties etc) (Scotland) Regulations SI 1984/1494, reg 3(2).
3 Mental Health (Scotland) Act 1984, s 98(1)(b).
4 Ibid, s 98(3)(a). The Commission emphasises that the doctor must act reasonably and give adequate information to the patient (*Annual Report of the Mental Welfare Commission for Scotland 1988* para 12.10).
5 Ibid, s 102(2).
6 Ibid, s 98(3)(b).
7 Ibid, s 98(4). The Medical Welfare Commission is likely to require (where long-term drug therapy is concerned) that the examinations by second opinion doctors and the issue of certificates by them should be carried out in the last two weeks of the three months following the first administration of medicines for the treatment of mental disorder.
8 Ibid, s 99(1)(b). Although there is no requirement in the Act, the Mental Welfare Commission now reviews the use of such treatments by way of another second opinion every three years in cases where a refusal of consent by a patient was overruled (*Annual Report of the Mental Welfare Commission for Scotland 1987*, para 6.12).
9 Mental Health (Scotland) Act 1984, s 99(1)(a).
10 Ibid, s 99(2).
11 Ibid, s 102(2).
12 Ibid, s 98(5).

4.4:6 Category 3: Where no consent is required

No consent is required for treatment given by the responsible medical officer or under his or her direction if it is treatment for mental disorder and not one of the treatments that falls into one of the two categories considered above. Thus, short-term drug treatment can be given without the patient's consent. There may be procedures that are normally associated with treatment but are not themselves treatment. These would require consent[1]. When treatment is given without consent it should nonetheless be explained to the patient as should the reason why his or her refusal of consent is being over-ruled[2].

There are also a number of situations where treatment in a situation of urgency can be given without consent or a second opinion. Except in the case of treatment immediately necessary to save a patient's life there is a limit even in these situations of urgency on the types of treatment that can be given.

The treatments that can be given without consent in situations of urgency are:

- Treatment which is immediately necessary to save a patient's life[3]. This is the only situation where a treatment that would otherwise fall into one of the two categories already considered can be given whatever the actual or possible side effects and long-term consequences.

- Treatment immediately necessary to prevent a serious deterioration of the patient's condition. The types of treatment allowed must not be 'irreversible'[4]. An 'irreversible' treatment is one that has unfavourable irreversible physical or psychological consequences[5].

- Treatment immediately necessary to alleviate serious suffering by the patient[6]. Again the types of treatment allowed must be not 'irreversible' and in addition the treatment must not be 'hazardous' in the sense that it must not entail significant physical hazard[7].

- Treatment immediately necessary to prevent the patient from behaving violently or being a danger to his or herself or to others[8]. Again the treatment must not be 'irreversible' or hazardous and, in addition, it must only amount to the minimum interference necessary.

So, faced with alternative forms of treatment, in the last two of these treatments, only the least invasive can be used[9]. Even that treatment cannot be used if it is irreversible or hazardous. The Act does not specify what types of treatment are envisaged.

The Mental Welfare Commission must be notified by the responsible medical officer within seven days of the treatment being given[10].

1 Mental Health (Scotland) Act 1984, s 103. The Mental Welfare Commission reports (*Annual Report of the Mental Welfare Commission for Scotland 1987*, para 6.6) that it has advised, having taken legal opinion, that venepuncture to take blood to monitor level of lithium carbonate where a patient was being treated with that drug was not 'treatment' even though it was highly desirable or even essential that it should accompany the use of that drug.
2 *Draft Code of Practice*, para 4.6 (see note 1 at 4.4:3 above).
3 Mental Health (Scotland) Act 1984, s 102(1)(a).
4 Ibid, s 102(1)(b).
5 Ibid, s 102(3).
6 Ibid, s 102(1)(c).
7 Ibid, s 102(3).
8 Ibid, s 102(1)(d).
9 It is in any event good practice that this should be so for all treatment (*Draft Code of Practice*, para 4.6) (see note 1 at 4.4:3 above).
10 Mental Health (Scotland) Act 1984, s 102(4). Giving treatment under these provisions is rare. It usually involves the giving of ECT in a situation of urgency prior to getting a second opinion to enable a course of ECT to be given (under s 98) (See *Annual Report of the Mental Welfare Commission for Scotland 1984*, para 9.14 and the Mental Welfare Commission's 'Part X Letter' (see note 2 at para 4.4:4 above)).

4.5 MONEY AND PROPERTY

4.5:1 Hospital's right to lay down conditions as to what property is kept in the hospital

In principle hospital patients are entitled to keep with them any personal possessions that they wish.

However, this is subject to two considerations. The managers of the hospital have a duty to protect patients and others[1]. They also have to run the hospital.

Dangerous or large articles

The hospital is entitled to refuse to allow patients to keep with them in the hospital dangerous articles, such as knives, drugs and other illicit material. It can also insist that property that is so large that it gets in the way of normal running of the hospital should not be kept there. In these circumstances the hospital can ask a relative or friend of the patient to keep the item in question[2].

Valuables

Hospitals are accustomed to keeping small valuable items like jewellery for patients. Where the patient is not capable of dealing with his or her property the managers of the hospital have a specific power to hold money or valuables on their behalf[3]. Where the patient is capable but wants such items kept, the hospital will make provision for this. The hospital secretary will take a note of the item and lock it up. A receipt should be given to the patient[4]. If the item is lost or damaged the health board (the public body responsible for hospitals) will be liable to compensate the patient for any loss only if 'negligence' on the part of the hospital brought about the loss. If the item is stolen it is unlikely that the health board will accept liability.

Any cash or cheques must be given or sent to the patient personally. Cheques must be made payable to the patient. In each hospital a personal bank account is kept for any patient who requires one[5].

1 See *Reid v Greater Glasgow Health Board* 1976 SLT (Notes) 33.
2 A difficulty may arise if the patient has no friends or relatives or none of these is prepared to take the patient's property. In such a case the appropriate course would be to contact the local social work department.
3 See 4.5:3 below for further details.
4 *Report of the Working Party on Incapax Patients' Funds*, Scottish Home and Health Department, 1985, Appendix III, para 3.1.
5 Apart from very small sums, money should be kept in interest-bearing accounts. The details are given in the *Report of the Working Party on Incapax Patients' Funds*, Scottish Home and Health Department para 43.

4.5:2 Searches

If the hospital staff want to search a patient's possessions in the hospital or search for something on the patient the position depends on whether the patient is a voluntary or compulsorily detained patient.

In the case of a voluntary patient the hospital can require the patient either to submit to a search for which there are reasonable grounds or alternatively leave the hospital[1].

In the case of a compulsorily detained patient this is clearly not possible since the patient must stay in the hospital. If the hospital staff have reasonable grounds for suspecting that patients may have with them material that may injure themselves or other patients then a search may be made of the possessions that the patient has in the hospital[2].

However, the patient's permission should always be obtained if possible. The Mental Welfare Commission has expressed the view that a search should be approved by the patient's consultant, that the patient should preferably be present and there should be at least two members of the hospital staff present[3].

The person of a compulsorily detained patient should not be searched without their permission. The only exception to this would be in an emergency where there are good grounds for believing that there is an immediate danger[4].

The Mental Welfare Commission has expressed the view that where a patient does give permission for a body search it should take place in private and if a search of bodily orifices is carried out on female patients it should be by qualified female nurses and in the presence of a female witness[5].

Material recovered as a result of a search should not be destroyed unless in itself it constitutes an immediate danger where no course of action other than destruction would be reasonable[6].

1 The legal basis for this is that they are entitled to determine the conditions on which patients voluntarily attend hospital so long as they are not unreasonable. If the patient, however, is a potential suicide risk then the hospital may run the risk of being liable for negligence if as a result of being required to leave the hospital a suicide or damage from an attempted suicide takes place. (Compare duty of police where a vulnerable person has been in their direct custody: *Wilson v Chief Constable of Lothian and Borders Police Force* 1989 SLT 97, Lord McCluskey). In this situation the same approach should be taken as that to a compulsorily detained patient.
2 In practice it is difficult to see what remedy the patient would have in any event (since there would be no damage and no time to get an interdict, i.e. a court order preventing this from happening). However, technically speaking, searching someone's belongings without their permission is trespass to moveable goods, unless it is done in circumstances which constitutes a defence to that, and damages could be payable.
3 *Annual Report of the Mental Welfare Commission for Scotland 1987* para 5.3.
4 The Mental Welfare Commission has stated that no search of the person of a compulsorily detained patient should take place without permission: *Annual Report of the Mental Welfare Commission for Scotland 1987* para 5.4. This is clearly good practice. However, there could arise an exceptional situation where immediate emergency justified it and so it would not amount to assault.
5 Ibid, para 5.4.
6 The Mental Welfare Commission has expressed a different view (*Annual Report of the Mental Welfare Commission for Scotland 1987*, para 5.3). Actually to destroy another's property, however, could in principle lead to a court action for damages.

4.5:3 The management of patients' finances etc

Going into hospital does not of itself affect the rights of patients to deal generally with their own money and property. The crucial question is whether the patient is capable of managing his or her own affairs. If the answer is yes, the position is exactly as it is for someone in the community (see para 3.4:2).

If, on the other hand, the patient is incapable of managing his or her own affairs there is one major difference from the position of someone in the community, who has to have a **curator** appointed to manage his or her affairs if informal arrangements are unsatisfactory. In the case of hospital patients, the hospital has power to keep and administer money and valuables for patients who are incapable, because of a mental disorder, of administering their own property and affairs[1].

For this to happen there must be no curator (and the hospital should take reasonable steps to try and find out if one has been appointed)[2]. The doctor in charge of the patient's treatment has to state that the patient is incapable of managing his or her own affairs because of mental disorder. This should be done in writing[3].

There is a system for dealing with patients' funds and small items of property. The day-to-day administration is normally done by charge nurses[4]. In practice, the money and property of the great majority of in-patients is administered by the hospital in conjunction with the health board[5].

Considerable attention has been paid to the system for this by the Mental Welfare Commission[6] and detailed guidance has been given in the *Report of a Working Party on Incapax Patients' Funds* (the Crosby Report)[7] set up by the **Scottish Home and Health Department**.

The job of management of the patient's affairs is to be done so the best can be done for the patient. The hospital has a duty[8] to provide health care free of charge. However, the purchase of items, and expenditure on things that enhance the quality of life, are appropriately done from a patient's own resources[9]. It is desirable that patients should get the items and have money spent on them as they would have done if they had themselves been capable of this.

The managers of the hospital are required to take into account not only the financial value but also the sentimental value to the patient of any item of property they are dealing with[10].

If it is felt that the hospital is not dealing with a patient's affairs correctly, the Mental Welfare Commission should be consulted[11].

The arrangement of having the hospital look after a patient's affairs is not designed to deal with cases where there is more than a modest amount of money and/or property.

The managers of the hospital have to inform the Mental Welfare Commission if the total value of the money and valuables amounts to more than £3,000 and obtain their agreement to the arrangement[12]. The Mental Welfare Commission will not normally agree to this if the value is in excess of £12,000. These figures are revised from time to time.

Where the amount is more than this a curator will normally have to be appointed (see para 3.4:3). If such an appointment is sought by a regional or islands council the managers of the hospital must be informed by the body in question within twenty-eight days of the appointment[13].

Immediate danger of property being lost or damaged

The position is the same as it is where property of a person in the community is concerned. Anyone can step in and act to save the property (see para 3.4:2 for details). The regional or islands council has a duty to take reasonable steps to try and avoid damage to property[14] (see para 3.4:2 for details).

1 Mental Health (Scotland) Act 1984, s 94(1).
2 If there is a curator the hospital cannot act: s 94(6).
3 A suitable form is given in the *Report of the Working Party on Incapax Patients' Funds*. Scottish Home and Health Department (1985).

4 *Report of the Working Party on Incapax Patients' Funds*, Scottish Home and Health Department (1985) paras 55–62.
5 In a survey carried out for the Crosby Report it was found that this was true in the case of 72 per cent. of patients classified as psychiatric or psycho-geriatric and 95 per cent. of patients classified as suffering from mental deficiency. (Appendix II, Table 2).
6 See in particular the *Annual Report of the Mental Welfare Commission for Scotland 1988* chapter 5.
7 Although its recommendations have the support of the Secretary of State for Scotland the *Annual Report of the Mental Welfare Commission for Scotland 1987* noted that so far they had not been implemented in full by health boards (para 5.9).
8 National Health Service (Scotland) Act 1978, ss 1, 36.
9 *Report of the Working Party on Incapax Patients' Funds*, Scottish Home and Health Department, p 16. However, it should be noted that the Mental Welfare Commission has stated its opinion that it is not appropriate to use accumulated funds for patient's clothing (*Annual Report of the Mental Welfare Commission for Scotland 1987* paras 5.7–5.10).
10 Mental Health (Scotland) Act 1984, s 94(3).
11 The hospital should have a procedure for dealing with complaints: *Report of the Working Party on Incapax Patients' Funds*, Scottish Home and Health Department, para 53.
12 Mental Health (Scotland) Act 1984, s 94(2). The amount changes from time to time by direction of the Secretary of State.
13 Ibid, s 92(1).
14 National Assistance Act 1948, s 49 as amended.

4.5:4 Social security and other forms of financial support

Mental disorder is likely to have an impact on financial resources. The main sources of support from state benefits are outlined in chapter 3 at para 3.4:6.

Apart from social security benefits many patients qualify for discretionary payments of pocket money. This is paid by the health board for the area which covers the hospital. The money comes from central government[1]. This money should not be seen as available for the purchase of basic clothing.

Sometimes patients are paid for work they do in the context of their treatment. What they earn is often referred to as 'therapeutic earnings'.

Going into hospital for an extended period of time results in certain social security benefits being reduced or stopped altogether. There is a DSS leaflet (NI 9) summarising the position. Copies of this are available from local social security offices and some post offices. It can also be obtained by post from DSS Leaflets Unit, PO Box 21, Stanmore, Middlesex, HA7 1AY.

The effect on main benefits likely to be being paid is

- Statutory sick pay (SSP)—This continues to be paid while a patient is in hospital

- Sickness benefit—In the majority of cases there is no effect for the first eight weeks in hospital. It is then reduced to a lower figure. The amount of reduction depends on whether the claimant has one or more dependants. There are a small number of cases where it is reduced immediately on going into hospital. These are where the patient has already been in hospital in the period in question for eight weeks and where the patient normally lives in a local authority home or similar place.

- Invalidity benefit—The position is the same as with sickness benefit.

- Special disablement allowance—the position is the same as with sickness benefit.

- Attendance allowance—This will be payable for only four weeks after going into hospital. If the patient is allowed home for a period of time, it may become payable again.

- Income support—Going into hospital generally results in the amount paid as benefit being reduced. The particular circumstances are important and the rules complicated (see DSS Leaflet NI 9).

Fares to hospital (see DSS Leaflet H 11)

National Health Service hospital patients (including those being treated for mental disorder) may be entitled to payment of all or part of the cost of fares to and from hospital.

Patients living in the Highlands or Islands can get paid fares if they have to travel more than thirty miles (or five miles by water), whatever their income.

For other patients entitlement depends on having a low income. This condition is satisfied if the patient is getting income support or family credit. People not receiving these benefits can still qualify if their income is low enough. The hospital will be able to give the necessary information.

If it is medically necessary for someone to travel with a patient who is entitled to payment for fares, the person travelling with them can also get paid.

Close relatives getting income support can get help with fares to make hospital visits. Inquiries should be made at the local social security office.

1 Mental Health (Scotland) Act 1984, s 114.

4.6 THE RIGHT TO PLAY A PART IN PUBLIC LIFE—THE RIGHT TO VOTE

People whom the courts would regard as 'insane' are not entitled to cast their vote. However, this does not mean that any person who is an in-patient cannot vote[1]. Insanity for this purpose means being in a state where the person cannot understand what he or she is doing—the same approach as in marriage law and the law of wills. The Mental Welfare Commission has specifically noted the importance of seeing that patients who wish to vote and are entitled to should be in a position to do so[2].

In any event the right to vote depends on being registered on the voters' roll. If a patient is already registered on the voters' roll that registration will be effective until a new roll is made up.

Rights of patients to get onto a new voters' roll being made up, were significantly altered in 1980. There is a distinction between the position of voluntary patients and the position of other patients.

Voluntary patients are entitled to be registered if they are able without assistance (other than assistance required because of physical incapacity) to make what is known as a 'patient's declaration'[3]. Forms are available from the managers of the hospital. The completed form must be witnessed by a member of the hospital staff and lodged with the electoral registration officer for the appropriate area by 16 December.

It is not possible to register in this way for the purpose of voting only in a local government election[4]. But a registration for the purpose of parliamentary elections qualifies the patient also to vote in local government elections. The patient's declaration can be cancelled by the patient at any time[5].

Once registered, a patient who is on the voter's roll need not vote in person. A postal vote can be arranged[6].

The patient's declaration must state either the address where the patient would be resident in the United Kingdom if he or she were not a patient or the address of a previous residence (other than a mental hospital) in the United Kingdom[7].

In addition to an address in the United Kingdom the patient's declaration must state[8]:

- the date of the declaration

- that on that date and, unless it is the qualifying date, on the qualifying date next following the patient is or will be a voluntary mental patient

- the address of the mental hospital in which the patient is a voluntary patient

- that on the date of the declaration the patient is a Commonwealth citizen or a citizen of the Republic of Ireland

- whether the patient had on the date of the declaration attained the age of eighteen, or (to cover the case when they will have by the qualifying date) the date of birth.

A small number of voluntary patients may not have or have had an address outside the hospital and will not be able to make a patient's declaration, or they cannot do so without assistance, or they cannot come within the other terms required (eg if they are a foreign resident). They will then not be able to vote.

Compulsory patients cannot make a patient's declaration. If they are already registered on a voter's roll (and not so mentally disordered as to be regarded as 'insane') they may get a postal vote.

1 Representation of the People Act 1983, ss 1(1)(b)(i), 2(1)(b)(i).
2 *Annual Report of the Mental Welfare Commission for Scotland 1987*, para 5.1.
3 Representation of the People Act 1983, s 7.
4 Ibid, s 7(9).
5 Ibid, s 7(6).
6 Ibid, s 19(1).
7 Ibid, s 7(4)(d)(iv).
8 Ibid, s 7(4).

5 The criminal courts and mentally disordered people

5.1 MENTAL DISORDER AND THE CRIMINAL COURTS

5.1:1 Introduction

This chapter looks briefly at what can happen when a mentally disordered person comes before the courts accused of a criminal offence. The criminal courts have various powers to deal with mentally disordered persons who come before them, and can, in certain cases, refer them to hospital, although this happens fairly infrequently[1].

This chapter deals only in outline with the alternative courses which may be available, as in most cases the mentally disordered person will need to have legal assistance from a solicitor[2].

The court may take any of the following actions in respect of a mentally disordered person coming before it:

- it may commit him or her to hospital before the trial commences
- it may find that the person is 'insane' and thus unable to stand trial
- a person may be acquitted of an offence because he or she was 'insane' at the time when it was committed
- a person may be committed to hospital on a temporary basis or for medical reports following his or her conviction
- a convicted person may be committed to hospital with or without an order made restricting his or her discharge
- either an accused or a convicted person may be remanded in custody or on bail for psychiatric reports
- a **guardianship order** (see chapter 3) may be made
- the person may be put on probation on condition that he or she receives medical treatment.

1 Scottish Mental Health In-Patient Statistics 1982, Table 4.
2 For further information see Renton and Brown, *Criminal Procedure According to the Laws of Scotland*, chapter 20.

5.1:2 Remand or assessment before trial

The **sheriff court** and the High Court can commit a person awaiting trial or sentence to hospital if the accused person is suffering from a mental disorder[1]. The written or oral evidence of just one doctor is needed. This doctor need not be a specialist in mental disorder.

Before making an order the court must be satisfied that a suitable hospital is willing to admit the accused person.

On admission the **responsible medical officer** at the admitting hospital must examine the patient. If he or she decides that the patient could have been admitted under the compulsory admission procedure previously discussed in chapter 2, then the patient remains in hospital until he or she is tried or sentenced. If the responsible medical officer believes the patient should not remain in hospital, the patient will be discharged and then the court may make any order which it could have made had it not sent the accused person to hospital.

1 Criminal Procedure (Scotland) Act 1975, ss 25, 330 (amended by Mental Health (Scotland) Act 1984, s 127(1), Sch 3, paras 24 and 31).

5.1:3 Insanity in bar of trial

If an accused person is so mentally disordered that he or she cannot instruct the solicitors defending him or her properly, then the court may make the finding of 'insanity in bar of trial'[1]. The aim is to avoid having a trial where the accused person cannot instruct his or her solicitor properly. However this may, as seen below, result in an accused person who is innocent being detained indefinitely.

The question of an accused person's mental fitness to stand trial can be raised by the defence. If it is not raised by the defence and it seems clear that the accused is unable to give instructions due to a mental disorder then the prosecution *must* raise the matter of insanity with the judge[2].

The court can ask at any point during the trial that the case be adjourned for medical reports. Two doctors must agree that the accused person suffers from mental illness or mental handicap or both. One doctor must be an approved specialist in psychiatry. The doctors may be called on to give their evidence personally.

When reports have been ordered, the defence must be given copies and must be allowed to arrange a private examination of the accused person by a doctor of their choice so that he or she can have a chance to dispute the reports.

Courts may, and often do, hear such medical evidence in the absence of the accused person[3].

If the court finds that an accused person is 'insane' and therefore unable to stand trial then, if the case was being dealt with by a judge and jury, the judge must order that the patient be detained in the **State Hospital** at Carstairs or, if there are special reasons, in another hospital[4]. This order has the same effect as a hospital order with a restriction on discharge of unlimited duration[5]. The order is known as a 'restriction order'.

A patient so committed may appeal to the sheriff for his or her discharge. He or she may also be discharged by the **Secretary of State**. The **managers of the hospital** and the responsible medical officer cannot discharge a patient who is under a restriction order.

For more detailed information on restriction orders see para 5.1:11.

Should a person appearing before a district court charged with an offence punishable with imprisonment appear to the court to be 'insane' or suffering from a lesser mental disorder the magistrate must transfer the case to the sheriff court[6]. It is desirable that this should be done at once and before the trial begins, but it may be only when the person gives evidence that the disorder becomes apparent.

That a person is insane and unable to stand trial does not mean that he or she is cleared of the crime. If the patient were to recover his or her sanity he or she could be brought back again to trial because they would then be able to instruct their own defence. In practice this hardly ever happens.

1 Criminal Procedure (Scotland) Act 1975, ss 174(1), 375(2).
2 Ibid, s 376(5).
3 Ibid, ss 174(5), 375(4).
4 Ibid, s 174(3).
5 Ibid, s 174(4).
6 Ibid, s 376(4).

5.1:4 What the courts mean by 'insanity'

In certain cases, as has been seen, a person will receive different treatment from the courts if he or she is regarded by them as 'insane'.

The decision as to whether an accused person is regarded by the law as insane is one of fact, and is not left to psychiatrists. There is no precise definition of insanity for this purpose. The courts have emphasised that what is required is 'an absolute alienation of reason in relation to the act charged'. In considering this, the question whether the accused person understood the nature and quality of what he or she had done and that it was legally and morally wrong, is an element to be taken into account, but it is not conclusive[1].

Loss of mental control from self-inflicted means, such as drink or drugs, does not constitute insanity.

Sheriff Gordon, the author of a major book on Scottish criminal law, has argued that the lack of any authoritative definition of a person's fitness to stand trial has had unfortunate results in Scotland. Generally the evidence of medical experts is relied on and only rarely does the judge put the matter to the jury.

There is a tendency for courts to interpret unfitness to plead very widely so that many people who are mentally disordered are regarded as unfit to plead merely because of the mental disorder. Such people may, in fact, be able to understand the case against them and instruct a lawyer. They will be deprived of a trial and committed to hospital.

It is in such people's interests that they should stand trial and be convicted (or acquitted) and then given appropriate sentences rather than that they be committed to hospital without time limit.

The Thomson Committee which reported on Scottish Criminal Procedure (Cmnd 6218/1975) proposed a test which would mean that only severely disordered people would be found unfit to stand trial: 'Is the accused incapable by reason of mental disorder... of understanding the charge and proceedings and of communicating adequately with his [or her] legal advisers?'[2].

1 For a further discussion on 'insanity' and the criminal law, see Gloag & Henderson *Introduction to the Law of Scotland*, 9th edn, pp 897. See in particular *Brennan v HM Advocate* 1977 SLT 151 and *HM Advocate v Kidd* 1961 JC 61.
2 Gordon, *Criminal Law* p 377. For a very thorough investigation into the way mentally disordered offenders are dealt with by the police, procurators fiscal and the courts, see

Chiswick, McIsaac and McLintock, *Prosecution of the Mentally Disturbed* (Aberdeen University Press, 1984).

5.1:5 Acquittal by reason of insanity

Where an accused person is to be tried by judge and jury he or she may sometimes be acquitted because he or she was 'insane' when the offence was committed[1]. This is because the law says that a person cannot be guilty of committing a criminal offence unless he or she *intended* to commit it. If the accused person was 'insane' and did not know what he or she was doing or that it was wrong, there would be no criminal 'intent', and the person would have to be found not guilty.

A defence of insanity at the time the offence was committed can be employed even if the accused person is no longer insane and is now fit to stand trial.

However, the defence is very rarely used. This is because if a jury acquits a person because he or she has been shown to have been insane at the time of the offence, then the court must order that the accused person be detained in the State hospital in Carstairs, notwithstanding the acquittal[2]. The same requirement does not bind the court in a summary case[3].

This order has the same effect as a hospital order with a restriction order of unlimited duration (see para 5.1:11). Only the Secretary of State for Scotland or the sheriff, following an appeal, may grant the subsequent discharge of the patient from hospital.

If an accused person is acquitted due to his or her insanity at the time of the act, then he or she cannot be tried again for the same offence.

1 Criminal Procedure (Scotland) Act 1975, s 174(2).
2 Ibid, s 174(3).
3 *Smith v M* 1983 SCCR 67 (Sh Ct).

5.1:6 Diminished responsibility

There is only one area of criminal law where a mental condition instead of being a complete defence has the effect of reducing the severity of the crime for which the accused person can be convicted. This is to do with unlawful killing.

Someone suffering from 'diminished responsibility' when killing another cannot be convicted of the crime of murder. Instead, if the facts are proved, they will be convicted of 'culpable homicide', that is killing under extenuating circumstances. 'Diminished responsibility' is difficult to define precisely. It means a mental state which does not amount to 'insanity' but '... an aberration, a weakness of mind ... some form of mental unsoundness ... a mind so affected that responsibility is diminished from full responsibility to partial responsibility. In other words the prisoner in question must be only partially accountable for his [or her] actions. There must be some form of mental disease[1]'.

While the idea of 'diminished responsibility' was introduced into the law to protect people from suffering the death penalty, it is still important since the sentence for murder is mandatory life imprisonment, and acquittal on the ground of insanity results in committal to the State Hospital on an indefinite basis. By contrast a conviction for culpable homicide allows the judge more discretion as to sentence.

1 *HMA v Savage* 1923 JC 49 at 51 per Lord Alness—the statement usually thought to be the classic definition.

5.1:7 Interim hospital orders on conviction

The interim hospital order is a new type of order brought in by the **1983 Act**[1]. These orders may be made where a person is convicted in the High Court or sheriff court of any offence punishable with imprisonment, other than murder[2]. Where a person is convicted of murder the court must impose a sentence of life imprisonment.

If the court is satisfied on the evidence of two doctors that an offender is suffering from a mental disorder which could be treated in the State Hospital at Carstairs, it may make a temporary hospital order before reaching a final decision on what sentence to pass.

The interim hospital order allows the offender to be admitted to the State Hospital or, if there are special reasons, another hospital. The first period of detention cannot exceed twelve weeks[3]. This twelve week period may be extended by the court for up to twenty-eight days at a time. The total length of detention must not exceed six months[4].

If a temporary hospital order is made the court must not make any other order for that conviction until it expires[5]. Thereafter the court has the same powers to deal with the offender as it had before it made the order[6].

The convicted person can appeal against the temporary hospital order. If he or she does not appeal or if his or her appeal is not successful, he or she has no right to appeal against later renewals of the order[7].

These new provisions are additional to the existing power of remand which the courts have (see para 5.1:8). The courts can only remand a convicted offender in custody for up to three weeks at a time for a medical examination and report[8].

1 Criminal Procedure (Scotland) Act 1975, ss 174A, 375A (added by the Mental Health (Amendment) (Scotland) Act 1983, s 34).
2 Criminal Procedure (Scotland) Act 1975, ss 174A(1), 375A(1).
3 Ibid, ss 174A(6), 375A(6)(a).
4 Ibid, ss 174A(6)(b), 375A(6)(a).
5 Ibid, ss 174A(4), 375A(5).
6 Ibid, ss 174A(9), 375A(10).
7 Ibid, s 280.
8 Ibid, ss 180(1), 381(1).

5.1:8 Remand after conviction

The courts may **remand** a person either in custody or on bail in order to get a psychiatric report before sentence[1].

This gives the court the chance to judge the accused person's physical and mental condition before sentencing him or her, but without requiring him or her to go to hospital. The accused person may be medically examined as a condition of bail[2]. The initial remand can be for up to three weeks. Remand may be renewed for periods of up to three weeks as necessary[3].

There is no right of appeal against remand orders or the extension of these orders by the court.

1 Criminal Procedure (Scotland) Act 1975, ss 180(1), 381(1)(a).

2 Ibid, ss 180(2), 381(2).
3 Ibid, ss 180(1), 381(1).

5.1:9 Detention in a hospital after conviction—hospital orders

Any person convicted of an offence punishable with imprisonment, other than murder, may be detained compulsorily in a mental hospital by the High Court[1] or by the sheriff court[2]. A hospital order may be made in the case of a person convicted in a district court only if he or she is remitted to the sheriff court for sentencing.

The court may make a restriction order with the hospital order if it is necessary to do so to protect the public from serious harm[3]. The effect of the restriction order is to put responsibility for the discharge of the patient with the Secretary of State. An appeal may also be made to the sheriff to discharge the order (see para 5.1:13). A restriction order may last either for a fixed length of time or for an indefinite period. In either case the Secretary of State may at any time direct that the patient shall no longer be subject to the special restrictions.

See para 5.1:11 which deals in detail with restriction orders.

1 Criminal Procedure (Scotland) Act 1975, s 175.
2 Ibid, s 376.
3 Ibid, ss 178(1), 379(1).

5.1:10 Hospital orders

The grounds for a hospital order are that the accused person must be suffering from a mental disorder of a nature or degree that would justify him or her being admitted under the application for compulsory hospital admission procedure discussed in chapter 2 (ie that the **statutory grounds for admission** apply in the accused person's case)[1]. The court must adjourn the case if further time is needed in the interests of the accused person for the evidence to be studied[2]. If the accused person wishes to dispute the medical report, arrangements may be made for a private medical examination[3].

A hospital order must not be made unless the court is satisfied that that is the most suitable method of dealing with the case[4]. The court must not require the accused person to be committed to the State Hospital unless it is satisfied on the medical evidence that special security is required[5].

The hospital must be ready to admit the patient within twenty-eight days[6]. Once admitted, the patient is generally treated as if on the date of the order he or she was admitted under the compulsory admission procedures outlined in chapter 2.

The patient can appeal to the sheriff for discharge if the hospital managers renew the authority to detain him or her; and the **Mental Welfare Commission** and responsible medical officer can also both discharge the patient. The patient cannot, however, be discharged by his or her **nearest relative**. If the patient is discharged, the court cannot stop this or impose another sentence.

1 Criminal Procedure (Scotland) Act 1975, ss 175(1), 376(1).
2 Ibid, ss 176(3), 377(3).

3 Ibid, ss 176(4), 377(4).
4 Ibid, ss 175(1)(b), 376(1)(b).
5 Ibid, ss 175(4), 376(7).
6 Ibid, ss 175(3), 376(6).

5.1:11 Restriction orders

A restriction order is automatically imposed where an accused person is found unfit to stand trial by virtue of insanity or is acquitted by a jury of an offence because of insanity.

The court may impose a restriction order in other circumstances[1]. A restriction order may be made where it seems to the court that because of the nature of the offence, the person's previous history and the risk that he or she would commit offences if allowed to go free, an order is necessary to protect the public from serious harm[2]. The doctor involved must give evidence in person before a restriction order can be made[3].

A patient under a restriction order can be discharged only following a successful appeal to the sheriff[4], (see para 5.1:13) or by the Secretary of State.

A patient under a restriction order cannot be discharged by the responsible medical officer, the nearest relative or the Mental Welfare Commission.

A restriction order may be made for a fixed period or an unlimited period.

If it is made for a fixed period, during that period the patient can be discharged only by the sheriff or by the Secretary of State (see para 5.1:12 below). After the fixed period expires he or she continues to be detained compulsorily but under the normal rules applying to patients detained following an application for admission.

In the case of patients under limited restriction orders, only the sheriff or Secretary of the State may discharge the patient.

1 Criminal Procedure (Scotland) Act 1975, ss 178(1), 379(1).
2 Ibid, ss 178(1), 379(1).
3 Ibid, ss 178(2), 379(2) (as amended by the Mental Health (Scotland) Act 1984, s 127(1), Sch 3, para 28).
4 Mental Health (Scotland) Act 1984, s 64.

5.1:12 The power of the Secretary of State to discharge patients under restriction orders

The Secretary of State may require a report from the responsible medical officer as often as he or she wishes and in any event at least once per year[1].

Following receipt of the reports, the Secretary of State may either decide to continue the patient's detention, discharge him or her absolutely, or agree to his or her conditional discharge.

See para 5.1:14 below for conditional discharge.

1 Mental Health (Scotland) Act 1984, s 62(2).

5.1:13 Appeal to the sheriff

A patient under a restriction order can appeal to the sheriff of the sheriffdom within which the hospital in which he or she is liable to be detained is situated[1].

A patient may appeal both between the sixth and twelfth month of detention[2] and within any later period of twelve months[3]. A form of legal aid known as 'assistance by way of representation' may be available for such an appeal (see chapter 7).

If the appeal succeeds the sheriff may either grant the patient an absolute discharge or may conditionally discharge the patient[4].

There is no appeal against the sheriff's decision to the sheriff principal but judicial review may be available[5].

1 Mental Health (Scotland) Act 1984, s 63(2). There is no appeal against the sheriff's decision.
2 Ibid, s 63(2)(a).
3 Ibid, s 63(2)(b).
4 Ibid, s 64.
5 *T v Secretary of State for Scotland* 1987 SCLR 65, and see para 2.5:4.

5.1:14 Conditional discharge

A patient who is conditionally discharged may leave the hospital and live outside the hospital but may be recalled to hospital by the Secretary of State for as long as the restriction order lasts[1].

The patient must also comply with such conditions (if any) as may be imposed at the time of the conditional discharge by the sheriff or subsequently by the Secretary of State[2]. The conditions may be varied by the Secretary of State[3].

Where a conditionally discharged patient is in breach of a condition of his or her discharge this can result in him or her being recalled to hospital. The patient may appeal against the recall within one month of the day on which he or she is returned to hospital[4].

A conditionally discharged patient who is not recalled may appeal against the conditional discharge in the period between the expiry of twelve months and two years beginning with the date on which he or she was conditionally discharged. The patient may also appeal within any subsequent two year period[5]. On hearing the appeal the sheriff can grant the absolute discharge of the patient or vary any conditions attached to the conditional discharge[6].

The right of appeal against continuing discharge could be very important. Otherwise a patient under a restriction order of unlimited duration could find him or herself conditionally discharged but liable to recall by the Secretary of State for life.

Legal aid may be available for an appeal against conditional discharge (see chapter 7).

1 Mental Health (Scotland) Act 1984, s 64(4)(a).
2 Ibid, s 64(4)(b).
3 Ibid, s 64(5).
4 Ibid, s 66(1).
5 Ibid, s 66(2).
6 Ibid, s 66(3).

5.1:15 The Mental Welfare Commission

The Mental Welfare Commission cannot discharge patients subject to restriction orders but it may recommend that a restricted patient be discharged[1]. It is also available for consultation and advice in connection with the patient's general welfare, treatment and property. Patients or relatives should not hesitate to contact the Mental Welfare Commission in connection with persons under restriction orders.

1 Mental Health (Scotland) Act 1984, s 3(3); see chapter 6.

5.1:16 Transfer from prison to hospital

A prisoner may be transferred from prison to hospital either before or after sentence.

Before trial or sentence

Before a patient awaiting trial or sentence can be transferred from prison to hospital the **statutory grounds for admission** to hospital must apply (see para 2.5:3). In addition the Secretary of State must ask the sheriff for an order to transfer the prisoner[1]. Such an order has the same effect as a hospital order linked to a restriction order with no time limit[2] (see para 5.1:11).

The order continues until the case is finished or the proceedings dropped[3]. However if the responsible medical officer later reports that the prisoner no longer needs treatment for mental disorder, then the Secretary of State may transfer him or her back to custody[4].

If the prisoner remains in hospital until sentence is passed and the court does not pass a custodial sentence (or a hospital, guardianship order or probation order) the patient will automatically continue to be detained in hospital as if he or she had been admitted as a result of an application for compulsory admission[5]. From this point onwards all the provisions described in chapter 2 concerning compulsory admission to hospital apply.

After sentence—transfer orders

Prisoners serving custodial sentences may be transferred to a hospital if the Secretary of State so directs[6]. The Secretary of State must be satisfied from medical reports that the prisoner could be admitted under the compulsory admission procedure[7].

Prisoners so transferred may appeal to the sheriff within one month of their transfer to hospital. The sheriff cannot set the prisoner free but may cancel the order transferring him or her to hospital. If the appeal succeeds then the prisoner would be returned to the prison he or she had come from[8].

The Secretary of State may also impose a restriction direction on the transfer order[9].

Restriction directions

A restriction direction has almost the same effect as a restriction order (see para 5.1:11). The only difference is that a restriction direction can last only as long as the prison sentence still left to serve[10]. So the prisoner who still has three years of a sentence to serve when he or she is transferred to hospital cannot have a five year restriction direction imposed on him or her. Only a restriction direction lasting a maximum of three years can be imposed.

A prisoner with a restriction direction may appeal to the sheriff against the direction. The right of appeal takes effect in the same way as the right to appeal against a restriction order (see para 5.1:13)[11]. If the prisoner succeeds in the appeal he or she may either be returned to the prison from which he or she came, or be released on licence or subject to supervision, or continue to be detained in hospital but without the restriction direction[12].

Discharge from hospital

The Secretary of State must keep the condition of prisoners transferred to hospital under review. If the Secretary of State is satisfied that

- a prisoner is not suffering from a mental disorder which requires in-patient hospital treatment or
- that it is not necessary for the patient's health or safety or for the protection of others that he or she should receive such treatment; and
- that he or she should not be required to return to hospital for further treatment

then the Secretary of State must either

- transfer the prisoner back to the prison or other institution from which he or she came, for the remainder of the sentence, or
- release the prisoner on licence or under supervision (if the institution from which he or she came would have had this power)[13].

If the Secretary of State believes that, although the prisoner is not at the time of the review suffering from a mental disorder, it may be appropriate for him or her to be recalled to hospital for treatment in the future, then he or she may decide that the prisoner shall continue to be detained in hospital[14].

Expiry of restriction direction

Within twenty-eight days before the restriction direction ceases to have effect (ie before the end of the prisoner's original sentence) the responsible medical officer must obtain an independent medical report on the condition of the prisoner. If he or she thinks it is necessary in the interests of the health and safety of the prisoner *or* for the protection of others that the prisoner should continue to be detained in hospital then he or she must report this to the managers of the hospital and to the Mental Welfare Commission[15]. The prisoner will then be treated as if a hospital order (without a restriction order) had been made on expiry of the restriction direction. (See para 5.1:10).

The prisoner can then appeal to the sheriff for discharge[16].

Unless the responsible medical officer sends such a report within the required time limits, the prisoner will be discharged on expiry of the restriction direction[17].

1 Mental Health (Scotland) Act 1984, s 70(1).
2 Ibid, s 70(3).
3 Ibid, s 73(1).
4 Ibid, s 73(2).
5 Ibid, s 73(3).
6 Ibid, s 71.
7 Ibid, s 71(1).
8 Ibid, s 71(5).
9 Ibid, s 72.
10 Ibid, s 74(3).
11 Ibid, s 63.
12 Ibid, s 65.

13 Ibid, s 74(1).
14 Ibid, s 74(2)(c).
15 Ibid, s 74(5).
16 Ibid, s 74(6).
17 Ibid, s 74(4).

5.1:17 Guardianship orders

The court may make a guardianship order in respect of a person convicted of an offence. This may be made in the same circumstances as a hospital order if the court is satisfied that the **medical and welfare grounds** for guardianship apply (para 3.1:3). The effect of such an order is the same as a guardianship order made by the sheriff (see para 3.1) except that the nearest relative of the prisoner has no power to terminate the guardianship[1].

1 Criminal Procedure (Scotland) Act 1975, ss 175, 176, 376 and 377.

5.1:18 Probation orders

The courts can also make a probation order in respect of a convicted offender. If the court is satisfied that the mental condition of an offender is such that he or she requires treatment for a mental disorder, then it may attach a condition to the probation order requiring him or her to be treated by a doctor for up to twelve months[1].

One of the following methods of treatment may be specified in the order

- treatment as an in-patient in hospital (but not the State Hospital)[2]
- out-patient hospital treatment[3] or
- treatment by such doctor as is specified in the order[4].

Before imposing such conditions of treatment the court must be satisfied that all necessary arrangements have been made[5]. The court cannot, for example, make in-patient treatment a condition of the probation order if it is not first satisfied that a bed is available in the hospital specified.

The conditions of treatment can be altered if the medical officer treating the patient believes the patient requires a different type of treatment or treatment at a different hospital[6].

Such a change in treatment can be made only if both the person on probation and the probation officer agree.

If the person on probation fails to comply with any of the requirements of the probation order (including the treatment conditions) he or she will be required to appear in court to explain this[7] or a warrant may be issued for his or her arrest. If no satisfactory answer is received, the court may fine or sentence the offender[8].

A person on probation is not to be regarded as in breach of the probation order only because he or she refuses to undergo surgical, ECT or other treatment, unless the court thinks it was reasonable that he or she should undergo it[9].

1 Criminal Procedure (Scotland) Act 1975, ss 184(1), 385(1).
2 Ibid, ss 184(2)(a), 385(2)(a).
3 Ibid, ss 184(2)(b), 385(2)(b).

4 Ibid, ss 184(2)(c), 385(2)(c).
5 Ibid, ss 184(3), 385(3).
6 Ibid, ss 184(5), 385(5) (substituted by the Mental Health (Amendment) (Scotland) Act 1983, s 36(2)).
7 Criminal Procedure (Scotland) Act 1975, ss 186(1), 387(1).
8 Ibid, ss 186(2), 387(2).
9 Ibid, ss 186(4), 387(4).

5.2 THE STATE HOSPITAL

The State Hospital at Carstairs Junction is the only hospital of its type in Scotland. The Secretary of State for Scotland has direct responsibility for this hospital which exists to provide treatment under conditions of special security for those patients who are deemed to have 'dangerous, violent or criminal propensities'[1]. These patients must be suffering from mental disorder as defined by the Mental Health (Scotland) Act 1984. This means that the State Hospital provides treatment for both mentally handicapped and mentally ill patients.

The patients in the State Hospital are compulsorily detained, not always as a result of criminal proceedings. Many are admitted from other mental hospitals in Scotland. Patients transferred from these hospitals are those patients considered to require a greater degree of security and supervision than local hospitals can provide.

A patient who is transferred to the State Hospital from another hospital has the right to appeal against the transfer within twenty-eight days. This right of appeal may be exercised either by the patient or his or her nearest relative. The appeal should be addressed to the sheriff for the area of the hospital from which the patient was transferred.

The sheriff must order that the patient be returned to the hospital from which he or she was transferred unless he or she is satisfied that the patient requires treatment under conditions of special security because of his or her dangerous, violent or criminal propensities, and that the patient cannot suitably be cared for in any other hospital[2].

Legal aid may be available to meet the costs of an appeal (see chapter 7).

Another category of patient admitted to the State Hospital covers people who have been transferred from prison or other penal institutions into the hospital while serving their sentences.

Clearly then, not all patients admitted to the State Hospital are admitted as a result of criminal activity. Many of the patients admitted to the hospital have no criminal record whatsoever.

The average length of stay in the State Hospital has in the past been seven years. This is in stark contrast to the average length of stay in other mental institutions in Scotland where the majority of these patients are discharged within four weeks of admission[3].

Because of the unique nature of the State Hospital, the Mental Welfare Commission has developed a policy of visiting the hospital more frequently than any other in Scotland.

The Mental Welfare Commission has the same responsibilities in respect of patients in the State Hospital as it has in respect of any other mentally

The State Hospital

disordered persons. It has no power to discharge a patient who is subject to a restriction order or a restriction direction, but it may recommend to the Secretary of State that a patient be discharged[4].

1 Mental Health (Scotland) Act 1984, s 90(1).
2 Ibid, s 29(4). See *Ferns v Management Committee and Managers of Ravenscraig Hospital* 1987 SLT (Sh Ct) 76. Evidence should be led from which the court can infer that no other hospital in Scotland is a suitable alternative to the State hospital (Sheriff Principal Caplan at p 80). (This point was not considered by 2nd Division of the Court of Session on appeal (1989 SLT 49)). See also Appendix 3.
3 Scottish Mental Health In-Patient Statistics 1984, Table 4.14.
4 Mental Health (Scotland) Act 1984, s 3(3).

6 Protection of patients' interests and the Mental Welfare Commission for Scotland

This chapter deals with the Mental Welfare Commission's constitution and general function as well as its specific powers and duties. It also deals with the question of complaints generally.

6.1 CONSTITUTIONAL AND GENERAL FUNCTIONS

The **Mental Welfare Commission** for Scotland is located at 25 Drumsheugh Gardens, Edinburgh EH3 7RB (Phone No 031-225 7034).

The job of the Commission is to protect mentally disordered people who are unable adequately to protect themselves or their interests[1]. This includes safeguarding the welfare and rights of detained patients and also of voluntary patients in hospitals. The Commission is also responsible for the welfare of mentally disordered people in the community, whether they are subject to a formal **guardianship order** or not.

The Commission will generally look into individual cases only when they are brought to its attention. Anyone—not just a doctor or a patient—can bring a case to the Commission's attention. The Commission can be contacted at the above address, by letter, telephone call or in person. (It is best to telephone to make an appointment first).

The Commission consists of at least ten members. Of these members at least three must be women, one must be a lawyer and three must be doctors[2]. Over the years it has been accepted that there should be a majority of non-medical members. This is to reassure detained patients that their continued detention does not rest exclusively in medical hands[3]. In order to assist the Commissioners in their work, the Commission now employs three medical officers and a social work officer.

In the past the Commission has seen its role largely in terms of responding to individual cases brought to its attention. Following the 1984 legislation it became clear to the Commission that both the public and Parliament wished it to be more active in initiating inquiries and seeking out general topics of concern for investigation and report. Since then, it has been active in identifying causes for concern. In recent *Annual Reports* it has reported on, among other things:

- Patients detained in the **State Hospital** who no longer require its facilities but for whom there is no suitable alternative place in a hospital

- The working of the consent to treatment regulations

- Alleged deficiencies of care in various hospitals
- Seclusion and time-out (procedures in hospitals for mentally disordered people used to counteract undesirable or problem behaviour of patients) and
- The provision of semi-secure and intensive psychiatric care units, (urging the **Secretary of State** to review his policy).

It has also played a vigorous role in arguing for an improvement in the care of mentally disordered people in hospitals. In its *Annual Report for 1986* it drew attention to the poor staffing levels in hospitals for both mental illness and mental handicap, and in October 1987 it took the exceptional step of issuing a press statement drawing attention to the 'scandalous conditions of general neglect' seen by Commissioners in parts of many hospitals.

It has, therefore, proved to be extremely active and an outspoken champion of the rights of mentally disordered people in hospital and in the community, and its *Annual Reports* are essential reading.

Any person who is concerned about the treatment or living conditions of a mentally disturbed person is urged to contact the Mental Welfare Commission at the above address.

1 Mental Health (Scotland) Act 1984, s 3(1). Contrast the situation in England, where the Mental Health Act Commission is concerned only with the welfare of compulsorily detained patients.
2 Ibid, s 2(2).
3 See *Does the Patient Come First?—An Account of the Work of the Mental Welfare Commission for Scotland between 1975 and 1980*, p 2 at para 2.

6.2 THE COMMISSION'S POWERS AND DUTIES

6.2:1 The discharge of compulsory patients

As mentioned in chapters 2 and 5, the Mental Welfare Commission has an independent power to discharge any patient except those subject to **restriction orders** or **restriction directions**. Even in those cases it can recommend to the Secretary of State that the patient be discharged[1].

The Commission must discharge a patient from hospital or from a guardianship order if it decides that his or her disorder is such that hospital treatment or guardianship is either no longer appropriate or no longer necessary[2].

In practice, however, it is rare for the Commission to exercise these powers. (Thus, in 1987–8 the Commission discharged just two patients from compulsory detention under s 18 of **the Act**, and none from short term detention (under s 26 of the Act). This is because the **responsible medical officer**, who is nearer to hand, has the same duties and in most cases the Commission has taken the view, after consultation with the responsible medical officer, that it is in the best interests of the patient's continuing treatment that he or she be discharged by the responsible medical officer.

Where it is felt that that hospital treatment or guardianship is no longer required and the responsible medical officer has failed to take action, the Commission should be contacted.

The Commission must also bring to the attention of the **managers of the hospital** any case where it considers a patient is being improperly detained[3].

By bringing the case to the attention of the hospital managers, the Commission provides the opportunity for the responsible medical officer to discharge the patient.

1 Mental Health (Scotland) Act 1984, s 3(3).
2 Ibid, ss 33(3), 50(3), and see paras 2.7 and 3.1:15.
3 Ibid, s 3(2)(d)(iii).

6.2:2 Looking into complaints

The Commission must investigate any case where it appears that a person with a mental disorder (whether in hospital or in the community) is being ill-treated or improperly detained or receiving inadequate care or treatment[1].

The Commission's policy is to visit at least once a year each of the fifty or so hospitals in Scotland which provide care to mentally disordered people. These visits can be unannounced, and hospital staff will have no prior notice of the intended visit. (During 1987 it made unannounced visits to two hospitals.) Most complaints come to the Commission's attention during these routine visits to hospitals by members of the Commission. Nevertheless any person may bring a complaint directly to the attention of the Commission.

In 1985 the Commission started a programme of 'community visits' to hostels, small group homes and day-care centres run by social work departments and voluntary agencies.

It is a matter for the Commission how a particular complaint is investigated. It may correspond freely with the patient (see chapter 4) and has the right to interview any patient in private[2].

Its medical commissioners may also examine any patient in private and inspect the patient's medical records[3].

The complaints received by the Commission may either be investigated on an informal basis or by setting up a committee of inquiry. The Commission can appoint an experienced lawyer to conduct an investigation[4]. It must appoint such a lawyer or one of the Commission's lawyer members to chair any committee of inquiry which it sets up[5]. Such committees of inquiry have some of the powers and privileges of courts and a person giving evidence before them may be examined under oath.

The Commission has powers to rectify any unsatisfactory situation which it uncovers or which is brought to its attention. These powers are restricted. But it does have the ability to give effective publicity. Indeed the Commission must

- bring to the attention of the managers of the hospital or the **regional or islands council** the facts of any cases where it feels that either of them ought to take action to secure the welfare of patients who are being inadequately treated or improperly detained or whose property is at risk[6]

- report to the Secretary of State, a **health board** or a regional or islands council on any matter which has been referred to it by any of these bodies[7]

- bring to the attention of the Secretary of State, a health board, a regional or islands council or any other body, any matter concerning the welfare of any people who are suffering from mental disorder which the Commission considers ought to be brought to their attention[8].

The Commission's powers and duties 109

1 Mental Health (Scotland) Act 1984, s 3(2)(a).
2 Ibid, s 3(5).
3 Ibid, s 3(6).
4 Ibid, s 3(8).
5 Ibid, s 3(9).
6 Ibid, s 3(2)(d).
7 Ibid, s 3(2)(e).
8 Ibid, s 3(2)(f).

6.2:3 Protection of property

The Commission is required to investigate any case where it is alleged that a mentally disordered person's property is at risk[1].

The Commission has in the past devoted much time and energy to the protection of patients' property and financial interests. Because the Commission has the powers of investigation and report referred to above, it can examine a wide range of financial difficulties encountered by patients.

The Commission's advice may be sought on such diverse financial matters as eligibility for social security benefits and the appointment of a person (known as a **curator bonis**—see chapter 3) to manage the property of a mentally disordered person.

It has the express power to petition either the local **sheriff court** or the **Court of Session** in Edinburgh for the appointment of a curator bonis where it is satisfied that any person is incapable by reason of mental disorder of adequately managing his or her property and affairs[2].

1 Mental Health (Scotland) Act 1984, s 3(2)(a).
2 Ibid, s 93.

6.2:4 Consent to treatment

The Commission plays an important role in those situations where a second opinion is required before treatment can be given (see para 4.4:5). It is perhaps not surprising, as the Commission has noted, that a small number of psychiatrists question the usefulness of the consent to treatment rules and are irritated by the Commission's thorough monitoring of them[1]. They remain bound by the rules, however, and the Commission will continue to enforce them for the protection of the public.

The Commission has highlighted various factors indicating the real importance of its role, and the role of its second opinion doctors as a safeguard.

It has for example

- given special consideration to whether guidance should be issued on the maximum number of ECTs (electro-conclusive therapy treatments) which should be allowed with further consultation with the Commission's second opinion doctors[2].

- noted that it has seen a number of cases where a plan of treatment for high dosage drugs, or a number of drugs simultaneously, was limited by the doctor giving the second opinion[3].

- observed that the Commissioners have come across a number of cases where patients who did not appear to be able to understand the nature and purpose of treatment proposed for them had been certified by their responsible medical officers as able to do so, and so able to give their consent. In many of these cases the Commission asked the responsible medical officers to review the patient's case, and on many occasions (although not always) this resulted in a subsequent request for a second opinion[4].

1 *Annual Report of the Mental Welfare Commission for Scotland 1986*, para 7.10.
2 Ibid, para 7.10.
3 Ibid, para 7.13.
4 Ibid, para 7.16.

6.2:5 Visiting

The Commission must regularly visit all patients who are compulsorily detained in hospital or who are subject to a guardianship order. It must allow all patients the opportunity of a private interview with the Commissioners. (Any other patient in the hospital can request such an interview if he or she has a matter to discuss which might be relevant to the Commissioners' work[1].)

The Commission must visit at least once a year all patients whose compulsory detention in hospital has been renewed after the first year of detention. However, it is not required to do so where the patient has appealed to the sheriff for discharge during the year in question[2].

Clearly the Commission has a wide responsibility and considerable power to assist people suffering from a mental disorder. Anyone concerned about the welfare of a person suffering from a mental disorder, whether as a patient or in the community, should get in touch with the Mental Welfare Commission and ask for assistance. This, of course, includes patients themselves.

1 Mental Health (Scotland) Act 1984, s 3(2)(b).
2 Ibid, s 3(2)(c).

6.3 COMPLAINTS

6.3:1 Introduction

A number of safeguards are built into the Act. These are of great significance for patients and those closely involved with them. There are rights of appeal to the sheriff such as against being compulsorily detained (see chapter 2). The Mental Welfare Commission exists to safeguard the interests of mental patients, and also of mentally disordered people in the community. It is usually an appropriate place for making complaints. The way the Commission looks into complaints is considered earlier in this chapter.

There are other complaint mechanisms that can, depending on the circumstances, be relevant to patients and those involved with them.

6.3:2 Hospital doctors and nurses

Complaints specifically about a hospital doctor or nurse can be made to the health board. The person to contact is the General Manager of the health board at the health board office. National Health Service hospital doctors and nurses are employed by the health boards.

Complaints can also be made at the hospital. This is often the sensible place to start. There will be a person nominated to receive complaints—usually the unit general manager. (In the case of a nurse it is sensible to complain to the charge nurse or sister of the ward first). The patient (or anyone else making the complaint) should be given a reply in writing. If he or she is still not satisfied, the hospital may in some cases arrange for the matter to be looked into by two independent doctors. Complainants cannot insist on the hospital using this procedure, but their request for it will be given serious consideration. If the procedure is adopted, the two independent doctors will, as a part of their consideration of the question, discuss the complaint with the complainant, who can have a relative or friend present. Following this procedure the complainant will receive a written response.

If a doctor or nurse has negligently looked after a patient, a court action on the basis of professional negligence may be possible. Legal advice on this would be essential.

6.3:3 The General Medical Council

Where 'serious professional misconduct' is alleged against a doctor a complaint can be made to the General Medical Council. This is the body with which all doctors are required to be registered if they practise in the National Health Service. The complaint should be made in writing to the Registrar, General Medical Council, 44 Hallam Street, London W1N 6AE.

General practitioners also come under the General Medical Council. They are not, however, health board employees.

6.3:4 General practitioners

Complaints against general practitioners can be made to the 'service committee' for the relevant health board. Complaints to this source must be made within six week of the event or within six months after the end of treatment (if that is earlier)[1]. The service committee can be contacted at the health board's office.

The service committee's job is to decide whether the doctor has complied with the terms of his or her contract to provide services for the National Health Service. Although the committee cannot consider questions of wrong diagnosis it can consider whether the doctor provided 'all proper and necessary treatment'. The committee makes a report to the **Secretary of State** via the **Scottish Home and Health Department**. This may then in appropriate cases be sent to the General Medical Council.

1 Meston 'Complaints against Medical Practitioners' 1989 SLT (News) 69–70.

6.3:5 Medical records

Medical records are not the property of patients. The patient has right to see his or her records only if they are held in a computer[1]. But this right can be withheld if, either

- a doctor certifies that to see the records would cause serious damage to the patient's mental or physical health[2], or

- a social worker certifies that it would cause this damage to the patient *or to anyone else*[3].

There is a similar limited right to see non-computerised records of social work departments. There is also a general right to see a medical report[4] supplied for employment or insurance purposes[5].

If there is a court case and medical records need to be seen patients can generally get an order from a court requiring the medical records to be produced for use in connection with the case[6].

1 Data Protection Act 1984, s 21.
2 Data Protection (Subject Access Modification) (Health) Regulations 1987, SI 1987/1903.
3 Data Protection (Subject Access Modification) (Social Work) Regulations 1987, SI 1987/1904.
4 Access to Personal Files Act 1987.
5 Access to Medical Reports Act 1988.
6 If the court orders the records to be produced the patient may see them: *McBride v Strathclyde Regional Council* (4 March 1983, Unreported) Court of Session Outer House.

7 Consulting a solicitor

7.1:1 Introduction

Many of the matters covered in this book are complex. The assistance of a solicitor in understanding them will frequently be helpful both to patients and to their relatives or friends. In many cases the advice received from a solicitor will cost little or nothing because of the existence of the state subsidised **advice and assistance** and **legal aid schemes**.

This chapter deals with:

- making contact with a solicitor
- advice and assistance
- legal aid
- clients who do not qualify for advice and assistance or legal aid.

7.1:2 Making contact with a solicitor

It is important before consulting a solicitor to ensure that he or she has suitable experience and that he or she undertakes legal aid work (ie work for persons whose financial resources qualify them to have part or all of the expenses of their case paid for under the state-funded legal aid schemes). Both the **Scottish Legal Aid Board** (listed under 'Legal Aid' in the telephone directory) and **Citizens Advice Bureaux** carry information on the types of work local solicitors are prepared to undertake. They also provide information about which solicitors do legal aid work.

In addition to this the Law Society of Scotland's *Directory of General Services* may be consulted at local public libraries, citizens advice bureaux, social work departments, tourist information centres, courts and many other outlets. This directory contains information on the type of work which the solicitors listed in the directory are prepared to handle, including whether they do legal aid work. Unfortunately this directory does not at present indicate which solicitors have experience of undertaking mental health law work.

The **sheriff clerk** at the local sheriff court may be worth consulting as he or she will be able to advise which solicitors have undertaken work of this type in the past.

Once a solicitor has been chosen it is best to telephone or go to his or her office to make an appointment. Some solicitors will not charge for the initial interview to assess the situation; the client should inquire when making the appointment. At the first meeting with the solicitor, the client can outline the problem and should also ask the solicitor for an estimate of what he or she will charge.

7.1:3 Advice and assistance

Under this scheme solicitors can give immediate advice and assistance, oral or written, on any matter of Scots law to applicants who are financially eligible to benefit under the scheme. Usually, the solicitor provides the advice in his or her office, but it may also be given elsewhere, for example in hospital or at the client's home, in a police station or outside the court. The advice may be given by post if the applicant lives a considerable distance from the nearest solicitor. Alternatively, where there is good reason, the applicant can authorise an adult to attend the solicitor's office on his or her behalf to apply for advice and assistance under the scheme.

Normally, the solicitor will complete an application form on behalf of the applicant at their first meeting. The solicitor will then be in a position to assess immediately whether or not the client is financially eligible to benefit under the scheme. To qualify under the scheme the applicant's disposable capital and disposable income must fall within certain limits. These limits are adjusted annually to take account of inflation.

7.1:4 Disposable capital

In assesssing an applicant's disposable capital the solicitor notes the total value of the applicant's assets, excluding the value of his or her home, furniture, clothing, car and tools of trade. Where advice and assistance are being sought in relation to a dispute over ownership of an asset, its value is also excluded.

The assets and savings of cohabitees or spouses living together are added in if they do not have opposed interests in the case. Deductions are permitted from this total for each dependant whom the applicant is supporting. This gives the applicant's disposable capital. If this sum exceeds a certain level the applicant will not be eligible for the scheme. (In 1989 this level was £890).

7.1:5 Disposable income

Details of the applicant's weekly income from all sources (net of income tax and national insurance contributions) for the seven days before the form was completed must also be provided. In the case of a husband and wife living together both parties' income (if any) must be declared if they have a common interest in the matter. Child benefit is included as income but fostering allowances is not. Clients in receipt of income support, family credit automatically qualify for free advice and assistance provided their capital after deduction of allowances for dependants is no more than £890.

Allowances against income are permitted for the spouse and all dependants whom the applicant is supporting. At the present time if the total weekly income after deduction of all allowances does not exceed £61 then the advice given is free provided the client qualifies in terms of the rules applying to capital. A scale of contributions applies to clients with a disposable income of over £61 starting with a contribution of £5 and increasing on a sliding scale to a maximum contribution of £70. If the client's disposable income is more than £128 then he or she is not eligible under the advice and assistance scheme.

Once payment of the contribution (if any) has been made or agreed with the solicitor, applicants who qualify under the income and capital rules of the scheme are entitled to £60 worth of legal advice. This figure may be substantially increased if the solicitor applies to the Scottish Legal Aid Board giving good reasons why this is necessary.

Even though advice and assistance have been given, (with or without a contribution) should money be recovered as a result of the advice and assistance, the cost of providing the advice and assistance will usually be deducted from the recovered sum, unless to do so would cause hardship or distress.

7.1:6 What the scheme covers

The advice and assistance scheme covers only the giving of legal advice. It cannot normally be used to meet the costs of any court action, although it can be used to advise clients whether or not they should be starting, or negotiating settlement of, court proceedings.

However, as from 1 August 1988 a special form of advice and assistance (assistance by way of representation) has been available to cover representation in appeals to sheriffs by patients against orders or renewals of orders to detain them compulsorily in a mental hospital (see chapter 2). Eligibility for assistance by way of representation is subject to the similar financial limits to those applying in advice and assistance cases.

7.1:7 Legal aid

If any court action is to be started, then legal aid should be applied for. This needs a separate quite lengthy form to be completed by the solicitor on the applicant's behalf. Applications for legal aid can take several months to be processed. For this reason a start should be made on the legal aid application as soon as possible.

To qualify for legal aid, applicants must meet certain financial requirements (similar to those under advice and assistance). They must also satisfy the Scottish Legal Aid Board that they have a good case in law. Because of this requirement the legal aid application must be carefully prepared by the solicitor and all the information requested by the solicitor and the Scottish Legal Aid Board in support of the application must be provided.

Legal aid may be granted free to an applicant, or with a contribution varying from £1 to several hundred pounds paid by the applicant. Contributions can usually be paid by instalments. If the applicant fails to pay an instalment of the contribution, the award of legal aid may be suspended or lost.

The solicitor consulted will advise whether or not to apply for legal aid in the particular circumstances of the case.

There is a separate application form for legal aid for summary criminal matters.

For further information see the publications of the Scottish Legal Aid Board available from their offices at 44 Drumsheugh Gardens, Edinburgh, EH3 7SW (Tel: 031 226 7061).

7.1:8 Those who do not qualify for advice and assistance or legal aid

If a client does not qualify for either advice and assistance or legal aid, he or she may of course instruct a solicitor on a private basis. In such cases it is advisable to ask for a quotation from the solicitor of the legal expenses likely to be incurred.

In many cases involving court proceedings it may not be possible to provide an exact quotation of the expenses. Nevertheless, it should always be possible to obtain some indication from the solicitor of what the expenses might be. A sensible arrangement would be to agree with the solicitor that he or she will not do work in excess of an agreed sum without the prior consent of the client.

The **Mental Welfare Commission**, in its *Annual Report for 1987*, reports a number of worrying cases where patients have engaged solicitors without being made fully aware that they may become liable for all or part of the legal expenses, which, if a court appearance is required, could run into hundreds of pounds. It is obviously essential that solicitors should use their best efforts to make a patient aware of his or her potential liability to pay the legal fees. If the patient appears too confused to understand this, the **nearest relative** should be consulted. Otherwise it might be questionable whether the patient was legally competent to enter into the contract to employ the solicitor.

If the solicitor refuses to give any estimate of the legal expenses there is nothing to prevent the client from going to another solicitor.

Appendix 1

Mental Health (Scotland) Act 1984

ARRANGEMENT OF SECTIONS

PART I APPLICATION OF ACT

Section
1. Application of Act: 'mental disorder'.

PART II MENTAL WELFARE COMMISSION

2. Mental Welfare Commission.
3. Functions and duties of the Mental Welfare Commission.
4. Proceedings and evidence at enquiries under section 3.
5. Duties of the Secretary of State and of local authorities in relation to the Mental Welfare Commission.
6. Appointment and payment of staff.

PART III LOCAL AUTHORITY SERVICES

7. Functions of local authorities.
8. Provision of after-care services.
9. Appointment of mental health officers.
10. Welfare of certain hospital patients.
11. The training and occupation of the mentally handicapped.

PART IV PRIVATE HOSPITALS

12. Registration of private hospitals.
13. Pre-requisites of registration.
14. Control of private hospitals.
15. Cancellation and continuance in certain circumstances of registration.
16. Offences against this Part of this Act and penalties.

PART V ADMISSION TO AND DETENTION IN HOSPITAL AND GUARDIANSHIP

Grounds for hospital admission

17. Patients liable to be detained in hospital.

Procedure for admission of patients: hospital

Section
18. Admission and detention of patients: hospital.
19. General provisions as to applications: hospital.
20. Medical recommendations: hospital.
21. Approval of applications by the sheriff: hospital.
22. Effect of applications: hospital.
23. Rectification of application and recommendations: hospital.
24. Emergency admission: hospital.
25. Detention of patients already in hospital.
26. Short term detention.

Care and treatment of patients: hospital

27. Leave of absence from hospital.
28. Return and re-admission of patients absent without leave: hospital.
29. Transfer of patients: hospital.

Duration of authority for detention and discharge of patients: hospital

30. Duration of authority: hospital.
31. Special provisions as to patients absent without leave: hospital.
32. Special provisions as to patients sentenced to imprisonment etc.: hospital.
33. Discharge of patients: hospital.
34. Restrictions on discharge by nearest relative: hospital.

Appeals: hospital

35. Appeals to the sheriff: hospital.

Grounds for reception into guardianship

36. Patients liable to be received into guardianship.

Procedure for reception of patients: guardianship

37. Reception of patients into guardianship.
38. General provisions as to applications: guardianship.
39. Medical recommendations: guardianship.
40. Approval of applications by the sheriff: guardianship.
41. Effect of applications: guardianship.
42. Rectification of application and recommendations: guardianship.

Care and treatment of patients: guardianship

43. Regulations as to guardianship.
44. Return of patients absent without leave: guardianship.
45. Transfer of patients: guardianship.
46. Transfer of guardianship in case of death, incapacity etc of guardian.

Duration of authority for guardianship and discharge of patients

47. Duration of authority: guardianship.
48. Special provisions as to patients absent without leave: guardianship.
49. Special provisions as to patients sentenced to imprisonment, etc: guardianship.

Section
50. Discharge of patients: guardianship.
51. Restrictions on discharge by nearest relative: guardianship.

Appeals: guardianship

52. Appeals to the sheriff: guardianship.

Functions of relatives of patients

53. Definition of 'relative' and 'nearest relative'.
54. Children and young persons in care of local authority.
55. Nearest relative of child under guardianship etc.
56. Appointment by sheriff of acting nearest relative.
57. Discharge and variation of orders under s 56.

Supplementary

58. Regulations for purposes of Part V.
59. Interpretation of Part V.

PART VI DETENTION OF PATIENTS CONCERNED IN CRIMINAL PROCEEDINGS ETC AND TRANSFER OF PATIENTS UNDER SENTENCE

Provisions for compulsory detention and guardianship of patients charged with offences etc

60. Effect of hospital orders.
61. Effect of guardianship orders.
62. Effect of restriction orders.
63. Right of appeal of restricted patients etc.
64. Right of appeal of patients subject to restriction orders.
65. Right of appeal of patients subject to restriction directions.
66. Further consideration of case of conditionally discharged patients.
67. Application of sections 63 to 66 to other persons treated as restricted patients.
68. Powers of Secretary of State in respect of patients subject to restriction orders.
69. Persons ordered to be kept in custody during Her Majesty's pleasure.

Transfer to hospital or guardianship of prisoners etc

70. Removal to hospital of persons in prison awaiting trial etc.
71. Removal to hospital of persons serving sentences of imprisonment and other prisoners.
72. Restriction on discharge of prisoners removed to hospital.
73. Further provisions as to persons removed to hospital while awaiting trial etc.
74. Further provisions as to prisoners under sentence.
75. Further provisions as to civil prisoners and persons detained under the Immigration Act 1971.

Supplementary

76. Interpretation of Part VI.

PART VII REMOVAL AND RETURN OF PATIENTS WITHIN UNITED KINGDOM ETC

Removal to and from England and Wales

Section
77. Removal of patients to England and Wales.
78. Position of nearest relative on removal to England and Wales.
79. Position of nearest relative on removal to Scotland.

Removal to and from Northern Ireland

80. Removal of patients to Northern Ireland.
81. Removal to Scotland of patients from Northern Ireland.

Other provisions as to removal

82. Removal of certain patients from Channel Islands and Isle of Man to Scotland.
83. Removal of alien patients.

Return of patients absent without leave

84. Patients absent from hospitals in Scotland.
85. Patients absent from hospitals in Northern Ireland.

Supplementary

86. Regulations for purposes of Part VII.
87. General provisions as to patients removed from Scotland.
88. Intimation of removal of patients to Scotland.
89. Interpretation of Part VII.

PART VIII STATE HOSPITALS

90. Provision of hospitals for patients requiring special security.
91. Administrative provisions.

PART IX PROTECTION OF PROPERTY OF PATIENTS

92. Duties of local authority in relation to property.
93. Power of Mental Welfare Commission to petition for appointment of curator bonis.
94. Powers of managers in relation to property of patients.
95. Reciprocal arrangements in relation to Northern Ireland as to exercise of powers.

PART X CONSENT TO TREATMENT

96. Preliminary.
97. Treatment requiring consent and a second opinion.
98. Treatment requiring consent or a second opinion.
99. Review of treatment.
100. Plans of treatment.
101. Withdrawal of consent.

Section
102. Urgent treatment.
103. Treatment not requiring consent.

PART XI MISCELLANEOUS AND GENERAL

Offences

104. False statements.
105. Ill-treatment of patients.
106. Protection of mentally handicapped females.
107. Protection of patients.
108. Assisting patients to absent themselves without leave etc.
109. Obstruction.

Miscellaneous provisions

110. Duty to give information to patients and nearest relatives.
111. Duty of managers to inform nearest relative of discharge of detained patient.
112. Religious persuasion of patients.
113. Duty of sheriff to give patient opportunity to be heard.
114. Provision for personal expenses of in-patients in hospital.
115. Correspondence of patients.
116. Review of decision to withhold postal packet.
117. Entry on premises and warrant to search for and remove patients.
118. Mentally disordered persons found in public places.
119. Code of practice.

Supplementary

120. Provisions as to custody, conveyance and detention.
121. Retaking of patients escaping from custody.
122. Protection for acts done in pursuance of this Act.
123. Inquiries.
124. General provisions as to regulations and orders.
125. Interpretation.
126. Preservation of amendments.
127. Consequential and transitional provisions and repeals.
128. Application to England and Wales.
129. Application to Northern Ireland.
130. Short title and commencement.

SCHEDULES:

Schedule 1—State Hospital Management Committees.
Schedule 2—Application of provisions of Part V to patients subject to hospital or guardianship orders.
Schedule 3—Consequential amendments.
Schedule 4—Transitional and savings provisions.
Schedule 5—Repeals.

PART I   APPLICATION OF ACT

1. Application of Act: 'mental disorder'

(1) The provisions of this Act shall have effect with respect to the reception, care and treatment of persons suffering, or appearing to be suffering, from mental disorder, to the management of their property and affairs, and to other related matters.

(2) In this Act—
    'mental disorder' means mental illness or mental handicap however caused or manifested;
    'mental impairment' means a state of arrested or incomplete development of mind not amounting to severe mental impairment which includes significant impairment of intelligence and social functioning and is associated with abnormally aggresive or seriously irresponsible conduct on the part of the person concerned; and cognate expressions shall be construed accordingly;
    'severe mental impairment' means a state of arrested or incomplete development of mind which includes severe impairment of intelligence and social functioning and is associated with abnormally aggressive or seriously irresponsible conduct on the part of the person concerned; and cognate expressions shall be construed accordingly;
and other expressions have the meanings assigned to them in section 125 of this Act.

(3) No person shall be treated under this Act as suffering from mental disorder by reason only of promiscuity or other immoral conduct, sexual deviancy or dependence on alcohol or drugs.

PART II   MENTAL WELFARE COMMISSION

2. Mental Welfare Commission

(1) There shall continue to be a body called the Mental Welfare Commission for Scotland (in this Act referred to as 'the Mental Welfare Commission') who shall perform the functions assigned to them by or under this Act.

(2) The Mental Welfare Commission shall consist of no fewer than 10 commissioners (including at least 3 women) of whom one shall be chairman, at least 3 shall be medical practitioners (in this Act referred to as 'medical commissioners'), and one shall be a person who has been for a period of at least 5 years either a member of the Faculty of Advocates or a solicitor.

(3) Five commissioners of whom at least one shall be a medical commissioner shall constitute a quorum of the Mental Welfare Commission.

(4) The commissioners shall be appointed by Her Majesty on the recommendation of the Secretary of State and shall hold and vacate office under the terms of the instrument under which they are appointed, but may resign office by notice in writing to the Secretary of State.

(5) Before making a recommendation under subsection (4) of this section the Secretary of State shall consult such bodies as appear to him to be concerned.

(6) No person who for the time being is employed in the civil service of the Crown whether in an established capacity or not, and whether for the whole or part of his time, shall be appointed to the Mental Welfare Commission.

(7) The Mental Welfare Commission may—
    (a) pay to the said commissioners such remuneration; and
    (b) make provision for the payment of such pensions, allowances or gratuities to or in respect of the said commissioners,

as the Secretary of State may, with the approval of the Treasury, determine; and such determination may make different provision for different cases or different classes of case.

(8) The following provisions of the National Health Service (Scotland) Act 1978 shall apply to the Mental Welfare Commission as they apply to a Health Board, that is to say—
- (a) sections 85(1), (2A), (4) and (6) (which contain provisions as to expenditure being met by the Secretary of State);
- (b) sections 85A(1) and (3) (which impose financial duties); and
- (c) section 86 (which provides for the auditing and examination of accounts).

(9) The Secretary of State may provide for the Mental Welfare Commission such officers and servants and such accommodation as the Commission may require.

(10) The Mental Welfare Commission shall be a body corporate and shall have a common seal.

(11) The proceedings of the Mental Welfare Commission shall not be invalidated by any vacancy in the membership of the Commission or any defect in the appointment of any commissioner.

3. Functions and duties of the Mental Welfare Commission

(1) It shall be the duty of the Mental Welfare Commission generally to exercise protective functions in respect of persons who may, by reason of mental disorder, be incapable of adequately protecting their persons or their interests, and, where those persons are liable to be detained in hospital or subject to guardianship under the following provisions of this Act, their functions as aforesaid shall include, in appropriate cases, the discharge of such patients in accordance with the said provisions.

(2) In the exercise of their functions as aforesaid, it shall be the duty of the Mental Welfare Commission—
- (a) to make enquiry into any case where it appears to them that there may be ill-treatment, deficiency in care or treatment, or improper detention of any person who may be suffering from mental disorder, or where the property of any such person may, by reason of his mental disorder, be exposed to loss or damage;
- (b) to visit regularly and, subject to paragraph (c) of this subsection, as often as they think appropriate, patients who are liable to be detained in a hospital or who are subject to guardianship and on any such visit to afford an opportunity, on request, for private interview to any such patient or, where the patient is in a hospital, to any other patient in that hospital;
- (c) in any case where—
    - (i) the authority for the detention of a patient—
        - (A) has been renewed for a period of one year under section 30 of this Act; and
        - (B) is renewed for a further period of one year under that section; and
    - (ii) the patient has not, during the period referred to in sub-paragraph (i)(A) of this paragraph—
        - (A) appealed to the sheriff under section 30(6) of this Act; or
        - (B) been visited by the Mental Welfare Commission under paragraph (b) of this sub-section,

    to visit the patient before the expiry of the period of one year referred to in sub-paragraph (i)(B) of this paragraph, unless the patient has previously been discharged, and on any such visit to afford an opportunity, on request, for private interview to any such patient;
- (d) to bring to the attention of the managers of any hospital or of any local authority the facts of any case in which in the opinion of the Mental Welfare Commission

it is desirable for the managers or the local authority to exercise any of their functions to secure the welfare of any patient suffering from mental disorder by—
  (i) preventing his ill-treatment;
  (ii) remedying any deficiency in his care or treatment;
  (iii) terminating his improper detention; or
  (iv) preventing or redressing loss or damage to his property;
(e) to advise the Secretary of State, a Health Board or a local authority on any matter arising out of this Act which has been referred to the Commission by the Secretary of State, the Health Board, or the local authority, as the case may be;
(f) to bring to the attention of the Secretary of State, a Health Board, a local authority or any other body any matter concerning the welfare of any persons who are suffering from mental disorder which the Commission consider ought to be brought to his or their attention.

(3) Where, in the course of carrying out any of their functions, the Mental Welfare Commission from the opinion that any patient who is—
(a) liable to be detained in a hospital; and
(b) either a restricted patient within the meaning of section 63 of this Act or a person mentioned in section 67(1) or (2) (persons treated as restricted patients) of this Act,
should be discharged, they shall recommend accordingly to the Secretary of State.

(4) On any visit by the Mental Welfare Commission in pursuance of paragraph (b) or (c) of subsection (2) of this section, the visitor shall be, or the visitors shall include, a medical commissioner or a medical officer of the Commission.

(5) For the purposes of subsection (2) of this section, the Mental Welfare Commission may interview, and a medical commissioner or a medical officer of the Commission may examine, any patient in private.

(6) A medical commissioner or a medical officer of the Mental Welfare Commission may require the production of and inspect the medical records of any patient.

(7) The Mental Welfare Commission shall in 1985 and in every year thereafter publish a report on their activities; and copies of each such report shall be submitted by the Commission to the Secretary of State who shall lay copies before Parliament.

(8) Subject to the provisions of subsection (4) of this section the Mental Welfare Commission may appoint—
  (a) any commissioner or committee of commissioners to carry out any of the functions of the Commission, other than those relating to the discharge of patients, under this Act,
  (b) a person, not being a commissioner—
    (i) to make by himself; or
    (ii) to act as chairman of any committee of commissioners appointed under paragraph (a) of this subsection to make,
  any enquiry which the Commission are obliged to make under subsection (2)(a) of this section.
and where any committee is so appointed the Commission may fix a quorum for that committee and otherwise regulate its proceedings.

(9) A person appointed under subsection (9)(b) of this section shall be—
(a) an advocate; or
(b) a solicitor,
of not less than 5 years standing.

(10) Any commissioner or committee or person appointed in pursuance of subsection (9) of this section shall exercise the functions so conferred in accordance with the directions of the Mental Welfare Commission.

4. Proceedings and evidence at enquiries under section 3

(1) For the purpose of any enquiry under section 3(1)(a) of this Act, the Mental Welfare Commission may, by notice in writing, require any person to attend at the time and place set forth in the notice to give evidence, but no person shall be required in obedience to such a notice to go more than 10 miles from his place of residence unless the necessary expenses of his attendance are paid or tendered to him.

(2) A person giving evidence at such an enquiry shall not be required to answer any questions which he would be entitled, on the ground of privilege or confidentiality, to refuse to answer if the enquiry were a proceeding in a court of law.

(3) The proceedings in any such enquiry shall have the privilege of a court of law.

(4) The chairman of, or person holding, the enquiry may administer oaths to witnesses and examine witnesses on oath, and may accept, instead of evidence on oath by any person, evidence on affirmation or a statement in writing by that person.

(5) Any person who refuses or wilfully neglects to attend in obedience to a notice under subsection (1) of this section or to give evidence shall be guilty of an offence and liable on summary conviction to a fine not exceeding level 1 on the standard scale.

5. Duties of the Secretary of State and of local authorities in relation to the Mental Welfare Commission

(1) The Secretary of State shall afford the Mental Welfare Commission all facilities necessary to enable them to carry out their functions in respect of any patient in a hospital other than a private hospital.

(2) The local authority concerned and the guardian of any person subject to guardianship under this Act, shall afford the Mental Welfare Commission all facilities necessary to enable them to carry out their functions in respect of such a patient.

6. Appointment and payment of staff

The Mental Welfare Commission may—
- (a) appoint officers and servants on such terms as to remuneration and conditions of service; and
- (b) make provision for the payment of—
    - (i) such remuneration to—
        - (A) any person appointed under section 3(9)(b) of this Act; and
        - (B) any medical practitioner or other person appointed for the purposes of the provisions mentioned in section 97(2) of this Act; and
    - (ii) such pensions, allowances or gratuities to or in respect of any officers, servants, persons and medical practitioners appointed under paragraph (a) or as mentioned in paragraph (b)(i) of this section,

as the Secretary of State may, with the consent of the Treasury, determine; and such determination may make different provision for different cases or different classes of case.

PART III LOCAL AUTHORITY SERVICES

7. Functions of local authorities

(1) In relation to persons who are or have been suffering from mental disorder a local authority may, with the approval of the Secretary of State and shall, to such extent as he may direct, make arrangements for any of the following purposes—

(a) the provision, equipment and maintenance of residential accommodation, and the care of persons for the time being resident in accommodation so provided;
(b) the exercise by the local authority of their functions under the following provisions of this Act in respect of persons under guardianship (whether under the guardianship of a local authority or of any other person);
(c) the provision of any ancillary or supplementary services;
(d) the supervision of persons suffering from mental handicap who are neither liable to detention in a hospital nor subject to guardianship.

(2) The reference in subsection (1)(a) of this section to the care of persons for the time being resident in accommodation provided by a local authority includes, in the case of persons so resident who are under the age of 16 years, the payment to those persons of such amounts as the local authority think fit in respect of their personal expenses where it appears to that authority that no such payment would otherwise be made.

8. Provision of after-care services

(1) A local authority shall provide after-care services for any persons who are or have been suffering from mental disorder.

(2) In providing after-care services under subsection (1) of this section a local authority shall co-operate with such health board or boards and such voluntary organisations as appear to the local authority to be concerned.

(3) The duty imposed by this section is without prejudice to any other power or duty which a local authority may have in relation to the provision of after-care services.

9. Appointment of mental health officers

(1) A local authority shall appoint a sufficient number of persons for the purpose of discharging in relation to their area the functions of mental health officers under this Act.

(2) Any officer appointed by a local authority to act as a mental health officer after the date of coming into force of section 64(4) of the Local Government (Scotland) Act 1973 (that is to say, 16th May 1975) but before 16th August 1983 shall be deemed to have been appointed under subsection (1) of this section as if that subsection and section 64(5)(bb) of the said Act of 1973 had come into force on 16th May 1975.

(3) On and after a day appointed by the Secretary of State by order, no person shall be appointed to act as a mental health officer under subsection (1) of this section unless he is approved by the local authority as having competence in dealing with persons who are suffering from mental disorder; and before appointing a person to act as a mental health officer, a local authority shall—
(a) ensure that the person has such qualifications, experience and competence in dealing with persons suffering from mental disorder; and
(b) have regard to such other matters,
as the Secretary of State may direct.

(4) No person appointed to act as a mental health officer before the appointed day shall continue so to act on or after the appointed day unless—
(a) he is approved by the local authority as having competence in dealing with persons who are suffering from mental disorder; and
(b) the local authority are satisfied that he has such qualifications, experience and competence in dealing with persons who are suffering from mental disorder as the Secretary of State may direct.

Note.—The appointed day under sub-s (3) is 1 April 1986: Mental Health (Scotland) Act 1984 (Appointed Day) Order 1986, SI 1986/374.

10. Welfare of certain hospital patients

(1) The provisions of this section shall apply to any patient suffering from mental disorder who is—
   (a) a child or young person in respect of whom the rights and powers of a parent are vested in a local authority by virtue of—
      (i) section 17 of the Social Work (Scotland) Act 1968; or
      (ii) section 3 of the Child Care Act 1980 (which relates to the assumption by a local authority of parental rights and duties in relation to a child in their care); or
      (iii) section 10 of the said Act of 1980 (which relates to the powers and duties of local authorities in England and Wales with respect to persons committed to their care);
   (b) a person who is under the guardianship of a local authority under the following provisions of this Act or under the provisions of the Mental Health Act 1983; or
   (c) a person the functions of whose nearest relative under this Act or under the Mental Health Act 1983 are for the time being transferred to a local authority.

(2) Where a patient to whom this section applies is admitted to any hospital or nursing home in Scotland (whether for treatment for mental disorder or for any other reason) then, without prejudice to their duties in relation to the patient apart from the provisions of this section, the authority having rights or functions in relation to him as aforesaid shall arrange for visits to be made to him on their behalf, and shall take such other steps in relation to the patient while in the hospital or nursing home as would be expected of a parent.

11. The training and occupation of the mentally handicapped

(1) Without prejudice to the operation of section 1 of the Education (Scotland) Act 1980 (which among other things imposes a duty on education authorities to provide educational facilities for pupils who suffer from disability of mind) it shall be the duty of the local authority to provide or secure the provision of suitable training and occupation for persons suffering from mental handicap who are over school age within the meaning of the Education (Scotland) Act 1980:
   Provided that this subsection shall not apply in the case of a person in a hospital.

(2) A local authority shall make such provision as they may think necessary for securing that transport is available for the conveyance of persons for the purpose of their training and occupation under this section; and accordingly section 45 of the National Health Service (Scotland) Act 1978 (which relates to the provision by the Secretary of State of ambulances and other means of transport), shall not have effect in relation to the conveyance of persons as aforesaid.

(3) Where a local authority makes arrangements with any voluntary organisation for the performance by that organisation of any services in connection with the duties of the local authority under this section, the local authority may make contributions to the funds of that voluntary organisation.

PART IV   PRIVATE HOSPITALS

12. Registration of private hospitals

(1) Every private hospital within the meaning of this Act shall be registered and the following provisions of this Part of this Act shall apply to the registration, conduct and inspection of such hospitals.

(2) In this Act 'private hospital' means any premises used or intended to be used for the reception of, and the provision of medical treatment for, one or more patients subject to detention under this Act (whether or not other persons are received and treated), not being—
- (a) a hospital vested in the Secretary of State;
- (b) a State hospital; or
- (c) any other premises managed by a Government department or provided by a local authority.

(3) Application for registration of premises as a private hospital shall be made in writing to the Secretary of State by or on behalf of the person proposing to carry on the hospital and the application shall be accompanied by a fee of £1.

(4) Subject to section 13 of this Act, the Secretary of State may register the premises named in the application as a private hospital and issue to the person proposing to carry on the hospital a certificate in that behalf (in this Act referred to as 'a certificate of registration').

(5) A certificate of registration shall specify the maximum number of persons who at any one time may receive care or treatment in the hospital to which the certificate relates, and such conditions as the Secretary of State may consider appropriate for regulating the category of patients who may be received into the hospital.

(6) A certificate of registration shall lapse on the expiration of a period of 5 years from the date of issue, but shall be renewable on a fresh application.

(7) A certificate of registration shall be kept fixed conspicuously in the hospital to which it relates and if this requirement is not complied with the person carrying on the hospital shall be guilty of an offence under this Part of this Act.

13. Pre-requisites of registration

(1) The Secretary of State shall not issue a certificate of registration unless he is satisfied—
- (a) that the person proposing to carry on the hospital is a fit person for this purpose, having regard to his age, conduct and any other relevant consideration;
- (b) that the premises are fit to be used for a private hospital;
- (c) that neither the hospital nor any premises to be used in connection therewith consist of or include works executed in contravention of section 12(1) of the Health Services Act 1976;
- (d) that the arrangements proposed for patients are suitable and adequate; and
- (e) that the medical and nursing staff proposed is adequate for the hospital and is suitably trained and qualified.

(2) Nothing in the foregoing provisions of this Part of this Act shall be construed as requiring the Secretary of State to issue a certificate of registration under section 12 of this Act.

14. Control of private hospitals

(1) Any person carrying on a private hospital shall—
- (a) keep the hospital open to inspection for the purposes of this section at all reasonable times;
- (b) keep such registers and records as the Secretary of State may from time to time by regulations prescribe, and keep such registers and records open to inspection;
- (c) ensure that any conditions specified in the certificate of registration are complied with;
- (d) afford to the Mental Welfare Commission all such facilities (including facilities for inspection of the hospital) as are necessary for the Commission to exercise their functions under this Act,

and any person who fails to comply with any requirement of this subsection shall be guilty of an offence under this Part of this Act.

(2) The Secretary of State shall ensure by regular inspection of any private hospital that that hospital is being properly carried on, and any person authorised in that behalf by the Secretary of State may, after producing, if asked to do so, some duly authenticated document showing that he is so authorised, enter any hospital for the purpose of any inspection in pursuance of this section and carry out that inspection.

(3) Any person authorised under subsection (2) of this section may interview any patient in private.

15. Cancellation and continuance in certain circumstances of registration

(1) Subject to the provisions of this section, the Secretary of State may, at any time, cancel a registration of a private hospital on any ground on which he might have refused an application for such a registration of that hospital, or on the ground that the person carrying on the hospital has been convicted of an offence under this Act.

(2) On the cancellation of a registration, the person who is or was carrying on the hospital shall forthwith deliver up the certificate to the Secretary of State, and if this requirement is not complied with the holder of the certificate shall be guilty of an offence under this Part of this Act.

(3) Where at the time of any cancellation of a registration under subsection (1) of this section any patient is liable to be detained on the premises concerned, the registration shall, notwithstanding the cancellation, continue in force until the expiration of a period of 28 days from the date of cancellation or until every such patient has ceased to be so liable, whichever first occurs.

16. Offences against this Part of this Act and penalties

(1) If any person carries on a private hospital which is not registered under this Part of this Act, he shall be guilty of an offence and shall be liable on summary conviction to a fine not exceeding the statutory maximum or on conviction on indictment to a fine.

(2) Any person guilty of an offence under this Part of this Act other than the offence specified in subsection (1) of this section shall be liable on summary conviction to a fine not exceeding level 1 on the standard scale and in the case of a continuing offence to a further fine not exceeding two pounds in respect of each day on which the offence continues after conviction.

PART V ADMISSION TO AND DETENTION IN HOSPITAL AND GUARDIANSHIP

Grounds for hospital admission

17. Patients liable to be detained in hospital

(1) A person may, in pursuance of an application for admission under section 18(1) of this Act, be admitted to a hospital and there detained on the grounds that—
   (a) he is suffering from mental disorder of a nature or degree which makes it appropriate for him to receive medical treatment in a hospital; and
      (i) in the case where the mental disorder from which he suffers is a persistent one manifested only by abnormally aggressive or seriously irresponsible conduct, such treatment is likely to alleviate or prevent a deterioration of his condition; or
      (ii) in the case where the mental disorder from which he suffers is a mental handicap, the handicap comprises mental impairment (where such treat-

ment is likely to alleviate or prevent a deterioration of his condition) or severe mental impairment; and
   (b) it is necessary for the health or safety of that person or for the protection of other persons that he should receive such treatment and it cannot be provided unless he is detained under this Part of this Act.

(2) Nothing in this Act shall be construed as preventing a patient who requires treatment for mental disorder from being admitted to any hospital or nursing home for that treatment in pursuance of arrangements made in that behalf without any application, recommendation or order rendering him liable to be detained under this Act, or from remaining in any hospital in pursuance of such arrangements if he has ceased to be so liable to be detained.

Procedure for admission of patients: hospital

18. Admission and detention of patients: hospital

(1) A patient may be admitted to a hospital and there detained for the period allowed by this Part of this Act in pursuance of an application in the prescribed form (in this Act referred to as 'an application for admission') approved by the sheriff and made in accordance with this Part of this Act.

(2) An application for admission shall be founded on and accompanied by 2 medical recommendations which shall be in the prescribed form and each such recommendation shall include the following statements, being statements of opinion, and the grounds on which each statement is based—
   (a) a statement of the form of mental disorder from which the patient is suffering, being mental illness or mental handicap or both; and
   (b) a statement as to which of the grounds set out in section 17(1) of this Act apply in relation to the patient.

(3) An application for admission shall be of no effect unless the patient is described in each of the medical recommendations as suffering from the same form of mental disorder, whether or not he is described in either of those recommendations as suffering also from the other form.

Note.—See *B v Forsey* 1988 SLT 572, HL (Appendix 3).
For prescribed forms, see The Mental Health (Prescribed Forms) (Scotland) Regulations 1984 SI 1984/1495 (Appendix 2).

19. General provisions as to applications: hospital

(1) Subject to the provisions of this section, an application for admission may be made either by the nearest relative of the patient or by a mental health officer; and every such application shall be addressed to the managers of the hospital to which admission is sought.

(2) The nearest relative of the patient shall not make an application for admission unless he has personally seen the patient within the period of 14 days ending with the date on which the proposed application is submitted to the sheriff for his approval.

(3) A local authority shall, if so required by the nearest relative of a patient residing in their area, direct a mental health officer as soon as practicable to take the patient's case into consideration with a view to making an application for admission in respect of the patient; and if in any such case that officer decides not to make an application he shall inform the nearest relative of his reasons in writng.

(4) A mental health officer shall make an application for admission in respect of a patient within the area of the local authority by whom that officer was appointed in

any case where he is satisfied that such an application ought to be made and is of the opinion, having regard to any wishes expressed by relatives of the patient and to any other relevant circumstances, that it is necessary or proper for the application to be made by him.

(5) A mental health officer who proposes to make an application for admission shall—
- (a) interview the patient within the period of 14 days ending with the date on which the proposed application is submitted to the sheriff for his approval and satisfy himself that detention in a hospital is, in all the circumstances of the case, the most appropriate way of providing the care and medical treatment which the patient needs; and
- (b) take such steps as are reasonably practicable to inform the nearest relative of the patient of the proposed application, and of his right to object thereto in accordance with the provisions of section 21 of this Act.

(6) A mental health officer shall make an application for admission in respect of a patient where—
- (a) he has received the 2 medical recommendations required for the purposes of such an application; and
- (b) he has been requested to do so by a medical practitioner who gave one of the medical recommendations,

and the application shall include—
- (i) a statement of the mental health officer's opinion as to whether or not the application should be granted; and
- (ii) a statement of the grounds on which that opinion is based.

(7) An application under this section by a mental health officer may be made outside the area of the local authority by whom he is appointed.

20. Medical recommendations: hospital

(1) The medical recommendations required for the purposes of an application for admission shall satisfy the following requirements—
- (a) such recommendations shall be signed on or before the date of the application and shall be given by medical practitioners (neither being the applicant) who have personally examined the patient separately, in which case not more than 5 days must have elapsed between the days on which the separate examinations took place, or, where no objection has been made by the patient or his nearest relative, together;
- (b) one of the recommendations shall be given by a practitioner approved for the purposes of this section by a Health Board as having special experience in the diagnosis or treatment of mental disorder and the other recommendation shall, if practicable, be given by the patient's general medical practitioner or another medical practitioner who has previous acquaintance with him;
- (c) neither recommendation shall be given by a practitioner on the staff of the hospital named in the application where the patient is to be accommodated under section 57 or 58 of the National Health Service (Scotland) Act 1978 (which relates to accommodation for private patients) or in a private hospital and, subject to subsection (2) of this section, where the patient is to be accommodated otherwise one only of the recommendations may be given by such a practitioner;
- (d) such recommendations shall contain a statement as to whether the person signing the recommendation is related to the patient and of any pecuniary interest that that person may have in the admission of the patient to hospital.

(2) Notwithstanding the provisions of paragraph (c) of subsection (1) of this section, both medical recommendations may be given by practitioners on the staff of the hospital named in the application where—

(a) compliance with the said paragraph (c) would result in a delay involving serious risk to the health or safety of the patient or to the safety of other persons;
(b) one of the practitioners giving the recommendations works at the hospital for less than half the time which he is bound by contract to devote to work in the health service; and
(c) if one of the practitioners is a consultant, the other does not work (whether at the hospital or elsewhere) in a grade in which he is under that consultant's directions.

(3) For the purposes of this section a general practitioner who is employed part-time in a hospital shall not be regarded as a practitioner on its staff.

21. Approval of applications by the sheriff: hospital

(1) An application for admission shall be submitted to a sheriff of the sheriffdom—
  (a) within which the patient is resident at the time when the application is submitted; or
  (b) where the patient is a resident patient in a hospital at the time when the application is submitted, within which the hospital is situated,
[...][1] within 7 days of the last date on which the patient was examined for the purposes of any medical recommendation accompanying the application.

(2) Subject to the following provisions of this section and to section 113 of this Act, the sheriff, in considering [whether to approve][2] an application submitted to him under this section—
  (a) may make such inquiries and hear such persons (including the patient) as he think fit; and
  (b) where an application is the subject of objection by the nearest relative of the patient, shall afford that relative and any witness that relative may call an opportunity of being heard; and
  (c) shall, where a mental health officer makes an application for admission in respect of a patient under section 19(6) of this Act and such application includes a statement of the mental health officer's opinion that the application should not be granted, afford the mental health officer an opportunity of being heard.

(3) The sheriff shall not withhold approval to an application submitted under this section without affording to the applicant and any witness the applicant may call an opportunity of being heard.

(4) Any proceedings under this section shall, where the patient or applicant so desires or the sheriff thinks fit, be conducted in private.

(5) The sheriff in the exercise of the functions conferred on him by this section shall have the like jurisdiction, and the like powers as regards the summoning and examination of witnesses, the administration of oaths, the awarding of expenses, and otherwise, as if he were acting in the exercise of his civil jurisdiction.

Note.—[1] Words in sub-s (1) deleted by the Law Reform (Miscellaneous Provisions) (Scotland) Act 1985, s 51.
[2] Words in sub-s (2) inserted by the Law Reform (Miscellaneous Provisions) (Scotland) Act 1985, s 51.
  For rules of procedure in the sheriff court in relation to applications to the sheriff under this section, see Act of Sederunt (Mental Health (Scotland) Act 1984) 1986, SI 1986/545.

22. Effect of applications: hospital

(1) Where an application for admission has been approved by the sheriff, that application shall be sufficient authority for the removal of the patient to the hospital named in the application and, when the application has been forwarded to the managers of the hospital, for the admission of the patient to that hospital at any time within a period of

7 days from the date on which the sheriff approved the application and for his detention there in accordance with the provisions of this Act.

(2) Where a patient has been admitted to a hospital in pursuance of an application under this Part of this Act, it shall be the duty of the managers of the hospital to notify—
   (a) the Mental Welfare Commission; and
   (b) the local authority for the area in which the hospital is situated (except where the admission is in pursuance of an application made by a mental health officer appointed by that authority),
of that admission together with a copy of the application and recommendations relating to the patient's admission within 7 days of its taking place.

(3) A local authority shall, on being notified under subsection (2) of this section, arrange for a mental health officer as soon as practicable and, in any event, not later than 7 days before the expiry of the period of 28 days beginning with the day on which the patient was admitted to a hospital—
   (a) to interview the patient whose admission has been notified to them; and
   (b) to provide the responsible medical officer and the Mental Welfare Commission with a report on the patient's social circumstances,
unless the mental health officer has done so under section 26(5) of this Act within the previous 28 days.

(4) Where a patient has been admitted as aforesaid the responsible medical officer shall—
   (a) within the period of 7 days ending on the 28th day after the patient's admission—
      (i) examine the patient or obtain from another medical practitioner a report on the condition of the patient; and
      (ii) consult such other person or persons who appear to him to be principally concerned with the patient's medical treatment; and
   (b) if he is satisfied, as a result of the examination or report, that—
      (i) the patient is not suffering from mental disorder of a nature or degree which makes it appropriate for him to be liable to be detained in a hospital for medical treatment; or
      (ii) it is not necessary for the health or safety of the patient or for the protection of other persons that he should receive such treatment,
      order the discharge of the patient; or
   (c) if he does not order the discharge of the patient, so inform the Mental Welfare Commission, the nearest relative of the patient, the local authority and the managers concerned.

23. Rectification of application and recommendations: hospital

(1) If within the period of 14 days beginning with the day on which a patient has been admitted to a hospital in pursuance of an application for admission, the application, or any medical recommendation given for the purposes of the application, is found to be in any respect incorrect or defective, the application or recommendation may, not later than 7 days after the expiration of the said period, with the approval of the sheriff, be amended by the person by whom it was signed; and upon such amendment being made the application or recommendation shall have effect, and shall be deemed always to have had effect, as if it had been originally made as so amended.

(2) Without prejudice to the provisions of subsection (1) of this section, if within the period first mentioned therein it appears to the managers of the hospital, that one of the 2 medical recommendations on which the application for admission is founded is insufficient to warrant the detention of the patient in pursuance of the application, they may within that period give notice in writing to that effect to the applicant and to the sheriff; and where any such notice is given in respect of a medical recommendation

that recommendation shall be disregarded, but the application shall be, and shall be deemed always to have been, sufficient if—

(a) a fresh medical recommendation complying with the relevant provisions of this Part of this Act (other than the provisions relating to the time of signature and the interval between examinations) is furnished to the managers and to the sheriff; and

(b) the sheriff is satisfied that that recommendation and the other recommendation on which the application is founded together comply with those provisions.

(3) Where the medical recommendations upon which an application for admission is founded are, taken together, insufficient to warrant the detention of the patient in pursuance of the application, a notice under subsection (2) of this section may be given in respect of either of those recommendations; but this subsection shall not apply in a case where the application is of no effect by virtue of section 18(3) of this Act.

24. Emergency admission: hospital

(1) In any case of urgent necessity a recommendation (in this Act referred to as 'an emergency recommendation') may be made by a medical practitioner in respect of a patient stating that by reason of mental disorder it is urgently necessary for his health or safety or for the protection of other persons, that he should be admitted to a hospital, but that compliance with the provisions of this Part of this Act relating to an application for admission before the admission of the patient to a hospital would involve undesirable delay.

(2) An emergency recommendation shall not be made unless, where practicable, the consent of a relative or of a mental health officer has been obtained; and the recommendation shall be accompanied by a statement that such a consent as aforesaid has been obtained or, as the case may be, by a statement of the reasons for the failure to obtain that consent.

(3) An emergency recommendation shall be sufficient authority for the removal of the patient to a hospital at any time within a period of 3 days from the date on which it was made and for his detention therein for a period not exceeding 72 hours from the time of his admission.

(4) An emergency recommendation shall be made only by a medical practitioner who has personally examined the patient on the day on which he signed the recommendation.

(5) Where a patient is admitted to a hospital in pursuance of this section, it shall, where practicable, be the duty of the managers without delay to inform the nearest relative of the patient, the Mental Welfare Commission and, except in the case of a patient referred to in section 25 of this Act, some responsible person residing with the patient.

(6) A patient who has been detained in a hospital under this section shall not be further detained under this section immediately after the expiry of the period of detention.

Note.—See *B v Forsey* 1988 SLT 572, HL (Appendix 3).

25. Detention of patients already in hospital

(1) An application for admission or an emergency recommendation may be made under this Part of this Act notwithstanding that the patient is already in a hospital; and

where the application or recommendation is made in such a case the patient shall be treated for the purposes of this Part of this Act as if he had been admitted to the hospital on the date on which the application was forwarded to the managers of the hospital, or, as the case may be, the recommendation was made.

(2) If, in the case of a patient who is already in a hospital receiving treatment for mental disorder and who is not liable to be detained therein under this Part of this Act, it appears to a nurse of the prescribed class—
- (a) that the patient is suffering from mental disorder to such a degree that it is necessary for his health or safety or for the protection of other persons for him to be immediately restrained from leaving the hospital; and
- (b) that it is not practicable to secure the immediate attendance of a medical practitioner for the purpose of making an emergency recommendation,

the patient may be detained in the hospital for a period of 2 hours from the time when he was first so detained or until the earlier arrival at the place where the patient is detained of a medical practitioner having power to make an emergency recommendation.

(3) Where a patient is detained under subsection (2) of this section the nurse shall as soon as possible record in writing—
- (a) the facts mentioned in paragraphs (a) and (b) of the said subsection (2);
- (b) the fact that the patient has been detained; and
- (c) the time at which the patient was first so detained.

(4) A record made by a nurse under subsection (3) of this section shall, as soon as possible after it is made, be delivered by the nurse, or by a person authorised by the nurse in that behalf, to the managers of the hospital; and a copy of the record shall, within 14 days of the date on which the managers received it, be sent to the Mental Welfare Commission.

(5) A patient who has been detained in a hospital under sub-section (2) of this section shall not be further detained thereunder immediately after the expiry of that period of detention.

(6) In subsection (2) of this section 'prescribed' means prescribed by an order made by the Secretary of State.

Note.—See the Mental Health (Prescription of Class of Nurses) (Scotland) Order 1984, SI 1984/1095.

26. Short term detention

(1) Where a patient is admitted to a hospital in pursuance of section 24 of this Act, he may be detained in that hospital after the expiry of the period of 72 hours referred to in subsection (3) of that section if—
- (a) a report on the condition of the patient has been furnished to the managers of the hospital; and
- (b) where practicable, consent to the continued detention has been given by the nearest relative of the patient or by a mental health officer.

(2) The report referred to in subsection (1)(a) of this section shall—
- (a) be given by a medical practitioner approved for the purposes of section 20(1)(b) of this Act who has personally examined the patient and shall include a statement that in the opinion of the medical practioner—
    - (i) the patient is suffering from mental disorder of a nature or degree which makes it appropriate for him to be detained in a hospital for at least a limited period; and
    - (ii) the patient ought to be so detained in the interests of his own health or safety or with a view to the protection of other persons;

(b) include, where consent to the continued detention has not been obtained, a statement of the reasons for not obtaining such consent; and
(c) contain a statement as to whether the person signing the report is related to the patient and of any pecuniary interest that that person may have in the admission of the patient to hospital.

(3) Subject to subsection (6) of this section, where a report is duly furnished under subsection (1) of this section the authority for the detention of the patient shall be thereby renewed for a further period of 28 days from the expiry of the period of 72 hours referred to in the said subsection (1).

(4) Where a patient is detained in a hospital in pursuance of this section, the managers of the hospital shall so inform—
   (a) the Mental Welfare Commission;
   (b) where practicable, the nearest relative of the patient (except where the nearest relative has consented under subsection (1)(b) of this section); and
   (c) the local authority (except in a case where a mental health officer appointed by that local authority has consented under subsection (1)(b) of this section),
not later than 7 days after the patient was detained.

(5) A local authority, on being informed under subsection (4) of this section of the admission of a patient, shall arrange for a mental health officer as soon as practicable and in any event not later than 7 days before the expiry of the period of 28 days referred to in subsection (3) of this section—
   (a) to interview the patient; and
   (b) to provide the responsible medical officer and the Mental Welfare Commission with a report on the patient's social circumstances.

(6) Any patient may, within the period for which the authority for his detention is renewed by virtue of a report furnished in respect of him under this section, appeal to the sheriff to order his discharge and the provisions of section 33(2) and (4) of this Act shall apply in relation to such an appeal.

(7) A patient who has been detained in a hospital under this section shall not be further detained under this section nor detained under section 24 of this Act immediately after the expiry of the period of detention under this section.

Care and treatment of patients: hospital

27. Leave of absence from hospital

(1) The responsible medical officer may grant to any patient who is for the time being liable to be detained in a hospital under this Part of this Act leave to be absent from the hospital.

(2) Leave of absence may be granted to a patient under this section either on specified occasions or for any specified period of not more than 6 months; and where leave is so granted for a specified period it may be extended for further such periods as aforesaid.

(3) Where it appears to the responsible medical officer that it is necessary so to do in the interests of the patient or for the protection of other persons, he may, upon granting leave of absence under this section, direct that the patient remain in custody during his absence; and where leave of absence is so granted the patient may be kept in the custody of any officer on the staff of the hospital, or of any other person authorised in writing by the managers of the hospital, or, if the patient is required in accordance with conditions imposed on the grant of leave of absence to reside in another hospital, of any officer on the staff of that other hospital.

(4) Where leave of absence is granted to a patient under this section or where a period of leave is extended by further leave and the leave or the extension is for a period of

more than 28 days, it shall be the duty of the responsible medical officer to inform the Mental Welfare Commission within 14 days of the granting of leave or of the extension, as the case may be, of the address at which the patient is residing and, on the return of the patient, to notify the Commission thereof within 14 days.

(5) In any case where a patient is absent from a hospital in pursuance of leave of absence granted under this section, and it appears to the responsible medical officer that it is necessary so to do in the interests of the health or safety of the patient or for the protection of other persons, that officer may, subject to subsection (6) of this section, by notice in writing given to the patient or to the person for the time being in charge of the patient, revoke the leave of absence and recall the patient to the hospital.

(6) A patient to whom leave of absence is granted under this section shall not be recalled under subsection (5) of this section after he has ceased to be liable to be detained under this Part of this Act.

28. Return and re-admission of patients absent without leave: hospital

(1) Where a patient who is for the time being liable to be detained under this Part of this Act in a hospital—
  (a) absents himself from the hospital without leave granted under section 27 of this Act; or
  (b) fails to return to the hospital on any occasion on which, or at the expiration of any period for which, leave of absence was granted to him under that section, or upon being recalled thereunder; or
  (c) absents himself without permission from any place where he is required to reside in accordance with conditions imposed on the grant of leave of absence under that section,
he may, subject to the provisions of this section, be taken into custody and returned to the hospital or place by any mental health officer, by any officer on the staff of the hospital, by any constable, or by any person authorised in writing by the managers of the hospital.

(2) Where the place referred to in subsection 1(c) of this section is a hospital other than the one in which the patient is for the time being liable to be detained, the references in that subsection to an officer on the staff of the hospital and to the managers of the hospital shall respectively include references to an officer on the staff of the first-mentioned hospital and to the managers of that hospital.

(3) A patient shall not be taken into custody under this section after the expiration of the period of 28 days beginning with the first day of his absence without leave and a patient who has not returned or been taken into custody under this section within the said period shall cease to be liable to be detained at the expiration of that period.

(4) A patient shall not be taken into custody under this section if the period for which he is liable to be detained is that specified in section 24(3), 25(2) or 26(3) of this Act and that period has expired.

29. Transfer of patients: hospital

(1) A patient who is for the time being liable to be detained in a hospital by virtue of an application for admission under this Part of this Act may be transferred by the managers of that hospital, as follows—
  (a) to another hospital with the consent of the managers of that hospital; or
  (b) into the guardianship of a local authority with the consent of that authority; or
  (c) into the guardianship of any person approved by a local authority with the consent of that person.

(2) Any transfer of a patient under the last foregoing subsection shall be intimated to his nearest relative and to the Mental Welfare Commission by the managers of the

hospital to which the patient is transferred or, as the case may be, by the local authority concerned within 7 days of the date of transfer.

(3) Where a patient is transferred in pursuance of this section, the provisions of this Part of this Act (including this subsection) shall apply to him as follows, that is to say—
  (a) where the patient, being liable to be detained in a hospital by virtue of an application for admission, is transferred to another hospital, as if the application were an application for admission to that other hospital, and as if the patient had been admitted to that other hospital at the time when he was originally admitted in pursuance of the application;
  (b) where the patient, being liable to be detained as aforesaid, is transferred into guardianship, as if the application were a guardianship application duly forwarded to the local authority at the time aforesaid.

(4) Where a patient is transferred to a State hospital under subsection (1)(a) of this section he or his nearest relative may, within 28 days of the date of the transfer, appeal by way of summary application to a sheriff of the sheriffdom within which the hospital from which the patient was transferred is situated against the decision of the managers of that hospital to transfer the patient; and on any such appeal the sheriff shall order the return of the patient to the hospital from which he was transferred unless he is satisfied that the patient, on account of his dangerous, violent or criminal propensities, requires treatment under conditions of special security, and cannot suitably be cared for in a hospital other than a State hospital.

Note.—See *F v Management Committee and Managers Ravenscraig Hospital* 1989 SLT 49 and *T v Secretary of State for Scotland* 1987 SCCR 65 (Appendix 3).

Duration of authority for detention and discharge of patients: hospital

30. Duration of authority: hospital

(1) Subject to the provisions of this Part of this Act, a patient admitted to a hospital in pursuance of an application for admission may be detained in a hospital for a period not exceeding 6 months beginning with the day on which he was so admitted, but shall not be so detained for any longer period unless the authority for his detention is renewed under the following provisions of this section.

(2) Authority for the detention of a patient may, unless the patient has previously been discharged, be renewed under this section—
  (a) from the expiration of the period referred to in subsection (1) of this section, for a further period of 6 months;
  (b) from the expiration of any period of renewal under paragraph (a) of this subsection, for a further period of one year, and so on for periods of one year at a time.

(3) The responsible medical officer shall within the period of 2 months ending on the day when a patient who is liable to be detained in a hospital under this Part of this Act would cease to be so liable under this section in default of the renewal of the authority for his detention—
  (a) examine the patient or obtain from another medical practitioner a report on the condition of the patient; and
  (b) consult such other person or persons who appear to him to be principally concerned with the patient's medical treatment,

Mental Health (Scotland) Act 1984

and thereafter assess the need for the detention of the patient to be continued; and if it appears to him that the grounds set out in section 17(1) of this Act apply to the patient he shall furnish to the managers of the hospital where the patient is liable to be detained and to the Mental Welfare Commission a report to that effect in the prescribed form, along with the report first mentioned if such a report has been obtained.

(4) Subject to subsection (6) of this section and section 33(2) and (4) of this Act, where a report is duly furnished to the managers of a hospital under subsection (3) of this section, the authority for the detention of the patient shall be thereby renewed for the period prescribed in that case by subsection (2) of this section.

(5) Where a report under this section is furnished to them in respect of a patient, the managers of the hospital shall, unless they discharge the patient, cause him and his nearest relative to be informed.

(6) Any patient may within the period for which the authority for his detention is renewed by virtue of a report furnished in respect of him under this section appeal to the sheriff to order his discharge and the provisions of section 33(2) and (4) of this Act shall apply in relation to such an appeal.

Note.—For prescribed form of report see the Mental Health (Prescribed Forms) (Scotland) Regulations 1984, SI 1984/1495 (Appendix 2).

31. Special provisions as to patients absent without leave: hospital

(1) If on the day on which, apart from this section, a patient would cease to be liable to be detained under this Part of this Act or within the period of one week ending with that day, the patient is absent without leave, he shall not cease to be so liable or so subject—
  (a) in any case, until the expiration of the period during which he can be taken into custody under section 28 of this Act, or the day on which he returns or is returned to the hospital or place where he ought to be, whichever is the earlier; and
  (b) if he returns or is returned as aforesaid within the period first mentioned in the foregoing paragraph, until the expiration of the period of one week beginning with the day on which he is returned or returns as aforesaid.

(2) Where the period for which a patient is liable to be detained is extended by virtue of this section, any examination and report to be made and furnished under subsection (3) of section 30 of this Act may be made and furnished within that period as so extended.

(3) Where the authority for the detention of a patient is renewed by virtue of this section after the day on which, apart from this section, that authority would have expired under section 30 of this Act, the renewal shall take effect as from that day.

32. Special provisions as to patients sentenced to imprisonment etc: hospital

(1) Where a patient who is liable to be detained in a hospital under this Part of this Act is detained in custody in pursuance of any sentence or order passed or made by a court in the United Kingdom (including an order committing or remanding him in custody) and is so detained for a period exceeding 6 months, he shall, at the end of that period, cease to be so liable.

(2) Where any such patient is detained in custody as aforesaid for a period not exceeding 6 months, or for successive periods that do not in the aggregate exceed 6 months, then—
  (a) if apart from this subsection the patient would have ceased to be liable to be detained as aforesaid on or before the day he is discharged from custody, he shall not cease to be so liable until the end of that day; and

(b) in any case, sections 28 and 31 of this Act shall apply in relation to the patient as if he had absented himself without leave on that day.

33. Discharge of patients: hospital

(1) Subject to the provisions of this and the next following section, a patient who is liable to be detained in a hospital under this Part of this Act shall cease to be so liable if an order in writing discharging him from detention (in this Act referred to as 'an order for discharge') is made in accordance with the following provisions of this section.

(2) An order for discharge may be made in respect of a patient by the responsible medical officer, the Mental Welfare Commission or, where an appeal has been taken under sections 26, 30 or 34 of this Act, by the sheriff:

Provided that such an order shall not be made by the responsible medical officer in respect of a patient detained in a State hospital without the consent of the managers of the hospital.

(3) The responsible medical officer or the Mental Welfare Commission shall make an order for discharge in respect of a patient where he is or they are satisfied that—
  (a) he is not suffering from mental disorder of a nature or degree which makes it appropriate for him to be liable to be detained in a hospital for medical treatment; or
  (b) it is not necessary for the health or safety of the patient or for the protection of other persons that he should receive such treatment.

(4) Where an appeal is made to the sheriff by a patient under sections 26, 30 or 34 of this Act, the sheriff shall order the discharge of the patient if he is satisfied that—
  (a) the patient is not at the time of the hearing of the appeal suffering from mental disorder of a nature or degree which makes it appropriate for him to be liable to be detained in a hospital for medical treatment; or
  (b) it is not necessary for the health or safety of the patient or for the protection of other persons that he should receive such treatment.

(5) Subject to the provisions of this section and section 34 of this Act, an order for discharge in respect of a patient may also be made by the managers of the hospital or by the nearest relative of the patient.

(6) An order for discharge made in respect of a patient by the managers of a hospital shall, with the consent of the responsible medical officer, take effect on the expiration of a period of 7 days from the date on which the order was made, and where the responsible medical officer does not so consent he shall furnish to the managers a report certifying that in his opinion the grounds set out in section 17(1) of this Act apply in relation to the patient.

Note.—See *AB and CB v E* 1987 SCLR 419 (Appendix 3).

34. Restrictions on discharge by nearest relative: hospital

(1) An order for the discharge of a patient who is liable to be detained in a hospital shall not be made by his nearest relative except after giving not less than 7 days' notice in writing to the managers of the hospital; and if within that period the responsible medical officer furnishes to the managers a report certifying that, in his opinion, the grounds set out in section 17(1) of this Act apply in relation to the patient—
  (a) any order for the discharge of the patient made by that relative in pursuance of the notice shall be of no effect; and
  (b) no further order for the discharge of the patient shall be made by that relative during the period of 6 months beginning with the date of the report.

(2) In any case where a report under subsection (1) of this section is furnished in respect of a patient, the managers shall cause the nearest relative of the patient to be

informed and that relative may, within the period of 28 days beginning with the day on which he is so informed, appeal to the sheriff to order the discharge of the patient and the provisions of section 33(2) and (4) of this Act shall apply in relation to such an appeal.

(3) An order for discharge in respect of a patient detained in a State hospital shall not be made by his nearest relative.

Note.—See *AB and CB v E* 1987 SCLR 419 (Appendix 3).

Appeals: hospital

35. Appeals to the sheriff: hospital

(1) Where an appeal lies to the sheriff in respect of a report on a patient under any of sections 26, 30 or 34 of this Act, the managers of the hospital where the patient is liable to be detained shall, when intimating that a report has been furnished in pursuance of any of the said sections, inform any person having a right so to appeal, whether the patient or his nearest relative or both, of that right and of the period within which it may be exercised.

(2) An appeal under any of the said sections shall be made by way of summary application to a sheriff of the sheriffdom—
   (a) within which the patient is resident at the time when the appeal is made; or
   (b) where the patient is a resident patient in a hospital at the time when the appeal is made, within which the hospital is situated.

(3) For the purpose of advising whether any appeal to the sheriff under any of the said sections should be made by or in respect of a patient who is liable to be detained under this Part of this Act, or of furnishing information as to the condition of a patient for the purposes of such an appeal or of advising the nearest relative of any such patient as to the exercise of any power to order the discharge of the patient, any medical practitioner authorised by or on behalf of the patient or by the nearest relative of the patient, as the case may be, may, at any reasonable time, visit the patient and may examine him in private.

(4) Any medical practitioner authorised for the purposes of subsection (3) of this section to visit and examine a patient may require the production of and inspect any records relating to the detention or treatment of the patient in any hospital.

Grounds for reception into guardianship

36. Patients liable to be received into guardianship

A person may, in pursuance of an application for reception into guardianship under section 37(1) of this Act, be received into guardianship on the grounds that—
   (a) he is suffering from mental disorder of a nature or degree which warrants his reception into guardianship; and
   (b) it is necessary in the interests of the welfare of the patient that he should be so received.

Procedure for reception of patients: guardianship

37. Reception of patients into guardianship

(1) A patient who has attained the age of 16 years may be received into guardianship for the period allowed by this Part of this Act, in pursuance of an application in the

prescribed form (in this Act referred to as 'a guardianship application') approved by the sheriff and made in accordance with the provisions of this Part of this Act.

(2) The person named as guardian in a guardianship application may be—
   (a) the local authority to whom the application is addressed; or
   (b) a person chosen by that authority; or
   (c) any other person who has been accepted as a suitable person to act in that behalf by that authority,

and any person chosen or accepted as aforesaid may be a local authority or any other person including the applicant.

(3) A guardianship application shall be founded on and accompanied by 2 medical recommendations in the prescribed form and a recommendtion by a mental health officer in such form; and
   (a) each medical recommendation shall include—
      (i) a statement of the form of mental disorder from which the patient is suffering being mental illness or mental handicap or both; and
      (ii) a statement that the ground set out in section 36(a) of this Act applies in relation to the patient,
   being statements of opinion, together with the grounds on which those statements are based;
   (b) the recommendation by the mental health officer shall include—
      (i) a statement, being a statement of opinion, that the ground set out in section 36(b) of this Act applies in relation to the patient, together with the grounds on which the statement is based; and
      (ii) a statement as to whether he is related to the patient and of any pecuniary interest that he may have in the reception of the patient into guardianship.

(4) A guardianship application shall be of no effect unless the patient is described in each of the medical recommendations as suffering from the same form of mental disorder, whether or not he is described in either of those recommendations as suffering also from the other form.

Note.—For prescribed forms, see the Mental Health (Prescribed Forms) (Scotland) Regulations 1984, SI 1984/1495 (Appendix 2).

38. General provisions as to applications: guardianship

(1) Subject to the provisions of this section, a guardianship application may be made either by the nearest relative of the patient or by a mental health officer; and every such application shall be addressed to the local authority for the area in which the patient resides.

(2) The nearest relative of the patient shall not make a guardianship application unless he has personally seen the patient within the period of 14 days ending with the date on which the proposed application is submitted to the sheriff for his approval.

(3) A local authority shall, if so required by the nearest relative of a patient residing in their area, direct a mental health officer as soon as practicable to take the patient's case into consideration with a view to making a guardianship application in respect of the patient; and if in any such case that officer decides not to make an application he shall inform the nearest relative of his reasons in writing.

(4) A mental health officer shall make a guardianship application in respect of a patient within the area of the local authority by whom that officer was appointed in any case where he is satisfied that such an application ought to be made and is of the opinion, having regard to any wishes expressed by relatives of the patient and to any other relevant circumstances, that it is necessary or proper for the application to be made by him.

(5) A mental health officer who proposes to make a guardianship application shall—
  (a) interview the patient within the period of 14 days ending with the date on which the proposed application is submitted to the sheriff for his approval; and
  (b) take such steps as are reasonably practicable to inform the nearest relative of the patient of the proposed application, and of his right to object thereto in accordance with the provisions of section 40 of this Act.

(6) An application under this section by a mental health officer may be made outside the area of the local authority by whom he is appointed.

39. Medical recommendations: guardianship

The medical recommendations required for the purposes of a guardianship application shall satisfy the following requirements—
  (a) such recommendations shall be signed on or before the date of the application and shall be given by medical practitioners (neither being the applicant) who have personally examined the patient separately, in which case not more than 5 days must have elapsed between the days on which the separate examinations took place, or, where no objection has been made by the patient or his nearest relative, together;
  (b) one of the recommendations shall be given by a practitioner approved for the purposes of this section by a Health Board as having special experience in the diagnosis or treatment of mental disorder and the other recommendation shall, if practicable, be given by the patient's general medical practitioner or another medical practitioner who has previous acquaintance with him;
  (c) such recommendations shall contain a statement as to whether the person signing the recommendation is related to the patient and of any pecuniary interest that that person may have in the reception of the patient into guardianship.

40. Approval of applications by the sheriff: guardianship

(1) A guardianship application shall be submitted to a sheriff of the sheriffdom—
  (a) within which the patient is resident at the time when the application is submitted; or
  (b) where the patient is a resident patient in a hospital at the time when the application is submitted, within which the hospital is situated,
[...]¹ within 7 days of the last date on which the patient was examined for the purposes of any medical recommendation accompanying the application, together with a statement of the willingness to act of the guardian named in the application.

(2) Subject to the following provisions of this section and to section 113 of this Act, the sheriff, in considering [whether to approve]² an application submitted to him under this section may make such inquiries and hear such persons (including the patient) as he thinks fit, and, where an application is the subject of objection by the nearest relative of the patient, shall afford that relative and any witness that relative may call an opportunity of being heard.

(3) The sheriff shall not withhold approval to an application so submitted without affording to the applicant and any witness the applicant may call an opportunity of being heard.

(4) Any proceedings under this section shall, where the patient or applicant so desires or the sheriff thinks fit, be conducted in private.

(5) Every such application shall, after it is approved by the sheriff, be forwarded to the local authority for the area in which the patient resides.

(6) The sheriff in the exercise of the functions conferred on him by this section shall have the like jurisdiction, and the like powers as regards the summoning and examin-

ation of witnesses, the administration of oaths, the awarding of expenses, and otherwise, as if he were acting in the exercise of his civil jurisdiction.

Note.—[1] Words in sub-s (1) deleted by the Law Reform (Miscellaneous Provisions) (Scotland) Act 1985, s 51.
[2] Words in sub-s (2) inserted by the Law Reform (Miscellaneous Provisions) (Scotland) Act 1985, s 51.
For rules of procedure in the sheriff court in relation to applications under this section, see Act of Sederunt (Mental Health (Scotland) Act 1984) 1986, SI 1986/545.

41. Effect of applications: guardianship

(1) Where a patient has been received into guardianship in pursuance of an application under this Part of this Act, the local authority concerned shall notify the Mental Welfare Commission of that reception together with a copy of the application and recommendations relating to the patient's reception within 7 days of its taking place.

(2) Where a guardianship application has been approved by the sheriff and forwarded to the local authority concerned within a period of 7 days from the date on which the sheriff approved the application, the application shall, subject to the following provisions of this section and to regulations made by the Secretary of State, confer on the authority or person named in the appliction as guardian, to the exclusion of any other person, the following powers—
  (a) power to require the patient to reside at a place specified by the authority or person named as guardian;
  (b) power to require the patient to attend at places and times so specified for the purpose of medical treatment, occupation, education or training;
  (c) power to require access to the patient to be given, at any place where the patient is residing, to any medical practitioner, mental health officer or other person so specified.

(3) Nothing in the provisions of subsection (2) of this section or of regulations made thereunder shall confer any power on a guardian in respect of a patient received into his guardianship to intromit with any property of that patient.

(4) No person who is appointed as a guardian of a patient under this Act shall administer corporal punishment to that patient, and any person who contravenes the provisions of this subsection shall be guilty of an offence and shall be liable on summary conviction to a fine not exceeding level 3 on the standard scale and the court shall intimate the conviction to the Mental Welfare Commission.

Note.—At December 1989 no regulations had been made under sub-s (2).

42. Rectification of application and recommendations: guardianship

(1) If within the period of 14 days beginning with the day on which a patient has been received into guardianship in pursuance of a guardianship application, the application, or any medical recommendation given for the purposes of the application, is found to be in any respect incorrect or defective, the application or recommendation may, not later than 7 days after the expiration of the said period, with the approval of the sheriff, be amended by the person by whom it was signed; and upon such amendment being made the application or recommendation shall have effect, and shall be deemed to have had effect, as if it had been originally made as so amended.

(2) Without prejudice to the provisions of subsection (1) of this section, if within the period first mentioned therein it appears to the designated medical officer that one of the medical recommendations on which the guardianship application is founded is insufficient to warrant reception into guardianship in pursuance of the application, he may give notice in writing to that effect within that period to the applicant and to the

sheriff; and where any such notice is given in respect of a recommendation that recommendation shall be disregarded, but the application shall be, and shall be deemed always to have been, sufficient if—
  (a) a fresh recommendation complying with the relevant provisions of this Part of this Act (other than the provisions relating to the time of signature and the interval between medical examinations) is furnished to the local authority concerned and to the sheriff; and
  (b) the sheriff is satisfied that that recommendation and the other recommendations on which the application is founded together comply with those provisions.

(3) Where the medical recommendations upon which an application under this Part of this Act is founded are, taken together, insufficient to warrant reception into guardianship in pursuance of the application, a notice under subsection (2) of this section may be given in respect of either of those recommendations; but this subsection shall not apply in a case where the application is of no effect by virtue of section 37(4) of this Act.

Care and treatment of patients: guardianship

43. Regulations as to guardianship

(1) Subject to the provisions of this Part of this Act, the Secretary of State may make regulations for regulating the exercise by the guardians of patients received into guardianship under this Part of this Act of their powers as such, and for imposing on such guardians, and upon any local authority concerned, such duties as he considers necessary or expedient in the interests of the patients.

(2) Regulations under this section may in particular make provision for requiring the patients to be visited, on such occasions or at such intervals as may be prescribed by the regulations, on behalf of such local authorities as may be so prescribed.

Note.—See the Mental Health (Specified Treatments, Guardianship Duties etc) (Scotland) Regulations 1984, SI 1984/ 1494 (Appendix 2).

44. Return of patients absent without leave: guardianship

(1) Where a patient who is for the time being subject to guardianship under this Part of this Act absents himself without the leave of the guardian from the place at which he is required by the guardian to reside, he may, subject to the provisions of this section, be taken into custody and returned to that place by the guardian, by any officer on the staff of a local authority, by any constable, or by any person authorised in writing by the guardian or a local authority.

(2) A patient shall not be taken into custody under this section after the expiration of the period of 28 days beginning with the first day of his absence without leave and a patient who has not returned or been taken into custody under this section within the said period shall cease to be subject to guardianship at the expiration of that period.

45. Transfer of patients: guardianship

(1) A patient who is for the time being subject to the guardianship of any person, including a local authority, by virtue of a guardianship application may be transferred by the local authority concerned into the guardianship of another such person with the consent of that other person; but no patient shall be so transferred except with the consent of his guardian, or, if that consent is refused, with the approval of the sheriff to the transfer.

(2) Any transfer of a patient under the last foregoing subsection shall be intimated to his nearest relative and to the Mental Welfare Commission by the local authority concerned within 7 days of the date of transfer.

(3) Where a patient is transferred under this section, the provisions of this Part of this Act (including this subsection) shall apply to him as if the person into whose guardianship he is transferred had been the person named in the guardianship application.

46. Transfer of guardianship in case of death, incapacity etc of guardian

(1) If any person (other than a local authority) having the guardianship of a patient received into guardianship under this Part of this Act—
   (a) dies; or
   (b) gives notice in writing to the local authority concerned that he desires to relinquish the functions of guardian,

the guardianship of the patient shall thereupon vest in the local authority concerned, but without prejudice to any power to transfer the patient into the guardianship of another person under section 45 of this Act.

(2) If any such person, not having given notice under subsection (1)(b) of this section, is incapacitated by illness or any other cause from performing the functions of guardian of the patient, those functions may, during his incapacity, be performed on his behalf by the local authority concerned, or by any other person approved for the purpose by that authority.

(3) Where the guardianship of a patient is transferred to a local authority or other person by or under subsection (1) of this section, section 45(3) of this Act shall apply as if the patient had been transferred into the guardianship of that authority or person in pursuance of that section.

Duration of authority for guardianship and discharge of patients

47. Duration of authority: guardianship

(1) Subject to the provisions of this Part of this Act, a patient received into guardianship in pursuance of a guardianship application, may be kept under guardianship for a period not exceeding 6 months beginning with the day on which he was so received, but shall not be so kept for any longer period unless the authority for his guardianship is renewed under the following provisions of this section.

(2) Authority for the guardianship of a patient may, unless the patient has previously been discharged, be renewed under this section—
   (a) from the expiration of the period referred to in subsection (1) of this section, for a further period of 6 months;
   (b) from the expiration of any period of renewal under paragraph (a) of this subsection, for a further period of one year, and so on for periods of one year at a time.

(3) Within the period of 2 months ending with the day on which a patient who is subject to guardianship under this Part of this Act would cease under this section to be so liable in default of the renewal of the authority for his guardianship—
   (a) the responsible medical officer shall examine the patient or obtain from another medical practitioner a report on the condition of the patient; and, if it appears to him that the ground set out in section 36(a) of this Act continues to apply in relation to the patient, he shall furnish to such mental health officer as the local authority concerned may direct a report to that effect in the prescribed form along with the report first mentioned if such a report has been obtained; and
   (b) that mental health officer shall consider whether the ground set out in section 36(b) of this Act continues to apply in relation to the patient; and, if it appears to him that it does continue so to apply, he shall furnish to the local authority concerned and to the Mental Welfare Commission a report to that effect in the prescribed form along with the report or reports furnished to him under paragraph (a) of this subsection.

(4) Subject to subsection (6) of this section and section 50(2) and (5) of this Act, where a report is duly furnished to a local authority under subsection (3) of this section, the authority for the guardianship of the patient shall be thereby renewed for the period prescribed in that case by subsection (2) of this section.

(5) Where a report under this section is furnished to them in respect of a patient, the local authority shall, unless they discharge the patient, cause him, his nearest relative and his guardian, to be informed.

(6) Any patient may within the period for which the authority for his guardianship is renewed by virtue of a report furnished in respect of him under this section appeal to the sheriff to order his discharge and the provisions of section 50(2) and (5) of this Act shall apply in relation to such an appeal.

Note.—For prescribed forms see the Mental Health (Prescribed Froms) (Scotland) Regulations 1984, SI 1984/1495 (Appendix 2).

48. Special provisions as to patients absent without leave: guardianship

(1) If on the day on which, under this Part of this Act apart from this section, a patient would cease to be subject to guardianship, or within the period of one week ending with that day, the patient is absent without leave, he shall not cease to be so subject—
- (a) in any case, until the expiration of the period during which he can be taken into custody under section 44 of this Act, or the day on which he returns or is returned to the place where he ought to be, whichever is the earlier; and
- (b) if he returns or is returned as aforesaid within the period first mentioned in the foregoing paragraph, until the expiration of the period of one week beginning with the day on which he is returned or returns as aforesaid.

(2) Where the period for which a patient is subject to guardianship is extended by virtue of this section, any examination and report to be made and furnished under section 47(3) of this Act may be made and furnished within that period as so extended.

(3) Where the authority for the guardianship of a patient is renewed by virtue of this section after the day on which, apart from this section, that authority would have expired under section 47 of this Act, the renewal shall take effect as from that day.

49. Special provisions as to patients sentenced to imprisonment, etc: guardianship

(1) Where a patient who is subject to guardianship under this Part of this Act is detained in custody in pursuance of any sentence or order passed or made by a court in the United Kingdom (including an order committing or remanding him in custody) and is so detained for a period exceeding 6 months, he shall, at the end of that period, cease to be so subject.

(2) Where any such patient is detained in custody as aforesaid for a period not exceeding 6 months, or for successive periods that do not in the aggregate exceed 6 months, then—
- (a) if apart from this subsection the patient would have ceased to be subject as aforesaid on or before the day he is discharged from custody, he shall not cease to be so subject until the end of that day; and
- (b) in any case, sections 44 and 48 of this Act shall apply in relation to the patient as if he had absented himself without leave on that day.

50. Discharge of patients: guardianship

(1) Subject to the provisions of this section and section 51 of this Act, a patient who is for the time being subject to guardianship under this Part of this Act shall cease to be so

subject if an order in writing discharging him from guardianship (in this Act referred to as 'an order for discharge') is made in accordance with the following provisions of this section.

(2) An order for discharge may be made in respect of a patient by the responsible medical officer, the Mental Welfare Commission or, where an appeal has been taken under sections 47 or 51 of this Act, by the sheriff.

(3) The responsible medical officer or the Mental Welfare Commission shall make an order for discharge in respect of a patient where he is or they are satisfied that he is not suffering from mental disorder of a nature or degree which warrants his remaining under guardianship.

(4) The local authority concerned or the Mental Welfare Commission shall make an order for discharge where they are satisfied that it is not necessary in the interests of the welfare of the patient that he should remain under guardianship.

(5) Where an appeal is made to the sheriff by a patient under sections 47 or 51 of this Act, the sheriff shall order the discharge of the patient if he is satisfied that—
   (a) the patient is not at the time of the hearing of the appeal suffering from mental disorder of a nature or degree which warrants his remaining under guardianship; or
   (b) it is not necessary in the interests of the welfare of the patient that he should remain under guardianship.

(6) Subject to the provisions of this section and section 51 of this Act, an order for discharge in respect of a patient may also be made by the nearest relative of the patient.

(7) A patient subject to guardianship shall cease to be so subject where the sheriff has approved under section 21 of this Act an application for his admission to a hospital.

51. Restrictions on discharge by nearest relative: guardianship

(1) An order for the discharge of a patient who is subject to guardianship shall not be made by his nearest relative except after giving not less than 14 days' notice in writing to the local authority concerned; and within that period—
   (a) if it appears to the local authority that the ground set out in section 36(b) of this Act continues to apply in relation to the patient they shall inform the responsible medical officer of the notice given by the nearest relative; and
   (b) if it appears to the responsible medical officer that the ground set out in section 36(a) of this Act continues to apply in relation to the patient he shall inform the local authority; and
   (c) the local authority shall inform the nearest relative of the views taken by them and by the responsible medical officer,
and in that event—
      (i) any order for the discharge of the patient made by that relative in pursuance of the notice shall cease to have effect; and
      (ii) no further order for the discharge of the patient shall be made by that relative during the period of 6 months beginning with the date on which that relative is so informed.

(2) In any case where the local authority informs the nearest relative under subsection (1) of this section that relative may, within the period of 28 days beginning with the day on which he is so informed, appeal to the sheriff to order the discharge of the patient, and the provisions of section 50(2) and (5) of this Act shall apply in relation to such an appeal.

Note.—For suggested form of discharge see Appendix 2.

Mental Health (Scotland) Act 1984

Appeals: guardianship

52. Appeals to the sheriff: guardianship

(1) Where an appeal lies to the sheriff under either of sections 47 or 51 of this Act, the local authority concerned shall when intimating that a report has been furnished in pursuance of the said section 47, or when informing the nearest relative under the said section 51, inform any person having a right so to appeal, whether the patient or his nearest relative, or both, of that right, and of the period within which it may be exercised.

(2) An appeal under either of the said sections shall be made by way of summary application to a sheriff of the sheriffdom within which the patient is resident at the time when the appeal is made.

(3) For the purpose of advising whether any appeal to the sheriff under either of the said sections should be made by or in respect of a patient who is subject to guardianship under this Part of this Act, or furnishing information as to the condition of a patient for the purposes of such an appeal or of advising the nearest relative of any such patient as to the exercise of any power to order the discharge of the patient, any medical practitioner authorised by or on behalf of the patient or by the nearest relative of the patient, as the case may be, may, at any reasonable time, visit the patient and may examine him in private.

Functions of relatives of patients

53. Definition of relative and nearest relative

(1) For the purposes of this section, 'relative' means any of the following, that is to say—
   (a) spouse;
   (b) child;
   (c) father or mother;
   (d) brother or sister;
   (e) grandparent;
   (f) grandchild;
   (g) uncle or aunt;
   (h) nephew or niece;

(2) In deducing relationships for the purposes of this section, an illegitimate person shall be treated as the legitimate child of his mother.

(3) In this Act, subject to the provisions of this section and to the following provisions of this Part of this Act, the 'nearest relative' means the person first listed in subsection (1) of this section who is caring for the patient, or was so caring immediately before the admission of the patient to a hospital or his reception into guardianship, failing whom the person first so listed, brothers and sisters of the whole blood being preferred to brothers and sisters of the half-blood, and the elder or eldest of two or more relatives listed in any paragraph of that subsection being preferred to the other or others of those relatives, regardless of sex.

(4) Where the person who, under subsection (3) of this section, would be the nearest relative of a patient—
   (a) in the case of a patient ordinarily resident in the United Kingdom, the Channel Islands or the Isle of Man, is not so resident; or
   (b) being the husband or wife of the patient, is permanently separated from the patient, either by agreement or under an order of a court, or has deserted or has been deserted by the patient for a period and the spouse concerned is still in desertion; or

(c) not being the husband, wife, father, or mother of the patient, is for the time being under 18 years of age,

the nearest relative of the patient shall be ascertained without regard to that person.

(5) In this section 'spouse' includes a person who is living with the patient as if he or she were the husband or wife of the patient, as the case may be (or, if the patient is for the time being an in-patient in a hospital, was so living until the patient was admitted), and has been or had been so living for a period of not less than 6 months; but a person shall not be treated by virtue of this subsection as the nearest relative of a married patient unless the husband or wife of the patient is disregarded by virtue of paragraph (b) of subsection (4) of this section.

(6) A person, other than a relative, with whom the patient ordinarily resides (or, if the patient is for the time being an in-patient in a hospital, last ordinarily resided before he was admitted), and with whom he has or had been ordinarily residing for a period of not less than five years, shall be treated for the purposes of this Part of this Act as if he were a relative but—
- (a) shall be treated for the purposes of subsection (3) of this section as if mentioned last in subsection (1) of this section; and
- (b) shall not be treated by virtue of this subsection as the nearest relative of a married patient unless the husband or wife of the patient is disregarded by virtue of paragraph (b) of subsection (4) of this section.

54. Children and young persons in care of local authority

In any case where the rights and powers of a parent of a patient, being a child or young person, are vested in a local authority or other person by virtue of—
- (a) section 17 of the Social Work (Scotland) Act 1968 (which relates to children in respect of whom parental rights have been assumed under section 16 of that Act); or
- (b) section 3 of the Child Care Act 1980 (which makes corresponding provisions in England and Wales); or
- (c) section 10 of the said Act of 1980 (which relates to the powers and duties of local authorities in England and Wales with respect to persons committed to their care);

that authority or person shall be deemed to be the nearest relative of the patient in preference to any person except the husband or wife (if any) of the patient, and except, in a case where the said rights and powers are vested in a local authority by virtue of subsection (2) of the said section 17 or subsection (1) of the said section 3, any parent of the patient not being the person on whose account the resolution mentioned in that subsection was passed.

55. Nearest relative of child under guardianship etc

(1) Where a patient who has not attained the age of 18 years—
- (a) is, by virtue of an order made by a court in the exercise of jurisdiction (whether under any enactment or otherwise) in respect of the guardianship of children, or by virtue of a deed or will executed by his father or mother, under the guardianship of a person not being his nearest relative under the foregoing provisions of this Act, or is under the joint guardianship of two persons of whom one is such a person as aforesaid; or
- (b) is, by virtue of an order made by a court in the exercise of such jurisdiction as aforesaid or in matrimonial proceedings, or by virtue of a separation agreement between his father and mother, in the custody of any such person,

the person or persons having the guardianship or custody of the patient shall, to the exclusion of any other person, be deemed to be his nearest relative.

(2) Section 53(4) of this Act shall apply in relation to a person who is, or who is one of

the persons, deemed to be the nearest relative of a patient by virtue of this section as it applies in relation to a person who would be the nearest relative under subsection (3) of that section.

(3) A patient shall be treated for the purposes of this section as being in the custody or guardianship of another person if he would be in the custody or guardianship of that other person apart from section 41(2) of this Act.

(4) In this section 'court' includes a court in England and Wales or Northern Ireland, and 'enactment' includes an enactment of the Parliament of Northern Ireland, a measure of the Northern Ireland Assembly and an Order in Council under Schedule 1 to the Northern Ireland Act 1974.

56. Appointment by sheriff of acting nearest relative

(1) The sheriff may, upon application made in accordance with the provisions of this section in respect of a patient, by order direct that the functions under this Act of the nearest relative of the patient shall, during the continuance in force of the order, be exercisable by the applicant, or by any other person specified in the application, being a person who, in the opinion of the sheriff, is a proper person to act as the nearest relative of the patient, and who is willing to do so.

(2) An order under this section may be made on the application of—
   (a) any relative (including the nearest relative) of the patient;
   (b) any other person with whom the patient is residing (or, if the patient is then an in-patient in a hospital, was last residing before he was admitted); or
   (c) a mental health officer,
but in relation to an application made by such an officer subsection (1) of this section shall have effect as if for the words 'the applicant' there were submitted the words 'the local authority'.

(3) An application for an order under this section may be made upon any of the following grounds, that is to say—
   (a) that the patient has no nearest relative within the meaning of this Act, or that it is not reasonably practicable to ascertain whether he has such a relative or who that relative is;
   (b) that the nearest relative of the patient is incapable of acting as such by reason of mental disorder or other illness;
   (c) where the application is made by the nearest relative of the patient, that he is unwilling or considers it undesirable to continue to act as such.

(4) While an order made under this section is in force, the provisions of this Part of this Act (other than this section and section 57 of this Act) shall apply in relation to the patient as if for any reference to the nearest relative of the patient there were substituted a reference to the person having the functions of that relative and (without prejudice to section 57 of this Act) shall so apply notwithstanding that the person who was the nearest relative of the patient when the order was made is no longer his nearest relative.

57. Discharge and variation of orders under s 56

(1) An order made under section 56 of this Act in respect of a patient may be discharged by the sheriff upon application made—
   (a) by the person having the functions of the nearest relative of the patient by virtue of the order;
   (b) by the nearest relative of the patient.

(2) An order made under the said section 56 in respect of a patient may be varied by the sheriff, on the application of the person having the functions of the nearest relative by virtue of the order or on the application of a mental health officer, by substituting

for the first-mentioned person a local authority or any other person who, in the opinion of the sheriff, is a proper person to exercise those functions, being an authority or person who is willing to do so.

(3) If the person having the functions of the nearest relative of a patient by virtue of an order under the said section 56 dies, the foregoing provisions of this section shall apply as if for any reference to that person there were substituted a reference to any relative of the patient, and until the order is discharged or varied under those provisions the functions of the nearest relative under this Part of this Act shall not be exercisable by any person.

(4) An order under the said section 56 shall, unless previously discharged under subsection (1) of this section, cease to have effect—
- (a) if the patient was on the date of the order liable to be detained in pursuance of an application for admission or subject to guardianship under this Part of this Act, or becomes so liable or so subject within the period of 3 months beginning with that date, when he ceases to be so liable or so subject (otherwise than on being transferred in pursuance of sections 29 or 45 of this Act);
- (b) if the patient was not on the date of the order and has not within the said period become so liable or so subject, at the expiration of that period.

(5) The discharge or variation under this section of an order made under the said section 56 shall not affect the validity of anything previously done in pursuance of the order.

Supplementary

58. Regulations for purposes of Part V

The Secretary of State may make regulations for prescribing anything which, under this Part of this Act, is required or authorised to be prescribed.

Note.—See the Mental Health (Prescribed Forms) (Scotland) Regulations 1984, SI 1984/1495 and the Mental Health (Specified Treatments, Guardianship Duties etc) (Scotland) Regulations 1984, SI 1984/1494 (Appendix 2).

59. Interpretation of Part V

(1) In this Part of this Act the expression 'responsible medical officer' means—
- (a) in relation to a patient who is liable to be detained in a hospital, any medical practitioner employed on the staff of that hospital who may be authorised by the managers to act (either generally or in any particular case or class of case or for any particular purpose) as the responsible medical officer;
- (b) in relation to a patient subject to guardianship, any medical practitioner authorised by the local authority to act (either generally or in any particular case or class of case or for any particular purpose) as the responsible medical officer.

(2) In relation to a patient who is subject to guardianship under this Part of this Act, any reference in this Act to the local authority concerned is a reference—
- (a) where a guardianship application is effective, to the local authority to whom that application is addressed;
- (b) where the patient has been transferred to guardianship by the managers of a hospital under section 29(1) of this Act, to the local authority who received him into guardianship or approved his guardian.

(3) In this Act the expression 'absent without leave' means absent from any hospital or other place and liable to be taken into custody and returned under section 28 or 44 of this Act, and kindred expressions shall be construed accordingly.

PART VI DETENTION OF PATIENTS CONCERNED IN CRIMINAL PROCEEDINGS ETC AND TRANSFER OF PATIENTS UNDER SENTENCE

Provisions for compulsory detention and guardianship of patients charged with offences etc.

60. Effect of hospital orders

(1) A hospital order made under section 175 or 376 of the Criminal Procedure (Scotland) Act 1975 shall be sufficient authority—
   (a) for a constable, a mental health officer, or any other person directed to do so by the court to convey the patient to the hospital specified in the order within a period of 28 days; and
   (b) for the managers of the hospital to admit at any time within that period, and thereafter to detain him in accordance with the provisions of this Act.

(2) A patient who is admitted to a hospital in pursuance of a hospital order shall be treated for the purposes of Part V of this Act (other than section 23) as if he had been so admitted on the date of the order in pursuance of an application for admission, except that the power to order the discharge of the patient under section 33 of this Act shall not be exercisable by his nearest relative; and accordingly the provisions of the said Part V specified in Part I of the Second Schedule to this Act shall apply in relation to him, subject to the exceptions and modifications set out in that Part and the remaining provisions of the said Part V shall not apply.

(3) Subject to the provisions of section 178(3) or 379(3) of the said Act of 1975, where a patient is admitted to a hospital in pursuance of a hospital order any previous application or hospital order by virtue of which he was liable to be detained in a hospital shall cease to have effect:
   Provided that, if the order first-mentioned or the conviction to which it relates is quashed on appeal, this subsection shall not apply and section 32 of this Act shall have effect as if during any period for which the patient was liable to be detained under the order he had been detained in custody as mentioned in that section.

(4) If within the period of 28 days referred to in subsection (1) of this section it appears to the Secretary of State that by reason of an emergency or other special circumstances it is not practicable for the patient to be received into the hospital specified in the order, he may give directions for the admission of the patient to such other hospital as appears to be appropriate in lieu of the hospital so specified; and where such directions are given the Secretary of State shall cause the person having the custody of the patient to be informed, and the hospital order shall have effect as if the hospital specified in the directions were substituted for the hospital specified in the order.

61. Effect of guardianship orders

(1) A guardianship order made under section 175 or 376 of the Criminal Procedure (Scotland) Act 1975 shall confer on the authority or person therein named as guardian the like powers as a guardianship application effective under Part V of this Act.

(2) A patient who is received into guardianship in pursuance of a guardianship order shall be treated for the purposes of Part V of this Act (other than section 42) as if he had been so received on the date of the order in pursuance of a guardianship application as aforesaid, except that the power to order the discharge of the patient under section 50 of this Act shall not be exercisable by his nearest relative; and accordingly the provisions of the said Part V specified in Part III of the Second Schedule to this Act

shall apply in relation to him subject to the exceptions and modifications set out therein, and the remaining provisions of the said Part V shall not apply.

(3) Where a patient is received into guardianship in pursuance of a guardianship order any previous application or order by virtue of which he was subject to guardianship shall cease to have effect:

Provided that, if the order first-mentioned or the conviction to which it relates is quashed on appeal, this subsection shall not apply and section 49 of this Act shall have effect as if during any period for which the patient was subject to guardianship under the order he had been detained in custody as mentioned in that section.

62. Effect of restriction orders

(1) The special restrictions applicable to a patient in respect of whom a restriction order made under section 178 or 379 of the Criminal Procedure (Scotland) Act 1975 is in force are as follows, that is to say—
  (a) none of the provisions of Part V of this Act relating to the duration, renewal and expiration of authority for the detention of patients shall apply, and the patient shall continue to be liable to be detained by virtue of the relevant hospital order until he is absolutely discharged under sections 63 to 68 of this Act;
  (b) the following powers shall be exercisable only with the consent of the Secretary of State, that is to say—
    (i) power to grant leave of absence to the patient under section 27 of this Act; and
    (ii) power to transfer the patient under section 29 of this Act;
    and if leave of absence is granted under the said section 27 the power to recall the patient under that section shall be vested in the Secretary of State as well as in the responsible medical officer; and
  (c) the power to take the patient into custody and return him under section 28 of this Act may be exercised at any time,

and in relation to any such patient the provisions of the said Part V specified in Part II of the Second Schedule to this Act shall have effect subject to the exceptions and modifications set out in that Part and the remaining provisions of Part V shall not apply.

(2) While a person is a restricted patient within the meaning of section 63 of this Act or a person to whom section 67 (persons treated as restricted patients) of this Act applies, the responsible medical officer shall at such intervals (not exceeding one year) as the Secretary of State may direct examine and report to the Secretary of State on that person; and every report shall contain such particulars as the Secretary of State may require.

(3) Without prejudice to the provisions of section 178(3) or 379(3) of the said Act of 1975, where a restriction order in respect of a patient ceases to have effect while the relevant hospital order continues in force, the provisions of section 60 of this Act and Part I of the Second Schedule to this Act shall apply to the patient as if he had been admitted to the hospital in pursuance of a hospital order (without a restriction order) made on the date on which the restriction order ceased to have effect.

63. Right of appeal of restricted patients etc

(1) In this section and in sections 64 to 67 of this Act—
  'restricted patient' means a patient who is subject to a restriction direction;
  'relevant hospital order' and 'relevant transfer direction', in relation to a restricted patient, mean the hospital order or transfer direction by virtue of which he is liable to be detained in a hospital.

(2) A restricted patient detained in a hospital may appeal by way of summary application to a sheriff of the sheriffdom within which the hospital in which he is liable to be detained is situated—

(a) in the period between the expiration of 6 months and the expiration of 12 months beginning with the date of the relevant hospital order or transfer direction; and
(b) in any subsequent period of 12 months,

to order his discharge under section 64 or 65 of this Act.

(3) The provisions of section 35(3) and (4) of this Act shall have effect in relation to an appeal under sections 63 to 67 of this Act as they have in relation to an appeal under Part V of this Act.

64. Right of appeal of patients subject to restriction orders

(1) Where an appeal to the sheriff is made by a restricted patient who is subject to a restriction order, the sheriff shall direct the absolute discharge of the patient if he is satisfied—
- (a) that the patient is not, at the time of the hearing of the appeal, suffering from mental disorder of a nature or degree which makes it appropriate for him to be liable to be detained in a hospital for medical treatment; or
- (b) that it is not necessary for the health or safety of the patient or for the protection of other persons that he should receive such treatment; and (in either case)
- (c) that it is not appropriate for the patient to remain liable to be recalled to hospital for futher treatment.

(2) Where in the case of any such patient as is mentioned in subsection (1) of this section the sheriff is satisfied as to the matters referred to in paragraph (a) or (b) of that subsection but not as to the matters referred to in paragraph (c) of that subsection he shall direct the conditional discharge of the patient.

(3) Where a patient is absoluely discharged under subsection (1) of this section he shall thereupon cease to be liable to be detained by virtue of the relevant hospital order, and the restriction order shall cease to have effect accordingly.

(4) Where a patient is conditionally discharged under subsection (2) of this section—
- (a) he may be recalled by the Secretary of State under section 68(3) of this Act as if he had been conditionally discharged under subsection (2) of that section; and
- (b) he shall comply with such conditions (if any) as may be imposed at the time of discharge by the sheriff or at any subsequent time by the Secretary of State.

(5) The Secretary of State may from time to time vary any condition imposed (whether by the sheriff or by him) under subsection (4) of this section.

(6) Where a restriction order in respect of a patient ceases to have effect after he has been conditionally discharged under subsection (2) of this section the patient shall, unless previously recalled, be deemed to be absolutely discharged on the date when the order ceases to have effect and shall cease to be liable to be detained by virtue of the relevant hospital order.

(7) The sheriff may defer a direction for the conditional discharge of a patient until such arrangements as appear to the sheriff to be necessary for that purpose have been made to his satisfaction; and where by virtue of any such deferment no direction has been given on an appeal before the time when the patient's case comes before the sheriff on a subsequent appeal, the previous appeal shall be treated as one on which no direction under this section can be given.

(8) This section is without prejudice to section 68 of this Act.

65. Right of appeal of patients subject to restriction directions

(1) Where an appeal to the sheriff is made by a restricted patient who is subject to a restriction direction, the sheriff—
- (a) shall notify the Secretary of State if, in his opinion, the patient would, if subject to a restriction order, be entitled to be absolutely or conditionally discharged under section 64 of this Act; and

(b) if he notifies the Secretary of State that the patient would be entitled to be conditionally discharged, may recommend that in the event of the patient's not being released on licence or discharged under supervision under subsection 2(b)(ii) of this section he should continue to be detained in a hospital.

(2) If the sheriff notifies the Secretary of State—
   (a) that the patient would be entitled to be absolutely discharged, the Secretary of State shall—
      (i) by warrant direct that the patient be remitted to any prison or other institution in which he might have been detained if he had not been removed to hospital, there to be dealt with as if he had not been so removed; or
      (ii) exercise any power of releasing the patient on licence or discharging the patient under supervision which would have been exercisable if the patient had been remitted to any prison or other institution in which he might have been detained if he had not been removed to hospital;
   (b) that the patient would be entitled to be conditionally discharged, the Secretary of State may—
      (i) by warrant direct that the patient be remitted to any prison or other institution in which he might have been detained if he had not been removed to hospital, there to be dealt with as if he had not been so removed; or
      (ii) exercise any power of releasing the patient on licence or discharging the patient under supervision which would have been exercisable if the patient had been remitted to any prison or other institution in which he might have been detained if he had not been removed to hospital; or
      (iii) decide that the patient should continue to be detained in a hospital,
and on his arrival in the prison or other institution or, as the case may be, his release or discharge as aforesaid, the transfer direction and the restriction direction shall cease to have effect.

66. Further consideration of case of conditionally discharged patient.

(1) Where a restricted patient has been conditionally discharged under sections 64 or 68(2) of this Act and is subsequently recalled under section 68(3) of this Act to hospital he may, within one month of the day on which he returns or is returned to hospital, appeal against such recall to a sheriff of the sheriffdom in which the hospital in which he is liable to be detained by virtue of the warrant under the said section 68(3) is situated.

(2) Where a restricted patient has been conditionally discharged as aforesaid but is not recalled to hospital he may appeal—
   (a) in the period between the expiration of 12 months and the expiration of 2 years beginning with the date on which he was conditionally discharged; and
   (b) in any subsequent period of 2 years,
to a sheriff of the sheriffdom in which he resides.

(3) If in any appeal under subsection (1) or (2) of this section the sheriff is satisfied as mentioned in section 64(1) or (2) of this Act, he shall uphold the appeal and—
   (a) where he is satisfied as mentioned in the said section 64(1), he shall direct the absolute discharge of the patient;
   (b) where he is satisfied as mentioned in the said section 64(2), he shall direct, or (as the case may be) continue, the conditional discharge of the patient; and, in either case, he may vary any condition to which the patient is subject in connection with his discharge or impose any condition which might have been imposed in connection therewith.

(4) Where a patient is absolutely discharged in an appeal under subsection (1) or (2) of this section he shall thereupon cease to be liable to be detained by virtue of the relevant hospital order, and the restriction order shall cease to have effect accordingly.

67. Application of sections 63 to 66 to other persons treated as restricted patients

(1) Sections 63, 64 and 66 of this Act shall apply to a person who—
  (a) is subject to—
    (i) a direction which by virtue of section 69(3) of this Act; or
    (ii) an order which by virtue of section 174(4) of the Criminal Procedure (Scotland) Act 1975,
    has the like effect as a hospital order and a restriction order; or
  (b) is treated as subject to a hospital order and a restriction order by virtue of section 80(2) of the Mental Health Act 1983 or section 81(2) of this Act,
as they apply to a restricted patient who is subject to a restriction order and references in the said sections 63, 64 and 66 to the relevant hospital order or restriction order shall be construed as references to the direction under section 69(1) of this Act or the order under section 174(3) of the Criminal Procedure (Scotland) Act 1975.

(2) Sections 63 and 65 of this Act shall apply to a person who is treated as subject to a transfer direction and a restriction direction by virtue of section 80(2) of the Mental Health Act 1983 or section 81(2) of this Act as they apply to a restricted patient who is subject to a restriction direction and references in the said sections 63 and 65 to the relevant transfer direction or the restriction direction shall be construed as references to the transfer direction or restriction direction to which that person is treated as subject by virtue of the said section 80(2) or 81(2).

68. Powers of Secretary of State in respect of patients subject to restriction orders

(1) If the Secretary of State is satisfied that a restriction order in respect of a patient is no longer required for the protection of the public from serious harm, he may direct that the patient shall cease to be subject to the special restrictions set out in section 62(1) of this Act; and, where the Secretary of State so directs, the restriction order shall cease to have effect and subsection (3) of that section shall apply accordingly.

(2) At any time while a restriction order is in force in respect of a patient, the Secretary of State may, if he thinks fit, by warrant discharge the patient from hospital, either absolutely or subject to conditions; and where a person is absolutely discharged under this subsection he shall thereupon cease to be liable to be detained by virtue of the relevant hospital order, and the restriction order shall cease to have effect accordingly.

(3) The Secretary of State may, at any time during the continuance in force of a restriction order in respect of a patient who has been conditionally discharged under subsection (2) of this section, and without prejudice to his further discharge as aforesaid, by warrant recall the patient to such hospital as may be specified in the warrant; and thereupon—
  (a) if the hospital so specified is not the hospital from which the patient was conditionally discharged, the hospital order and the restriction order shall have effect as if the hospital specified in the warrant were substituted for the hospital specified in the hospital order;
  (b) in any case, the patient shall be treated for the purposes of section 28 of this Act as if he had absented himself without leave from the hospital specified in the warrant, and if the restriction order was made for a specified period, that period shall not in any event expire until the patient returns to the hospital or is returned to the hospital under that section.

(4) If a restriction order ceases to have effect in respect of a patient after the patient has been conditionally discharged under this section, the patient shall, unless previously

recalled under the last foregoing subsection, be deemed to be absolutely discharged on the date when the order ceases to have effect, and shall cease to be liable to be detained by virtue of the relevant hospital order accordingly.

(5) The Secretary of State may, if satisfied that the attendance at any place in Great Britain of a patient who is subject to a restriction order is desirable in the interests of justice or for the purposes of any public inquiry, direct him to be taken to that place; and where a patient is directed under this subsection to be taken to any place he shall, unless the Secretary of State otherwise directs, be kept in custody while being so taken, while at that place, and while being taken back to the hospital in which he is liable to be detained.

69. Persons ordered to be kept in custody during Her Majesty's pleasure

(1) The Secretary of State may by warrant direct that any person who, by virtue of any enactment to which this subsection applies, is required to be kept in custody during Her Majesty's pleasure or until the directions of Her Majesty are known shall be detained in a State hospital or such other hospital as he may specify and, where that person is not already detained in the hospital, give directions for his removal there.

(2) The enactments to which subsection (1) of this section applies are section 16 of the Courts-Martial (Appeals) Act 1968, section 116 of the Army Act 1955, section 116 of the Air Force Act 1955, and section 63 of the Naval Discipline Act 1957.

(3) A direction under this section in respect of any person shall have the like effect as an order referred to in section 174(3) of the Criminal Procedure (Scotland) Act 1975.

Transfer to hospital or guardianship of prisoners etc.

70. Removal to hospital of persons in prison awaiting trial etc

(1) If in the case of a person committed in custody while awaiting trial or sentence it appears to the Secretary of State that the grounds are satisfied upon which an application may be made for his admission to a hospital under Part V of this Act he may apply to the sheriff for an order that that person be removed to and detained in such hospital (not being a private hospital) as may be specified in the order; and the sheriff, if satisfied by reports from 2 medical practitioners (complying with the provisions of this section) that the grounds are satisfied as aforesaid may make an order accordingly.

(2) An order under this section (in this Act referred to as 'a transfer order') shall cease to have effect at the expiration of the period of 14 days beginning with the date on which it is made, unless within that period the person with respect to whom it was made has been received into the hospital specified therein.

(3) A transfer order with respect to any person shall have the like effect as a hospital order made in his case together with a restriction order in respect of him made without limit of time.

(4) Of the medical practitioners whose reports are taken into account under subsection (1) of this section, at least one shall be a practitioner approved for the purposes of section 20 of this Act by a Health Board as having special experience in the diagnosis or treatment of mental disorder.

(5) A transfer order shall specify the form or forms of mental disorder, being mental illness or mental handicap or both, from which the patient is found by the sheriff to be suffering; and no such order shall be made unless the patient is described by each of the practitioners whose evidence is taken into account as aforesaid as suffering from the same form of mental disorder, whether or not he is also described by either of them as suffering from the other form.

71. Removal to hospital of persons serving sentences of imprisonment and other prisoners

(1) If in the case of a person to whom this section applies the Secretary of State is satisfied by the like reports as are required for the purposes of section 70 of this Act that the grounds are satisfied upon which an application may be made for his admission to a hospital under Part V of this Act the Secretary of State may make a direction (in this Act referred to as 'a transfer direction') in respect of him.

(2) This section apples to the following persons, that is to say—
  (a) persons serving sentences of imprisonment;
  (b) civil prisoners, that is to say, persons committed by court to prison in respect of a civil debt;
  (c) persons detained under the Immigration Act 1971.

(3) Subsections (2), (4) and (5) of section 70 of this Act shall apply for the purposes of this section and of any transfer direction given by virtue of this section as they apply for the purposes of that section and of any transfer order thereunder, with the substitution for any references to the sheriff of a reference to the Secretary of State.

(4) A transfer direction with respect to any person shall have the like effect as a hospital order made in his case.

(5) Where a transfer direction is given in respect of any person that person may, within one month of his transfer to a hospital thereunder, appeal to the sheriff to cancel the direction, and the sheriff shall cancel the direction unless he is satisfied that the grounds are satisfied upon which an application may be made for the admission of the person to a hospital under Part V of this Act; and, if a transfer direction is so cancelled, the Secretary of State shall direct that the person be remitted to any prison or other institution in which he might have been detained if he had not been removed to hospital, there to be dealt with as if he had not been so removed.

(6) Subsections (2), (3) and (4) of section 35 of this Act shall apply to an appeal under subsection (5) of this section in like manner as they apply to an appeal referred to in that section.

(7) References in this section to a person serving a sentence of imprisonment include references—
  (a) to a person detained in pursuance of any sentence or order for detention made by a court in criminal proceedings (other than an order under section 174 or 255 of the Criminal Procedure (Scotland) Act 1975, or under any enactment to which section 69 of this Act applies);
  (b) to a person committed by a court to a prison or other institution to which the Prisons (Scotland) Act 1952, applies in default of payment of any fine to be paid on his conviction.

72. Restriction on discharge of prisoners removed to hospital

(1) Where a transfer direction is given in respect of any person, the Secretary of State, if he thinks fit, may by warrant direct that that person shall be subject to the special restrictions set out in section 62(1) of this Act.

(2) A direction under this section (in this Act referred to as 'a restriction direction') shall have the like effect as a restriction order in respect of the patient made under section 178 or 379 of the Criminal Procedure (Scotland) Act 1975.

73. Further provisions as to persons removed to hospital while awaiting trial etc

(1) Subject to the following provisions of this section any transfer order made in respect of a person under section 70(1) of this Act shall cease to have effect if the

proceedings in respect of him are dropped or when his case is disposed of by the court to which he was committed, or by which he was remanded, but without prejudice to any power of that court to make a hospital order or other order under section 174A, 175, 178, 375A, 376 or 379 of the Criminal Procedure (Scotland) Act 1975 in his case.

(2) Where a transfer order has been made in respect of any such person as aforesaid, then, if the Secretary of State is notified by the responsible medical officer at any time before that person is brought before the court to which he was committed, or by which he was remanded, that he no longer requires treatment for mental disorder, the Secretary of State may by warrant direct that he be remitted to any place where he might have been detained if he had not been removed to hospital, there to be dealt with as if he had not been so removed, and on his arrival at the place to which he is so remitted the transfer order shall cease to have effect.

(3) Where a transfer order in respect of any person ceases to have effect under subsection (1) of this section, then unless his case has been disposed of by the court—
   (a) passing a sentence of imprisonment (within the meaning of section 175(7) or 376(10) of the said Act of 1975) on him; or
   (b) making a probation order under section 183, 184, 384 or 385 of the said Act of 1975 in relation to him; or
   (c) making a hospital order or guardianship order in his case,
he shall continue to be liable to be detained in the hospital in which he was detained under the transfer order as if he had been admitted thereto, on the date on which that order ceased to have effect, in pursuance of an application for admission made under Part V of this Act, and the provisions of this Act shall apply accordingly.

74. Further provisions as to prisoners under sentence

(1) Where a transfer direction and a restriction direction have been given in respect of a person serving a sentence of imprisonment and the Secretary of State is satisfied—
   (a) that the person is not suffering from mental disorder of a nature or degree which makes it appropriate for him to be liable to be detained in a hospital for medical treatment; or
   (b) that it is not necessary for the health or safety of the person or for the protection of other persons that he should receive such treatment; and (in either case)
   (c) that it is not appropriate for the person to remain liable to be recalled to hospital for further treatment,
he shall—
   (i) by warrant direct that the person be remitted to any prison or other institution in which he might have been detained if he had not been removed to hospital, there to be dealt with as if he had not been so removed; or
   (ii) exercise any power of releasing the person on licence or discharging the person under supervision, which would have been exercisable if he had been remitted to any prison or other institution in which he might have been detained if he had not been removed to hospital,
and on his arrival in the prison or other institution, or as the case may be his release or discharge as aforesaid, the transfer direction and the restriction direction shall cease to have effect.

(2) Where in the case of any such person as is mentioned in subsection (1) of this section the Secretary of State is satisfied as to the matter referred to in paragraph (a) or (b) of that subsection but not as to the matters referred to in paragraph (c) of that subsection he may—
   (a) by warrant direct that the person be remitted to any prison or other institution in which he might have been detained if he had not been removed to a hospital, there to be dealt with as if he had not been removed; or
   (b) exercise any power of releasing the person on licence or discharging the person under supervision, which would have been exercisable if he had been remitted

to any prison or other institution in which he might have been detained if he had not been removed to a hospital; or

(c) decide that the person should continue to be detained in a hospital,

and on his arrival in the prison or other institution or, as the case may be, his release or discharge as aforesaid, the transfer direction and the restriction direction shall cease to have effect.

(3) A restriction direction given in respect of a person serving a sentence of imprisonment shall cease to have effect on the expiration of the sentence.

(4) Subject to the following provisions of this section, where a restriction direction ceases to have effect in respect of a person that person shall be discharged unless a report is furnished in respect of him under subsection (5) of this section.

(5) Within a period of 28 days before a restriction direction ceases to have effect in respect of a person, the responsible medical officer shall obtain from another medical practitioner a report on the condition of the patient in the prescribed form and thereafter shall assess the need for the detention of the patient to be continued; and, if it appears to him that it is necessary in the interests of the health or safety of the patient or for the protection of other persons that the patient should continue to be liable to be detained in hospital, he shall furnish to the managers of the hospital where the patient is liable to be detained and to the Mental Welfare Commission a report to that effect in the prescribed form along with the report first mentioned.

(6) Where a report is duly furnished under subsection (5) of this section, the patient shall be treated as if he had been admitted to the hospital in pursuance of a hospital order (without a restriction order) made on the date on which the restriction direction ceased to have effect, but the provisions of section 30(5) and (6) and of section 35 of this Act shall apply to him in like manner as they apply to a patient the authority for whose detention in hospital has been renewed in pursuance of subsction (4) of the said section 30.

(7) Subject to subsection (8) of this section, references in this section to the expiration of a person's sentence are references to the expiration of the period during which he would have been liable to be detained in a prison or other institution if the transfer direction had not been given and if he had not forfeited remission of any part of the sentence after his removal in pursuance of the direction.

(8) For the purposes of subsection (2) of section 37 of the Prisons (Scotland) Act 1952 (which subsection provides for discounting from the sentence of certain prisoners periods while they are unlawfully at large) a patient who, having been transferred in pursuance of a transfer direction from any such institution as is referred to in that subsection, is at large, in circumstances in which he is liable to be taken into custody under any provision of this Act, shall be treated as unlawfully at large and absent from that institution.

(9) In this section 'prescribed' means prescribed by regulations made by the Secretary of State.

Note.—For prescribed forms, see the Mental Health (Prescribed Forms) (Scotland) Regulations 1984, SI 1984/1495 (Appendix 2).

75. Further provisions as to civil prisoners and persons detained under the Immigration Act 1971

(1) Subject to subsection (2) of this section, a transfer direction given in respect of any such person as is described in paragraph (b) or (c) of section 71(2) of this Act shall cease to have effect on the expiration of the period during which he would, but for his removal to a hospital, be liable to be detained in the place from which he was removed.

(2) Where a transfer direction and a restriction direction have been given in respect of any such person as is mentioned in subsection (1) of this section and the Secretary of State is satisfied—
- (a) that the person is not suffering from mental disorder of a nature or degree which makes it appropriate for him to be liable to be detained in a hospital for medical treatment; or
- (b) that it is not necessary for the health or safety of the person or for the protection of other persons that he should receive such treatment; and (in either case),
- (c) that it is not appropriate for the person to remain liable to be recalled to hospital for further treatment,

he shall—
- (i) by warrant direct that the person be remitted to any prison or other institution in which he might have been detained if he had not been removed to a hospital, there to be dealt with as if he had not been so removed; or
- (ii) exercise any power of releasing the person on licence or discharging the person under supervision, which would have been exercisable if he had been remitted to any prison or other institution in which he might have been detained if he had not been removed to a hospital,

and on his arrival in the prison or other institution, or as the case may be, his release or discharge as aforesaid, the transfer direction and the restriction direction shall cease to have effect.

(3) Where in the case of any such person as is mentioned in subsection (2) of this section the Secretary of State is satisfied as to the matters referred to in paragraph (a) or (b) of that subsection but not as to the matters referred to in paragraph (c) of that subsection he may—
- (a) by warrant direct that the person be remitted to any prison or other institution in which he might have been detained if he had not been removed to a hospital, there to be dealt with as if he had not been so removed; or
- (b) exercise any power of releasing the person on licence or discharging the person under supervision, which would have been exercisable if he had been remitted to any prison or other institution in which he might have been detained if he had not been removed to hospital; or
- (c) decide that the person should continue to be detained in hospital,

and on his arrival in the prison or other institution or, as the case may be, his release or discharge as aforesaid, the transfer direction and the restriction direction shall cease to have effect.

Supplementary

76. Interpretation of Part VI

(1) In the following provisions of this Part of this Act, that is to say—
- (a) section 60(2) and (3);
- (b) section 61;
- (c) section 62(1); and
- (d) section 68

and in section 178(3) or 379(3) of the Criminal Procedure (Scotland) Act 1975 any reference to a hospital order, a guardianship order or a restriction order in respect of a patient subject to a hospital order shall be construed as including a reference to any order or direction under this Part of this Act having the like effect as the first-mentioned order; and the exceptions and modifications set out in the Second Schedule to this Act in respect of the provisions of Part V of this Act described in that Schedule accordingly include those which are consequential on the provisions of this subsection.

(2) References in this Part of this Act to persons serving a sentence of imprisonment shall be construed in accordance with section 71(7) of this Act.

PART VII REMOVAL AND RETURN OF PATIENTS WITHIN UNITED KINGDOM ETC

Removal to and from England and Wales

77. Removal of patients to England and Wales

(1) If it appears to the Secretary of State, in the case of a patient who is for the time being liable to be detained or subject to guardianship under this Act, that it is in the interests of the patient to remove him to England and Wales, and that arrangements have been made for admitting him to a hospital or, as the case may be, for receiving him into guardianship there, the Secretary of State may authorise his removal to England and Wales and may give any necessary directions for his conveyance to his destination.

(2) Where a patient who is liable to be detained under this Act by virtue of an application, order or direction under any enactment in force in Scotland is removed under this section and admitted to a hospital in England and Wales, he shall be treated as if on the date of his admission he had been so admitted in pursuance of an application made, or an order or direction made or given, on that date under the corresponding enactment in force in England and Wales, and, where he is subject to an order or direction under any enactment in this Act restricting his discharge, as if he were subject to an order or direction under the corresponding enactment in force in England and Wales.

(3) Where a patient who is subject to guardianship under this Act by virtue of an application or order under any enactment in force in Scotland is removed under this section and received into guardianship in England and Wales, he shall be treated as if on the date on which he arrives at the place where he is to reside he had been so received in pursuance of an application or order under the corresponding enactment in force in England and Wales and as if the application had been accepted or, as the case may be, the order had been made on that date.

(4) Where a patient removed under this section was immediately before his removal liable to be detained under this Act by virtue of a transfer direction given while he was serving a sentence of imprisonment (within the meaning of section 71(7) of this Act) imposed by a court in Scotland, he shall be treated as if the sentence had been imposed by a court in England and Wales.

(5) Where a person so removed as aforesaid was immediately before his removal subject to a restriction order or a restriction direction, being an order or direction of limited duration, the restriction order or restriction direction to which he is subject by virtue of subsection (2) of this section shall expire on the date on which the first-mentioned order or direction would have expired if he had not been so removed.

(6) In this section references to a hospital in England and Wales shall be construed as references to a hospital within the meaning of Part II of the Mental Health Act 1983.

78. Position of nearest relative on removal to England and Wales

(1) Where a patient is removed from Scotland to England and Wales in pursuance of arrangements under this Part of this Act, and at the time of his removal there is in force an order under Part V of this Act directing that the functions of his nearest relative

under this Act shall be exercisable by a person other than the nearest relative within the meaning of the said Part V, the order, so far as it so directs, shall, on the patient's admission to a hospital or reception into guardianship in England and Wales, have effect as if it were an order made by a county court under Part II of the Mental Health Act 1983, and accordingly may be discharged or varied by the county court under that Act and not by the sheriff under this Act.

(2) Where a patient is removed as aforesaid and the person who, apart from any such order, is treated by virtue of any of the provisions of sections 53 to 57 of this Act as the nearest relative within the meaning of Part V of this Act would not be treated by virtue of section 26 of the said Act of 1983 as the nearest relative within the meaning of Part II of that Act, that person shall, after the admission of the patient to a hospital or his reception into guardianship in England and Wales, be treated as the nearest relative within the meaning of Part II of the said Act of 1983, subject, however, to any order made or treated by the foregoing subsection as made, by the county court under section 29 of that Act and without prejudice to the operation of the other provisions of Part II of that Act with respect to the nearest relative of a patient.

(3) An order of the sheriff under section 56 of this Act may be proved by a certificate under the hand of the sheriff clerk.

79. Position of nearest relative on removal to Scotland

(1) Where a patient is removed from England and Wales to Scotland in pursuance of arrangements under the Mental Health Act 1983, and at the time of his removal there is in force an order under Part II of that Act directing that the functions of his nearest relative under that Act shall be exercisable by a person other than the nearest relative within the meaning of that Part of that Act, the order, so far as it so directs, shall, on his admission to a hospital or reception into guardianship in Scotland, have effect as if it were an order made by a sheriff under Part V of this Act, and accordingly may be discharged or varied by the sheriff under this Act and not by the county court under that Act.

(2) Where a patient is removed as aforesaid and the person who, apart from any such order, is treated by virtue of sections 26 to 28 of the said Act of 1983 as the nearest relative within the meaning of Part II of that Act would not be treated by virtue of section 53 of this Act as the nearest relative within the meaning of Part V of this Act, that person shall, after the admission of the patient to a hospital or his reception into guardianship in Scotland, be treated as the nearest relative within the meaning of Part V of this Act, subject, however, to any order made, or treated by the foregoing subsection as made, by the sheriff under section 56 of this Act and without prejudice to the operation of the other provisions of Part V of this Act with respect to the nearest relative of a patient.

(3) An entry made in a book or other document required to be kept for the purposes of section 12 of the County Courts Act 1984 (which relates to the keeping of records of proceedings of county courts) and relating to an order of a county court under section 29 or section 52 or 53 of the Mental Health Act 1959 or section 30 of the Mental Health Act 1983, or a copy of such an entry purporting to be signed and certified as a true copy by the registrar of the county court, shall, in Scotland, be evidence of the like matters and to the like extent as in England and Wales.

Removal to and from Northern Ireland

80. Removal of patients to Northern Ireland

(1) If it appears to the Secretary of State, in the case of a patient who is for the time being liable to be detained or subject to guardianship under this Act, that it is in the

interests of the patient to remove him to Northern Ireland, and that arrangements have been made for admitting him to a hospital or, as the case may be, for receiving him into guardianship there, the Secretary of State may authorise his removal to Northern Ireland and may give any necessary directions for his conveyance to his destination.

(2) Subject to the provisions of subsection (4) of this section, where a patient who is liable to be detained under this Act by virtue of an application, order or direction under any enactment in force in Scotland is removed under this section and admitted to a hospital in Northern Ireland, he shall be treated as if on the date of his admission he had been so admitted in pursuance of an application made, or an order or direction made or given, on that date under the corresponding enactment in force in Northern Ireland, and, where he is subject to an order or direction under any enactment in this Act restricting his discharge, as if he were subject to [a restriction order or a restriction direction][1] under the corresponding enactment in force in Northern Ireland.

(3) Where a patient who is subject to guardianship under this Act by virtue of an application or order under any enactment in force in Scotland is removed under this section and received into guardianship in Northern Ireland, he shall be treated as if on the date on which he arrives at the place where he is to reside he had been so received in pursuance of an application or order under the corresponding enactment in force in Northern Ireland, and as if the application had been accepted or, as the case may be, the order had been made on that date.

(4) Where a person removed under this section was immediately before his removal liable to be detained by virtue of an application for admission under this Act, he shall, on his admission to a hospital in Northern Ireland, be treated as if—[he were detained for treatment under Part II of the Mental Health (Northern Ireland) Order 1986 by virtue of a report under Article 12(1) of that Order made on the date of his admission.][2]

(5) Where a patient removed under this section was immediately before his removal liable to be detained under this Act by virtue of a transfer direction given while he was serving a sentence of imprisonment (within the meaning of section 71(7) of this Act) imposed by a court in Scotland, he shall be treated as if the sentence had been imposed by a court in Northern Ireland.

(6) Where a person removed under this section was immediately before his removal subject to a restriction order or a restriction direction, being an order or direction of limited duration, the [restriction order or restriction direction][3] to which he is subject by virtue of subsection (2) of this section shall expire on the date on which the first-mentioned order or direction would have expired if he had not been so removed.

(7) In this section 'hospital' has the same meaning as in the Mental Health [(Northern Ireland) Order 1986][4].

Note.—[1] Words in sub-s (2) substituted by the Mental Health (Northern Ireland Consequential Amendments) Order 1986, SI 1986/596, art 3(2).
[2] Words in sub-s (4) substituted by ibid, art 3(3).
[3] Words in sub-s (6) substituted by ibid, art 3(4).
[4] Words in sub-s (7) substituted by ibid, art 3(5).

81. Removal to Scotland of patients from Northern Ireland

(1) If it appears to the responsible authority, in the case of a patient who is for the time being liable to be detained or subject to guardianship under the Mental Health [(Northern Ireland) Order 1986 (otherwise than by virtue of art 42, 43 or 45 of that Order)][1], that it is in the interests of the patient to remove him to Scotland, and that arrangements have been made for admitting him to a hospital or, as the case may be,

for receiving him into guardianship there, the responsible authority may authorise his removal to Scotland and may give any necessary directions for his conveyance to his destination.

(2) Subject to the provisions of [subsections 4 and 4A][2] of this section, where a patient who is liable to be detained under this Act by virtue of an application, order or direction under any enactment in force in Northern Ireland is removed under this section and admitted to a hospital in Scotland, he shall be treated as if on the date of admission he had been so admitted in pursuance of an application forwarded to the managers of the hospital, or an order or direction made or given, on that date under the corresponding enactment in force in Scotland and, where he is subject to [a restriction order or restriction direction under that order][2], restricting his discharge, as if he were subject to a restriction order or a restriction direction under the corresponding enactment in force in Scotland.

(3) Where a patient who is subject to guardianship under [the Mental Health (Northern Ireland) Order 1986][3] by virtue of an application or order under any enactment in force in Northern Ireland is removed under this section and received into guardianship in Scotland, he shall be treated as if on the date on which he arrives at the place where he is to reside he had been so received in pursuance of an application or order under the corresponding enactment in force in Scotland and as if the application had been forwarded or, as the case may be, the order had been made on that date.

[(4) Where a person removed under this section was immediately before his removal liable to be detained for treatment by virtue of a report under Article 12(1) or 13 of the Mental Health (Northern Ireland) Order 1986, he shall be treated on his admission to a hospital in Scotland as if he had been admitted thereto in pursuance of an application for admission forwarded to the managers of that hospital on the date of his admission.

(4A) Where a person removed under this section was immediately before his removal liable to be detained by virtue of an application for assessment under Article 4 of the Mental Health (Northern Ireland) Order 1986, he shall be treated on his admission to a hospital in Scotland, as if he had been admitted thereto in pursuance of an emergency recommendation made on the date of his admission.][4]

(5) Where a patient removed under this section was immediately before his removal liable to be detained under the Mental Health [(Northern Ireland) Order 1986][5], by virtue of a transfer direction given while he was serving a sentence of imprisonment (within the meaning of [Article 53(5) of that order][5] imposed by a court in Northern Ireland, he shall be treated as if the sentence had been imposed by a court in Scotland.

(6) Where a patient removed under this section was immediately before his removal subject to [a restriction order or restriction direction][6] of limited duration, the restriction order or restriction direction to which he is subject by virtue of subsection (2) of this section shall expire on the date on which the first-mentioned [a restriction order or restriction direction][6] would have expired if he had not been so removed.

(7) In this section 'the responsible authority' means the Department of Health and Social Services for Northern Ireland or, in relation to a patient who is subject to [a restriction order or restriction direction][7], the Secretary of State.

Note.—[1] Words in sub-s (1) substituted by the Mental Health (Northern Ireland Consequential Amendments) Order 1986, SI 1986/596 art 3(6).
  [2] Words in sub-s (2) substituted by ibid, art 3(7).
  [3] Words in sub-s (3) substituted by ibid, art 3(8).
  [4] Sub-s (4) substituted by and sub-s 4A inserted by ibid, art 3(9).
  [5] Words in sub-s (5) substituted by ibid, art 3(10).
  [6] Words in sub-s (6) substituted by ibid, art 3(11).
  [7] Words in sub-s (7) substituted by ibid, art 3(12).

Other provisions as to removal

82. Removal of certain patients from Channel Islands and Isle of Man to Scotland

(1) The Secretary of State may by warrant direct that any offender found by a court in any of the Channel Islands or in the Isle of Man to be insane or to have been insane at the time of the alleged offence, and ordered to be detained during Her Majesty's pleasure, be removed to a hospital in Scotland.

(2) A patient removed under this section shall, on his reception into the hospital in Scotland, be treated as if he had been removed to that hospital in pursuance of an order under section 174 of the Criminal Procedure (Scotland) Act 1975.

(3) The Secretary of State may by warrant direct that any patient removed under this section from any of the Channel Islands or from the Isle of Man be returned to the Island from which he was so removed, there to be dealt with according to law in all respects as if he had not been removed under this section.

83. Removal of alien patients

If it appears to the Secretary of State, in the case of any patient who is neither a British citizen nor a Commonwealth citizen having the right of abode in the United Kingdom by virtue of section 2(1)(b) of the Immigration Act 1971 and who is receiving treatment for mental illness as an in-patient in a hospital in Scotland, that proper arrangements have been made for the removal of that patient to a country or territory outside the United Kingdom, the Isle of Man and the Channel Islands and for his care or treatment there, and that it is in the interests of the patient to remove him, the Secretary of State may by warrant authorise the removal of the patient from the place where he is receiving treatment as aforesaid, and may give such directions as the Secretary of State thinks fit for the conveyance of the patient to his destination in that country or territory and for his detention in any place or on board any ship or aircraft until his arrival at any specified port or place in any such country or territory.

Return of patients absent without leave

84. Patients absent from hospitals in Scotland

(1) Subject to the provisions of this section, any person who, under section 28 or section 121 of this Act or under the said section 28 as applied by section 32 of this Act may be taken into custody in Scotland, may be taken into custody in, and returned to Scotland from, any other part of the United Kingdom or the Channel Islands or the Isle of Man.

(2) For the purposes of the enactments referred to in subsection (1) of this section, in their application by virtue of this section to England and Wales, Northern Ireland, the Channel Islands or the Isle of Man, the expression 'constable' includes an English constable, an officer or constable of the Royal Ulster Constabulary, a member of the police in Jersey, an officer of police within the meaning of section 43 of the Larceny (Guernsey) Law 1958, or any corresponding law for the time being in force, or a constable in the Isle of Man, as the case may be.

(3) For the purposes of the said enactments in their application by virtue of this section to England and Wales or Northern Ireland, any reference to a mental health officer shall be construed as including a reference—
    (a) In England and Wales, to any approved social worker within the meaning of the Mental Health Act 1983,
    (b) in Northern Ireland, to any [approved social worker within the meaning of the Mental Health (Northern Ireland) Order 1986]

(4) This section shall not apply to any person who is subject to guardianship.

Note.—Words in sub-s (3)(b) substituted by the Mental Health (Northern Ireland Consequential Amendments) Order 1986/596 art 3(13).

85. Patients absent from hospitals in Northern Ireland

Any person (other than a person subject to guardianship) who—
  (a) under [Article 29 or 132 of the Mental Health (Northern Ireland) Order 1986] (which provide respectively for the retaking of patients absent without leave and for the retaking of patients escaping from custody); or
  (b) under the said [Article 29 as applied by art 31 of the said Order] (which makes special provision as to persons sentenced to imprisonment);
may be taken into custody in Northern Ireland, may be taken into custody in, and returned to Northern Ireland from, Scotland by a mental health officer, by any constable or by any person authorised by or by virtue of the [said Order] to take him into custody.

Note.—Words in above section substituted by the Mental Health (Northern Ireland Consequential Amendments) Order 1986, s 1 1986/596, art 3(14).

Supplementary

86. Regulations for purposes of Part VII

Section 58 of this Act shall have effect as if references therein to Part V of this Act included references to this Part of this Act and to Part VI of the Mental Health Act 1983, so far as the said Parts apply to patients removed to Scotland thereunder.

87. General provisions as to patients removed from Scotland

(1) Where a patient liable to be detained or subject to guardianship by virtue of an application, order or direction under Part V or Part VI of this Act is removed from Scotland in pursuance of arrangements under this Part of this Act, the application, order or direction shall cease to have effect when he is duly received into a hospital or other institution, or placed under guardianship, in pursuance of those arrangements.

(2) The Secretary of State shall, where he authorises the removal from Scotland of a patient under any of the provisions of this Part of this Act, send notification of that authorisation to the Mental Welfare Commission and to the nearest relative of the patient not less than 7 days before the date of the removal of the patient.

88. Intimation of removal of patients to Scotland

(1) Where a patient is admitted to a hospital in Scotland or received into guardianship there in pursuance of arrangements under this Part of this Act, or under Part VI of the Mental Health Act 1983, the responsible medical officer shall, within 28 days of such admission or reception as aforesaid, furnish to the managers of the hospital, or, as the case may be, the local authority concerned, a report in the prescribed form stating the form of mental disorder, being mental illness or mental handicap or both, from which, in the opinion of the responsible medical officer, the patient is suffering; and for the purposes of this Act the reason for his admission or reception as aforesaid, and for his being liable to detention or subject to guardianship, shall be that he is suffering from the form or forms of mental disorder so stated.

(2) Where a patient has been admitted to a hospital or received into guardianship as aforesaid, the managers of the hospital or the local authority concerned, as the case may be, shall send notification to the Mental Welfare Commission of that admission or reception together with a copy of the report relating to the patient, made in

pursuance of the last foregoing subsection, within 7 days of the receipt by them of that report.

Note.—For prescribed form see the Mental Health (Prescribed Forms) (Scotland) Regulations 1984, SI 1984/1495 (Appendix 2).

89. Interpretation of Part VII

(1) Where a patient is treated by virtue of this Part of this Act as if he had been removed to a hospital in Scotland in pursuance of a direction under Part VI of this Act, that direction shall be deemed to have been given on the date of his reception into the hospital.

(2) In relation to a patient who has been received into guardianship in Scotland in pursuance of arrangements under this Part of this Act or under Part VI of the Mental Health Act 1959 or under Part VI of the Mental Health Act 1983, any reference in this Act to the local authority concerned shall be construed as a reference to the local authority for the place where he was received into guardianship as aforesaid.

PART VIII STATE HOSPITALS

90. Provision of hospitals for patients requiring special security

(1) The Secretary of State shall provide such hospitals as appear to him to be necessary for persons subject to detention under this Act who require treatment under conditions of special security on account of their dangerous, violent or criminal propensities.

(2) Hospitals provided by the Secretary of State under this section are in this Act referred to as 'State hospitals'.

91. Administrative provisions

(1) Subject to the following provisions of this section, the State hospitals shall be under the control and management of the Secretary of State.

(2) The Secretary of State may by order constitute in accordance with the provisions of Schedule 1 to this Act a committee to manage, on his behalf and subject to such directions as he may give, a State hospital; and a committee so constituted shall be called a State Hospital Management Committee.

(3) The Secretary of State may by order dissolve a State Hospital Management Committee and any such order may contain such provision as he considers necessary or expedient in connection with the dissolution of the Committee and the winding up of its affairs including provision for the transfer of employment of staff, property, rights and liabilities.

(4) A State Hospital Management Committee may—
  (a) pay to its members such remuneration; and
  (b) make provision for the payment of such pensions, allowances or gratuities to or in respect of its members,
as the Secretary of State may, with the approval of the Treasury, determine; and such determination may make different provision for different cases or different classes of case.

(5) A State Hospital Management Committee may appoint such officers and servants on such terms as to remuneration and conditions of service as the Secretary of State may, with the approval of the Treasury, determine; and such determination may make different provision for different cases or different classes of case.

(6) Section 79(1) of the National Health Service (Scotland) Act 1978 (which enables the Secretary of State to acquire land for the purposes of that Act) shall have effect as if the reference to the purposes of that Act included a reference to the purposes of this Part of this Act and as if the reference to any hospital vested in the Secretary of State included a reference to any State hospital.

PART IX   PROTECTION OF PROPERTY OF PATIENTS

92. Duties of local authority in relation to property

(1) Where a local authority is satisfied—
   (a) that any person in their area is incapable, by reason of mental disorder, of adequately managing and administering his property and affairs;
   (b) that a curator bonis ought to be appointed in respect of that person; and
   (c) that no arrangements have been made or are being made in that behalf,
they shall petition the court for such appointment as aforesaid; and, where that person is a patient in a hospital or has been placed under guardianship, the authority shall, on the grant of any such petition, so inform the managers of the hospital or, as the case may be, the guardian within 28 days therefrom.

(2) In relation to persons suffering from mental disorder, section 48 of the National Assistance Act 1948 (which imposes a duty on certain local authorities to provide protection for property of persons admitted to hospitals, etc.) shall have effect as if—
   (a) in subsection (1) the reference to a person admitted as a patient to hospital included a reference to a person admitted to a private hospital within the meaning of this Act or subject to guardianship thereunder; and
   (b) references to moveable property in subsections (1) and (2) included a reference to heritable property.

93. Power of Mental Welfare Commission to petition for appointment of curator bonis

Where the Mental Welfare Commission are satisfied—
   (a) that any person is incapable, by reason of mental disorder, of adequately managing and administering his property and affairs;
   (b) that a curator bonis ought to be appointed in respect of that person; and
   (c) that no arrangements have been made or are being made in that behalf,
they may petition the court for such appointment as aforesaid; and, where that person is a patient in a hospital or has been placed under guardianship, the Commission shall, on the grant of any such petition, so inform the managers of the hospital or, as the case may be, the local authority concerned within 28 days therefrom.

94. Powers of managers in relation to property of patients

(1) The managers of any hospital may receive and hold money and valuables on behalf of any person who is liable to be detained in that hospital under this Act or who is receiving treatment for mental disorder as a patient in the hospital, where the medical officer in charge of his treatment has stated that in his opinion that person is incapable, by reason of his mental disorder, of managing and administering his property and affairs; and a receipt or discharge given by the managers for any such money or valuables as aforesaid shall be treated as a valid receipt or discharge given by that person.

(2) The managers shall not, under subsection (1) of this section, receive or hold on behalf of any one person without the consent of the Mental Welfare Commission money or valuables exceeding in the aggregate such sums as the Secretary of State may from time to time direct.

(3) Where the managers of the hospital hold money or valuables on behalf of a person in pursuance of subsection (1) of this section, they may expend that money or dispose of those valuables for the benefit of that person and in the exercise of the powers conferred by this subsection the managers shall have regard to the sentimental value that any article may have for the patient, or would have but for his mental disorder.

(4) Without prejudice to the generality of subsection (3) of this section, where the managers of a hospital have received money on behalf of a person in pursuance of subsection (1) of this section, being either—
- (a) money becoming payable to that person during his lifetime under an insurance policy on his life, or
- (b) money becoming payable to him as proposer under an insurance policy following the death of the person insured,

they may arrange for part or all of the money to be used to refund premiums paid on the policy by another person on behalf of the first-mentioned person, if they are satisfied that such other person is legally entitled to such refund.

(5) The managers of a hospital may in pursuance of their functions under this section make application for a special death certificate for the purposes of the First Schedule to the Industrial Assurance and Friendly Societies Act 1948 and of Schedule 5 to the Friendly Societies Act 1974.

(6) The managers of a hospital shall not act on behalf of any person in pursuance of the foregoing provisions of this section where a curator bonis, tutor, judical factor, [receiver or controller or any person having the powers of a receiver or controller] has been appointed for that person under the law in force in Scotland, England and Wales or Northern Ireland, as the case may be; and where such an appointment as aforesaid has been made the managers shall account for any intromission under this section to any such curator bonis, tutor, judicial factor, [receiver or controller or any person having the powers of a receiver or controller][1] as aforesaid.

Note.—Words in sub-s (6) substituted by the Mental Health (Northern Ireland Consequential Amendments) Order 1986, SI 1986/596, art 3(15).

95. Reciprocal arrangements in relation to Northern Ireland as to exercise of powers

(1) Where a curator bonis, tutor or judicial factor has been appointed under the law in force in Scotland for any person suffering from mental disorder, the provisions of that law shall apply in relation to the property and affairs of that person in Northern Ireland unless [he is a patient in relation to whom powers have been exercised under Part VIII of the Mental Health (Northern Ireland) Order 1986, or a person as to whom powers are exercisable and have been exercised under Article 97(2) of that Order.]

(2) [Part VIII of the Mental Health (Northern Ireland) Order 1986 shall apply in relation to the property and affairs in Scotland of a patient in relation to whom powers have been exercised under that Part, or a person as to whom powers are exercisable and have been exercised under Article 97(2) of that Order, as it applies in relation to his property and affairs in Northern Ireland.] unless a curator bonis, tutor or judicial factor has been appointed for him in Scotland.

(3) In this section references to property do not include references to land or interests in land:
   Provided that this subsection shall not prevent the receipt of rent or other income arising from land or interests in land.

Note.—Words in sub-s (1) substituted by the Mental Health (Northern Ireland Consequential Amendments) Order 1986, SI 1986/596, art 3(16).
Words in sub-s (2) substituted by ibid, art 3(17).

PART X   CONSENT TO TREATMENT

96. Preliminary

(1) This Part of this Act applies to any patient liable to be detained under this Act except—
   (a) a patient who is liable to be detained by virtue of an emergency recommendation;
   (b) a patient who is liable to be detained by virtue of sections 25(2), 117 or 118 of this Act or section 177 or 378 of the Criminal Procedure (Scotland) Act 1975;
   (c) a patient who has been conditionally discharged under sections 64 or 68(2) of this Act and has not been recalled to hospital.

(2) Any certificate for the purposes of this Part of this Act shall be in such form as may be prescribed by regulations made by the Secretary of State.

Note.—For prescribed forms see the Mental Health (Prescribed Forms) (Scotland) Regulations 1984, SI 1984/1495 (Appendix 2).

97. Treatment requiring consent and a second opinion

(1) This section applies to the following forms of medical treatment for mental disorder—
   (a) any surgical operation for destroying brain tissue or for destroying the functioning of brain tissue; and
   (b) such other forms of treatment as may be specified for the purposes of this section by regulations made by the Secretary of State.

(2) Subject to section 102 of this Act, a patient shall not be given any form of treatment to which this section applies unless he has consented to it and—
   (a) a medical practitioner (not being the responsible medical officer) appointed for the purposes of this Part of this Act by the Mental Welfare Commission and two other persons (not being medical practitioners) appointed for the purposes of this paragraph by the Commission have certified in writing that the patient is capable of understanding the nature, purpose and likely effects of the treatment in question and has consented to it; and
   (b) the medical practitioner referred to in paragraph (a) of this subsection has certified in writing that, having regard to the likelihood of the treatment alleviating or preventing a deterioration of the patient's condition, the treatment should be given.

(3) Before giving a certificate under subsection (2)(b) of this section the medical practitioner concerned shall consult such person or persons who appear to him to be principally concerned with the patient's medical treatment.

(4) Where any person has given a certificate under subsection (2)(a) or (b) of this section he shall send a copy thereof to the Mental Welfare Commission within 7 days of the day on which the certificate was given.

(5) A medical practitioner or other person appointed as is mentioned in subsection (2)(a) of this section may, for the purpose of exercising his functions under this Part of this Act or (as the case may be) subsection (2)(a) of this section, at any reasonable time—

(a) in private visit and interview any patient; and
(b) in the case of a medical practitioner, examine any patient and require the production of and inspect any records relating to the treatment of the patient.

(6) Before making any regulations for the purposes of this section the Secretary of State shall consult such bodies as appear to him to be concerned.

Note.—For other forms of treatment specified by regulations see the Mental Health (Specified Treatments, Guardianship Duties etc) (Scotland) Regulations 1984, SI 1984/1494 (Appendix 2).

For the prescribed forms see the Mental Health (Prescribed Forms) (Scotland) Regulations 1984, SI 1984/1495 (Appendix 2).

98. Treatment requiring consent or a second opinion

(1) This section applies to the following forms of medical treatment for mental disorder—
   (a) such forms of treatment as may be specified for the purposes of this section by regulations made by the Secretary of State; and
   (b) the administration of medicine to a patient by any means (not being a form of treatment specified under paragraph (a) of this subsection or section 97 of this Act) at any time during a period for which he is liable to be detained as a patient to whom this Part of this Act applies if 3 months or more have elapsed since the first occasion in that period when medicine was administered to him by any means for his mental disorder.

(2) The Secretary of State may by order vary the length of the period mentioned in subsection (1)(b) of this section.

(3) Subject to section 102 of this Act, a patient shall not be given any form of treatment to which this section applies unless—
   (a) he has consented to that treatment and either the responsible medical officer or a medical practitioner appointed for the purposes of this Part of this Act by the Mental Welfare Commission has certified in writing that the patient is capable of understanding its nature, purpose and likely effects and has consented to it; or
   (b) a medical practitioner (not being the responsible medical officer) appointed as aforesaid has certified in writing that the patient is not capable of understanding the nature, purpose and likely effects of that treatment or has not consented to it but that, having regard to the likelihood of its alleviating or preventing a deterioration of his condition, the treatment should be given.

(4) Before giving a certificate under subsection (3)(b) of this section the medical practitioner concerned shall consult such person or persons who appear to him to be principally concerned with the patient's medical treatment.

(5) Where any person has given a certificate under subsection (3)(a) or (b) of this section he shall send a copy thereof to the Mental Welfare Commission within 7 days of the day on which the certificate was given.

(6) Before making any regulations for the purposes of this section the Secretary of State shall consult such bodies as appear to him to be concerned.

Note.—For regulations made by Secretary of State see the Mental Health (Specified Treatments, Guardianship Duties, etc) (Scotland) Regulations 1984, SI 1984/1494 (Appendix 2).

For forms relative to sub-s 3(a), (b) see the Mental Health (Prescribed Forms) (Scotland) Regulations 1984, SI 1984/1495 (Appendix 2).

99. Review of treatment

(1) Where a patient is given treatment in accordance with section 97(2) or 98(3)(b) of this Act a report on the treatment and the patient's condition shall be given by the responsible medical officer to the Mental Welfare Commission—

(a) on the next occasion on which the responsible medical officer furnishes a report in respect of the patient under section 30 of this Act; and
(b) at any other time if so required by the Mental Welfare Commission.

(2) The Mental Welfare Commission may at any time give notice to the responsible medical officer directing that, subject to section 102 of this Act, a certificate given in respect of a patient under section 97(2) or 98(3)(b) of this Act shall not apply to treatment given to him after a date specified in the notice, and sections 97 and 98 of this Act shall then apply to any such treatment as if that certificate had not been given.

100. Plans of treatment

Any consent or certificate under section 97 or 98 of this Act may relate to a plan of treatment under which the patient is to be given (whether within a specified period or otherwise) one or more of the forms of treatment to which that section applies.

101. Withdrawal of consent

(1) Where the consent of a patient to any treatment has been given for the purposes of section 97 or 98 of this Act, the patient may, subject to section 102 of this Act, at any time before the completion of the treatment withdraw his consent, and those sections shall then apply as if the remainder of the treatment were a separate form of treatment.

(2) Without prejudice to the application of subsection (1) of this section to any treatment given under a plan of treatment to which a patient has consented, a patient who has consented to such a plan may, subject to section 102 of this Act, at any time withdraw his consent to further treatment, or to further treatment of any description, under the plan.

102. Urgent treatment

(1) Sections 97 and 98 of this Act shall not apply to any treatment—
 (a) which is immediately necessary to save a patient's life; or
 (b) which (not being irreversible) is immediately necessary to prevent a serious deterioration of his condition; or
 (c) which (not being irreversible or hazardous) is immediately necessary to alleviate serious suffering by the patient; or
 (d) which (not being irreversible or hazardous) is immediately necessary and represents the minimum interference necessary to prevent the patient from behaving violently or being a danger to himself or to others.

(2) Sections 99(2) and 101 of this Act shall not preclude the continuation of any treatment or of treatment under any plan pending compliance with sections 97 and 98 of this Act if the responsible medical officer considers that the discontinuance of the treatment or of treatment under the plan would cause serious suffering to the patient.

(3) For the purposes of this section treatment is irreversible if it has unfavourable irreversible physical or psychological consequences and hazardous if it entails significant physical hazard.

(4) Where a patient is given treatment under this section the responsible medical officer shall, within 7 days of the day on which the treatment is given, notify the Mental Welfare Commission as to—
 (a) which of paragraphs (a) to (d) of subsection (1) of this section applied in relation to the patient; and
 (b) the nature of the treatment given to the patient.

103. Treatment not requiring consent

The consent of a patient shall not be required for any medical treatment given to him for the mental disorder from which he is suffering, not being treatment falling within section 97 or 98 of this Act, if the treatment is given by or under the direction of the responsible medical officer.

PART XI MISCELLANEOUS AND GENERAL

Offences

104. False statements

(1) Any person who makes any statement or entry which is false in a material particular in any appliction, recommendation, report, record or other document required or authorised to be made for any of the purposes of this Act or, with intent to deceive, makes use of any such entry or statement which he knows to be false, shall be guilty of an offence.

(2) Any person guilty of an offence under this section shall be liable—
  (a) on summary conviction, to imprisonment for a term not exceeding 6 months or to a fine not exceeding the statutory maximum, or both; or
  (b) on conviction on indictment, to imprisonment for a term not exceeding 2 years or to a fine, or both.

105. Ill-treatment of patients

(1) It shall be an offence for any person being an officer on the staff of or otherwise employed in a hospital or nursing home, or being a manager of a hospital or a person carrying on a nursing home—
  (a) to ill-treat or wilfully neglect a patient for the time being receiving treatment for mental disorder as an in-patient in that hospital or nursing home; or
  (b) to ill-treat or wilfully neglect, on the premises of which the hospital or nursing home forms part, a patient for the time being receiving such treatment there as an out-patient.

(2) It shall be an offence for any individual to ill-treat or wilfully neglect a patient who is for the time being subject to his guardianship under this Act or otherwise in his custody or care.

(3) Any person guilty of an offence against this section shall be liable—
  (a) on summary conviction, to imprisonment for a term not exceeding 6 months or to a fine not exceeding the statutory maximum or both;
  (b) on conviction on indictment, to imprisonment for a term not exceeding 2 years or to a fine, or both.

106. Protection of mentally handicapped females

(1) It shall be an offence, subject to the exception mentioned in this section—
  (a) for a man to have unlawful sexual intercourse with a woman who is protected by the provisions of this section;
  (b) for any person to procure or encourage any woman who is protected by the provisions of this section to have unlawful sexual intercourse;
  (c) for the owner or occupier of any premises or any person having or assisting in the management or control of premises to induce any woman who is protected by the provisions of this section to resort to or be upon such premises for the purpose of unlawful sexual intercourse with any man.

(2) A person shall not be guilty of an offence against this section if he did not know and had no reason to suspect that the woman in respect of whom he is charged was protected by the provisions of this section.

(3) Any person guilty of an offence under this section shall be liable on conviction on indictment to imprisonment for a term not exceeding 2 years or to a fine.

(4) Section 18 of the Sexual Offences (Scotland) Act 1976 (which relates to warrants to search where there is reasonable cause to suspect that a woman or girl is being unlawfully detained for immoral purposes) shall apply in the case of a woman who is protected by the provisions of this section in the same manner as that section applies in the case of a girl who is under the age of 16 years.

(5) If on the trial of an indictment for rape the jury are satisfied that the accused is guilty of an offence against paragraph (a) of subsection (1) of this section, but are not satisfied that he is guilty of rape, the jury may acquit him of rape and find him guilty of such offence as aforesaid, and in that event he shall be liable to be punished as if he had been convicted on an indictment for such offence as aforesaid.

(6) A woman is protected by the provisions of this section if she is suffering from a state of arrested or incomplete development of mind which includes significant impairment of intelligence and social functioning.

(7) In this section 'woman' includes girl.

107. Protection of patients

(1) Without prejudice to the last foregoing section, it shall be an offence, subject to the exception mentioned in this section,—
   (a) for a man who is an officer on the staff or is otherwise employed in a hospital or nursing home, or who is a manager of a hospital or who is a person carrying on a nursing home to have unlawful sexual intercourse with a woman who is for the time being receiving treatment for mental disorder as an in-patient in that hospital or nursing home, or to have such intercourse on the premises of which the hospital or nursing home forms part with a woman who is for the time being receiving such treatment there as an out-patient;
   (b) for a man to have unlawful sexual intercourse with a woman suffering from mental disorder who is subject to his guardianship under this Act or is otherwise in his custody or care under this Act or in the care of a local authority under the Social Work (Scotland) Act 1968 or resident in a house provided by a local authority under that Act.

(2) It shall not be an offence under this section for a man to have sexual intercourse with a woman if he does not know and has no reason to suspect her to be a person suffering from mental disorder.

(3) In this section any reference to having unlawful sexual intercourse with a woman shall include a reference to committing a homosexual act as defined in section 80(6) of the Criminal Justice (Scotland) Act 1980.

(4) Any person guilty of an offence under this section shall be liable on conviction on indictment to imprisonment for a term not exceeding 2 years or to a fine.

108. Assisting patients to absent themselves without leave etc

(1) any person who induces or knowlingly assists any other person—
   (a) being liable to be detained in a hospital or being subject to guardianship under this Act, to absent himself without leave; or
   (b) being in legal custody by virtue of section 120 of this Act, to escape from such custody,
shall be guilty of an offence.

(2) Any person who knowingly harbours a patient who is absent without leave or is otherwise at large and liable to be retaken under this Act, or gives him any assistance with intent to prevent, hinder or interfere with his being taken into custody or returned to the hospital or other place where he ought to be, shall be guilty of an offence.

(3) Any person guilty of an offence against this section shall be liable—

(a) on summary conviction, to imprisonment for a term not exceeding 6 months or to a fine not exceeding the statutory maximum or both;
(b) on conviction on indictment, to imprisonment for a term not exceeding 2 years or to a fine, or both.

109. Obstruction

(1) Any person who refuses to allow the inspection of any premises, or without reasonable cause refuses to allow the visiting, interviewing or examination of any person, by a person authorised in that behalf by or under this Act, or to produce for the inspection of any person so authorised any document or record the production of which is duly required by him, or otherwise obstructs any such person in the exercise of his functions, shall be guilty of an offence.

(2) Without prejudice to the generality of the last foregoing subsection, any person who insists on being present when requested to withdraw by a person authorised as aforesaid to interview or examine a person in private, shall be guilty of an offence.

(3) Any person guilty of an offence against this section shall be liable on summary conviction to imprisonment for a term not exceeding 3 months or to a fine not exceeding level 3 on the standard scale, or both.

Miscellaneous provisions

110. Duty to give information to patients and nearest relatives

(1) The managers of a hospital in which a patient is detained under the provisions of this Act, or in the case of a patient subject to guardianship, the local authority concerned shall take such steps as are practicable to ensure that the patient understands—
(a) under which of those provisions he is for the time being detained or subject to guardianship and the effect of that provision; and
(b) what rights of appeal to the sheriff are available to him in respect of his detention or guardianship under that provision; and
(c) that he may make representations to the Mental Welfare Commission,
and those steps shall be taken as soon as practicable after the commencement of the patient's detention or his reception into guardianship, or any renewal of the authority for his detention or guardianship.

(2) The managers of a hospital in which a patient is detained as aforesaid shall also take such steps as are practicable to ensure that the patient understands the effect, so far as relevant in his case, of—
(a) sections 33 and 34 of this Act; and
(b) Part X and sections 115, 116 and 119 of this Act;
and those steps shall be taken as soon as practicable after the commencement of the patient's detention in the hospital.

(3) The steps to be taken under this section shall include giving the requisite information both orally and in writing.

(4) The managers of a hospital in which a patient is detained as aforesaid or, as the case may be, the local authority concerned in relation to a patient subject to guardianship as aforesaid shall, except where the patient otherwise requests, take such steps as are practicable to furnish the person (if any) appearing to them to be his nearest relative with a copy of any information given to him in writing under subsection (1) and (2) above; and those steps shall be taken when the information is given to the patient or within a reasonable time thereafter.

(5) Section 56(4) of this Act shall have effect as if subsection (4) of this section were contained in part V of this Act.

111. Duty of managers to inform nearest relative of discharge of detained patients

(1) Where a patient liable to be detained in a hospital under this Act is to be discharged otherwise than by virtue of an order for discharge made by his nearest relative, the managers of the hospital shall, subject to subsection (2) of this section, take such steps as are practicable to inform the person (if any) appearing to them to be the nearest relative of the patient; and that information shall, if practicable, be given at least seven days before the date of discharge.

(2) Subsection (1) of this section shall not apply if the patient or his nearest relative has requested that information about the patient's discharge should not be given under this section.

(3) Section 56(4) of this Act shall have effect as if this section were contained in Part V of this Act.

112. Religious persuasion of patients

In any arrangements that may be made for the detention of a patient or his reception into guardianship in pursuance of this Act, regard shall be had to the religious persuasion to which the patient belongs or appears to belong.

113. Duty of sheriff to give patient opportunity to be heard

(1) In any appeal to the sheriff under this Act, or in any proceedings relating to an application for admission to a hospital or for reception into guardianship, the sheriff shall give the patient an opportunity to be heard, either—
  (a) in person (unless cause to the contrary has been shown); or
  (b) by means of a representative.

(2) Where it is established to the satisfaction of the sheriff that it would be prejudicial to the patient's health or treatment if he were present during any such appeal or proceedings, the sheriff may exclude the patient (but not his representative) from the whole or part of that appeal or those proceedings.

Note.—See Act of Sederunt (Mental Health (Scotland) Act 1984) 1986, SI 1986/545.

114. Provision for personal expenses of in-patients in hospital

(1) The Secretary of State may pay to persons who are receiving treatment as in-patients (whether liable to be detained or not) in any hospital, other than a private hospital, being a hospital wholly or mainly used for the treatment of persons suffering from mental disorder, such amounts as he thinks fit in respect of their occasional personal expenses where it appears to him that they would otherwise be without resources to meet those expenses.

(2) For the purposes of the National Health Service (Scotland) Act 1978, the making of payments under this section to persons for whom services are provided under that Act shall be treated as included among those services.

115. Correspondence of patients

(1) Any postal packet addressed to any person by a patient detained in a hospital under this Act and delivered by him for dispatch may be withheld from the Post Office—
  (a) if that person has requested that communications addressed to him by the patient should be withheld; or
  (b) subject to subsection (3) of this section, if the hospital is a State hospital and the managers of the hospital consider that the postal packet is likely—
    (i) to cause distress to the person to whom it is addressed or to any other person (not being a person on the staff of the hospital); or

(ii) to cause danger to any person,
and any request for the purposes of paragraph (a) of this subsection shall be made by a notice in writing given to the managers of the hospital, the responsible medical officer or the Secretary of State.

(2) Subject to subsection (3) of this section a postal packet addressed to a patient detained in a State hospital under this Act may be withheld from the patient if, in the opinion of the managers of the hospital, it is necessary to do so in the interests of the safety of the patient or for the protection of other persons.

(3) Subsections (1)(b) and (2) of this section do not apply to any postal packet addressed by a patient to, or sent to a patient by or on behalf of—
  (a) any Minister of the Crown or member of either house of Parliament;
  (b) the Mental Welfare Commission, any Commissioner thereof or any person appointed by them under section 3(9)(b) of this Act;
  (c) the Parliamentary Commissioner for Administration, the Health Service Commissioner for Scotland, or the Commissioner for Local Administration in Scotland;
  (d) any judge or clerk of court;
  (e) a Health Board, the Common Services Agency for the Scottish Health Service or a local council established under section 7 of the National Health Service (Scotland) Act 1978;
  (f) a local authority within the meaning of section 235 of the Local Government (Scotland) Act 1973;
  (g) the managers of the hospital in which the patient is detained;
  (h) any legally qualified person instructed by the patient to act as his legal advisor; or
  (i) the European Commission on Human Rights or the European Court of Human Rights.

(4) The managers of the hospital may open and inspect any postal packet for the purposes of determining whether it is one to which subsection (1) or (2) of this section applies and, if so, whether or not it should be withheld under that subsection; and the power to withhold a postal packet under either of those subsections includes power to withhold anything contained in it.

(5) Where a postal packet or anything contained in it is withheld under subsection (1) or (2) of this section the managers of the hospital shall record that fact in writing and shall, within 7 days of the date on which they withheld the postal packet or anything contained in it, notify the Mental Welfare Commission of—
  (a) the name of the patient concerned; and
  (b) the nature of the postal packet or contents withheld; and
  (c) the reason for withholding the postal packet or contents.

(6) Where a postal packet or anything contained in it is withheld under subsection (1)(b) or (2) of this section the managers of the hospital shall within 7 days give notice of that fact to the patient and, in a case under subsection (2) of this section, to the person (if known) by whom the postal packet was sent; and any such notice shall be in writing and shall contain a statement of the effect of section 116 of this Act.

(7) The functions of the managers of a hospital under this section shall be discharged on their behalf by a person on the staff of the hospital appointed by them for that purpose, and different persons may be appointed to discharge different functions.

(8) The Secretary of State may make regulations with respect to the exercise of the powers conferred by this section.

(9) In this section and in section 116 of this Act 'postal packet' has the same meaning as in the Post Office Act 1953; and the provisions of this section and section 116 of this Act shall have effect notwithstanding anything in section 56 of that Act.

116. Review of decision to withhold postal packet

(1) The Mental Welfare Commission shall review any decision to withhold a postal packet or anything contained in it under subsection (1)(b) or (2) of section 115 of this Act if an application in that behalf is made—
- (a) in a case under the said subsection (1)(b), by the patient; or
- (b) in a case under the said subsection (2), either by the patient or by the person by whom the postal packet was sent;

and any such application shall be made within 6 months of the receipt by the applicant of the notice referred to in subsection (6) of that section.

(2) On an application under subsection (1) of this section the Commission may direct that the postal packet or anything contained in it which is the subject of the application shall not be withheld and the managers of the hospital in which the patient is detained shall comply with any such direction.

(3) The Secretary of State may by regulations make provision with respect to the making and determination of applications under subsection (1) of this section, including provision for the production to the Mental Welfare Commission of any postal packet which is the subject of such an application.

117. Entry on premises and warrant to search for and remove patients

(1) Where a mental health officer or a medical commissioner has reasonable cause to believe that a person suffering from mental disorder—
- (a) has been or is being ill-treated, neglected or kept otherwise than under control, in any place; or
- (b) being unable to care for himself, is living alone or uncared for in any place,

he may, on production of some duly authenticated document showing that he is so authorised, demand admission at all reasonable times and, if admission is not refused, may enter and inspect that place.

(2) If it appears to a justice of the peace on sworn information in writing by such officer or commissioner as aforesaid, that admission when demanded in pursuance of subsection (1) of this section has been refused or that a refusal of such admission is apprehended, he may issue a warrant authorising any constable named therein to enter, if need be by force, any premises specified in the warrant, and to remove, if it appears proper so to do, any person suffering from mental disorder to whom subsection (1) of this section applies to a place of safety with a view to the making of an application or emergency recommendation in respect of him under Part V of this Act, or of other arrangements for his treatment or care.

(3) If it appears to a justice of the peace on sworn information in writing by any constable or other person who is authorised by or under this Act or under section 88 of the Mental Health Act 1983, to take a patient to any place, or to take into custody or retake a patient who is liable to be so taken or retaken—
- (a) that there is reasonable cause to believe that that patient is to be found on any premises; and
- (b) that admission to the premises has been refused or that a refusal of such admission is apprehended,

the justice may issue a warrant authorising any constable named therein to enter the premises, if need be by force, and to remove the patient.

(4) A patient who is removed to a place of safety in the execution of a warrant issued under this section may be detained there for a period not exceeding 72 hours.

(5) In the execution of a warrant issued under subsection (2) of this section, the constable to whom it is addressed shall be accompanied by a medical practitioner, and in the execution of a warrant issued under subsection (3) of this section the constable to whom it is addressed may be accompanied—

(a) by a medical practitioner;
(b) by any person authorised by or under this Act or section 88 of the Mental Health Act 1983, to take or retake the patient.

(6) It shall not be necessary in any information or warrant under subsection (2) of this section to name the person concerned.

(7) In this section—
(a) any reference to a justice of the peace includes a reference to the sheriff and to a stipendiary magistrate; and
(b) 'place of safety' means a hospital as defined by this Act or residential home for persons suffering from mental disorder or any other suitable place the occupier of which is willing temporarily to receive the patient; but shall not include a police station unless by reason of emergency there is no place as aforesaid available for receiving the patient.

118. Mentally disordered persons found in public places

(1) If a constable finds in a place to which the public have access a person who appears to him to be suffering from mental disorder and to be in immediate need of care or control, the constable may, if he thinks it necessary to do so in the interests of that person or for the protection of other persons, remove that person to a place of safety within the meaning of the last foregoing section.

(2) A person removed to a place of safety under this section may be detained there for a period not exceeding 72 hours for the purpose of enabling him to be examined by a medical practitioner and of making any necessary arrangements for his treatment or care.

(3) Where a patient is removed as aforesaid, it shall, where practicable, be the duty of the constable who has so removed him without delay to inform some responsible person residing with the patient and the nearest relative of the patient of that removal.

119. Code of practice

(1) The Secretary of State shall prepare, and from time to time revise, a code of practice—
(a) for the guidance of medical practitioners, managers and staff of hospitals and mental health officers in relation to the detention and discharge of patients in and from hospitals under this Act; and
(b) for the guidance of medical practitioners and members of other professions in relation to the medical treatment of patients suffering from mental disorder.

(2) Before preparing the code or making any alteration in it the Secretary of State shall consult such bodies as appear to him to be concerned.

(3) The Secretary of State shall lay copies of the code and of any alteration in the code before Parliament; and if either House of Parliament passes a resolution requiring the code or any alteration in it to be withdrawn the Secretary of State shall withdraw the code or alteration and, where he withdraws the code, shall prepare a code in substitution for the one which is withdrawn.

(4) No resolution shall be passed by either House of Parliament under subsection (3) of this section in respect of a code or alteration after the expiration of the period of 40 days beginning with the day on which a copy of the code or alteration was laid before that House; but for the purposes of this subsection no account shall be taken of any time during which Parliament is dissolved or prorogued or duing which both Houses are adjourned for more than four days.

(5) The Secretary of State shall publish the code as for the time being in force.

Supplementary

120. Provisions as to custody, conveyance and detention

(1) Any person required or authorised by or by virtue of this Act to be conveyed to any place or to be kept in custody or detained in a place of safety or at any place to which he is taken under section 68(5) of this Act shall, while being so conveyed, detained or kept, as the case may be, be deemed to be in legal custody.

(2) A constable or any other person required or authorised by or by virtue of this Act to take any person into custody, or to convey or detain any person shall, for the purposes of taking him into custody or conveying or detaining him, have all the powers, authorities, protection and privileges which a constable has within the area for which he acts as constable.

(3) In this section 'convey' includes any other expression denoting removal from one place to another.

121. Retaking of patients escaping from custody

(1) If any person being in legal custody by virtue of section 120 of this Act escapes, he may, subject to the provisions of this section, be retaken—
   (a) in any case, by the person who had his custody immediately before the escape, or by any constable or mental health officer;
   (b) if at the time of the escape he was liable to be detained in a hospital, or subject to guardianship under this Act, by any other person who could take him into custody under section 28 or 44 of this Act if he had absented himself without leave.

(2) A person who escapes as aforesaid when liable to be detained or subject to guardianship as mentioned in paragraph (b) of subsection (1) of this section (not being a person subject to a restriction order under Part VI of this Act or an order or direction having the like effect as such an order) shall not be retaken under this section after the expiration of the period within which he could be retaken under section 28 or 44 of this Act if he had absented himself without leave on the day of the escape; and subsection (3) of the said section 28 and subsection (2) of the said section 44 shall apply, with the necessary modifications, accordingly.

(3) A person who escapes while being taken to or detained in a place of safety under section 117 or 118 of this Act shall not be retaken under this section after the expiration of the period of 72 hours beginning with the time when he escapes or the period during which he is liable to be so detained whichever expires first.

(4) This section, so far as it relates to the escape of a person liable to be detained in a hospital, shall apply in relation to a person who escapes—
   (a) while being taken to a hospital in pursuance of an application for admission approved by the sheriff;
   (b) while being taken to or from a hospital in pursuance of section 29 of this Act, or of any order, direction or authorisation under Parts VI and VII of this Act; or
   (c) while being taken to or detained in a place of safety in pursuance of an order under Part VI of this Act pending his admission to a hospital,

as if he were liable to be detained in that hospital and, if he had not previously been received therein, as if he had been so received.

(5) In computing for the purposes of sections 22 and 60 of this Act the periods therein mentioned relating to the removal, admission or reception of patients, no account shall be taken of any time during which the patient is at large and liable to be retaken by virtue of this section.

(6) Section 31 (in the case of a patient who is liable to be detained in a hospital) and

section 48 (in the case of a patient who is subject to guardianship) of this Act shall, with any necessary modifications, apply in relation to a patient who is at large and liable to be retaken by virtue of this section as it applies in relation to a patient who is absent without leave within the meaning of section 28 or section 44 of this Act respectively, and references therein to the said section 28 or the said section 44 (as the case may be) shall be construed accordingly.

122. Protection for acts done in pursuance of this Act

(1) No person shall be liable, whether on the ground of want of jurisdiction or on any other ground, to any civil or criminal proceedings to which he would have been liable apart from this section in respect of any act purporting to be done in pursuance of this Act or any regulations thereunder, unless the act was done in bad faith or without reasonable care.

(2) Outwith Scotland, section 139 of the Mental Health Act 1983 (which relates to protection for acts done in pursuance of that Act) shall apply in respect of any act purporting to be done in pursuance of this Act or any regulations thereunder as it applies in relation to an act purporting to be done in pursuance of that Act or any regulations or rules thereunder.

Note.—See *Skinner v Robertson* 1980 SLT (Sh Ct) 43 and *B v Forsey* 1988 SLT 572, HL (Appendix 3).

123. Inquiries

The Secretary of State may cause an inquiry to be held in any case where he thinks it advisable to do so in connection with any matter arising under this Act, and subsections (2) to (9) of section 210 of the Local Government (Scotland) Act 1973 (which relates to the holding of local inquiries) shall apply to any inquiry held under this Act.

124. General provisions as to regulations and orders

(1) Any power of the Secretary of State to make regulations or orders under this Act shall be exercisable by statutory instrument.

(2) Any statutory instrument containing regulations made under this Act shall be subject to annulment in pursuance of a resolution of either House of Parliament.

125. Interpretation

(1) In this Act, unless the context otherwise requires, the following expressions have the meanings hereby respectively assigned to them, that is to say—
'absent without leave' has the meaning assigned to it by section 59 of this Act;
'application for admission' and 'guardianship application' have the meanings respectively assigned to them by sections 18 and 37 of this Act;
'health service' has the meaning given by section 108(1) of the National Health Service (Scotland) Act 1978;
'hospital' means—
(a) any hospital vested in the Secretary of State under the National Health Service (Scotland) Act 1978;
(b) any private hospital registered under Part IV of this Act; and
(c) any State hospital;
'hospital order' and 'guardianship order' have the meanings respectively assigned to them by section 175 or 376 of the Criminal Procedure (Scotland) Act 1975;
'local authority' has the same meaning as in the Social Work (Scotland) Act 1968;
'managers of a hospital' means—
(a) in relation to a hospital vested in the Secretary of State under the National

Health Service (Scotland) Act 1978, the Health Board responsible for the administration of that hospital;

(b) in relation to a private hospital registered under Part IV of this Act, the person or persons carrying on the hospital;

(c) in relation to a State hospital, the Secretary of State or, if the Secretary of State has appointed a State Hospital Management Committee to manage that hospital, that Committee, or, if the management of that hospital has been delegated to a Health Board or to the Common Services Agency for the Scottish Health Service, that Board or Agency, as the case may be;

'medical practitioner' means a registered medical practitioner within the meaning of Schedule 1 to the Interpretation Act 1978;

'medical treatment' includes nursing, and also includes care and training under medical supervision;

'mental health officer' means an officer of a local authority appointed to act as a mental health officer for the purposes of this Act;

'nearest relative', in relation to a patient, has the meaning assigned to it in Part V of this Act;

'patient' (except in Part IX of this Act) mans a person suffering or appearing to be suffering from mental disorder;

'private hospital' has the meaning assigned to it in Part IV of this Act;

'responsible medical officer' has the meaning assigned to it by section 59 of this Act;

'restriction direction' has the meaning assigned to it by section 72 of this Act;

'restriction order' means an order made under section 178 or 379 of the Criminal Procedure (Scotland) Act 1975;

'standard scale' means the standard scale defined in section 75 of the Criminal Justice Act 1982;

'State hospital' has the meaning assigned to it in Part VIII of this Act;

'statutory maximum' means the statutory maximum defined in section 74(2) of the Criminal Justice Act 1982;

'transfer direction' has the meaning asigned to it by section 71 of this Act;

'transfer order' has the meaning assigned to it by section 70 of this Act;

'voluntary organisation' means a body the activities of which are carried on otherwise than for profit, but does not include any public or local authority.

(2) Unless the context otherwise requires, any reference in this Act to any other enactment is a reference thereto as amended, and includes a reference thereto as extended or applied by or under any other enactment, including this Act.

(3) Without prejudice to the last foregoing subsection, any reference in this Act to an enactment of the Parliament of Northern Ireland, or to an enactment which that Parliament has power to amend, shall be construed, in relation to Northern Ireland, as reference to that enactment as amended by any Act of that Parliament, whether passed before or after this Act.

(4) In relation to a person who is liable to be detained or subject to guardianship by virtue of an order or direction under Part VI of this Act or under section 174, 175, 178, 375, 376 or 379 of the Criminal Procedure (Scotland) Act 1975, any reference in this Act to any enactment contained in Part V of this Act shall be construed as a reference to that enactment as it applies to that person by virtue of the said Part VI or any of the provisions of the said sections.

(5) Any reference, however expressed, in this Act to a patient admitted to or detained in, or liable to be admitted to or detained in, a hospital or received, or liable to be received, into guardianship under this Act (other than under Part V thereof) or under Part VI of this Act shall include a reference to a patient who is admitted to or detained in, or liable to be admitted to or detained in, a hospital or received or liable to be received into guardianship under the Criminal Procedure (Scotland) Act 1975.

126. Preservation of amendments

(1) Notwithstanding the repeal by this Act of the Mental Health (Scotland) Act 1960 ('the 1960 Act')—
  (a) the definition of 'nursing home' in section 10 of the Nursing Homes Registration (Scotland) Act 1938 (which defines, *inter alia*, the expression 'nursing home') shall continue to have effect with the amendment made by section 15(2) of the 1960 Act (which substituted a new paragraph (ii) for paragraphs (ii) and (iii)) but subject to the amendment made to that definition, in consequence of this Act, by Schedule 3 to this Act; and
  (b) the amendments made by Schedule 4 of the 1960 Act shall, insofar as not otherwise repealed, continue to have effect but subject to any amendments made to them, in consequence of this Act, by Schedule 3 to this Act or by any other enactment.

(2) Notwithstanding the repeal by this Act of the Mental Health (Amendment) (Scotland) Act 1983 ('the 1983 Act')—
  (a) paragraph (bb) of section 64(5) of the Local Government (Scotland) Act 1973 (which was inserted by section 7(2) of the 1983 Act) shall continue to have effect but subject to the amendment made, in consequence of this Act, by Schedule 3 to this Act;
  (b) Sections 174, 174A, 175, 176, 178, 184, 280, 375A, 376, 377, 379, 385, 443, and 462 of, and paragraph 4(b) of Schedule 5 to, the Criminal Procedure (Scotland) Act 1975 shall continue to have effect with the amendments made by the 1983 Act but subject to any amendments made, in consequence of this Act, by Schedule 3 to this Act;
  (c) paragraph 5 of Schedule 5 to the Employment Protection (Consolidation) Act 1978 (which was added by Schedule 2 to the 1983 Act) shall continue to have effect; and
  (d) section 80 of the Mental Health Act 1983 shall continue to have effect with the amendments made by paragraph 1 of Schedule 2 to the 1983 Act.

127. Consequential and transitional provisions and repeals

(1) Schedule 3 (consequential amendments) and Schedule 4 (transitional and saving provisions) to this Act shall have effect but without prejudice to the operation of sections 15 to 17 of the Interpretation Act 1978 (which relate to the effect of repeals).

(2) The enactments specified in Schedule 5 to this Act are hereby repealed to the extent mentioned in the third column of that Schedule.

128. Application to England and Wales

The following provisions of this Act shall extend to England and Wales, that is to say—
  section 10;
  section 68(5);
  section 77;
  section 78;
  section 84 and, so far as applied by that section, sections 28, 32 and 121;
  section 108, except so far as it relates to patients subject to guardianship;
  section 120;
  section 122(2);
  section 127 and Schedules 2 and 5 so far as they relate to enactments extending to England and Wales;
but except as aforesaid, and except so far as it relates to the interpretation or commencement of the said provisions, this Act shall not extend to England and Wales.

129. Application to Northern Ireland

The following provisions of this Act shall extend to Northern Ireland, that is to say—
sections 80 and 81;
section 84 and, so far as applied by that section, sections 28, 32 and 121;
section 85;
section 95;
section 108, except so far as it relates to patients subject to guardianship;
section 120;
section 122(2);
section 127 and Schedules 2 and 5 so far as they relate to enactments extending to Northern Ireland;
but except as aforesaid, and except so far as it relates to the interpretation or commencement of the said provisions, this Act shall not extend to Northern Ireland.

130. Short title and commencement

This Act may be cited as the Mental Health (Scotland) Act 1984 and shall come into force on 30th September 1984.

SCHEDULES

SCHEDULE 1

STATE HOSPITAL MANAGEMENT COMMITTEES
PART I

Constitution

1. A State Hospital Management Committee shall be a body corporate and shall have a common seal.

2. A State Hospital Management Committee shall consist of a chairman appointed by the Secretary of State and such number of other members so appointed as the Secretary of State thinks fit.

3. Not less than one half of the members of a State Hospital Management Committee shall be persons other than medical practitioners.

4. The application of the seal of a State Hospital Management Committee to any document shall be attested by at least one member of the Committee and by the person for the time being acting as secretary of the Committee.

5. Every document purporting to be an instrument issued by a State Hospital Management Committee and to be sealed and attested as aforesaid or to be duly signed on behalf of the Committee, shall be received in evidence and shall be deemed to be such an instrument without further proof, unless the contrary is shown.

PART II

Supplementary Provisions

6. Regulations may make provision—
    (a) as to the appointment, tenure and vacation of office of the chairman and other members of a State Hospital Management Committee;
    (b) as to the delegation of functions to committees or sub-committees composed, as to a majority, of members of a State Hospital Management Committee; and

(c) as to the procedure of a State Hospital Management Committee, its committees and sub-committees.

7. The proceedings of a State Hospital Management Committee shall not be invalidated by any vacancy in membership or by any defect in the appointment of any member thereof.

8. The following provisions of the National Health Service (Scotland) Act 1978 shall apply to a State Hospital Management Committee as they apply to a Health Board, that is to say—
    (a) section 77 (which gives default powers to the Secretary of State);
    (b) section 78 (which gives emergency powers to the Secretary of State);
    (c) sections 85(1), (2A), (4) and (6) (which contain provisions as to expenditure being met by the Secretary of State);
    (d) sections 85A(1) and (3) (which impose financial duties); and
    (e) section 86 (which provides for the auditing and examination of accounts).

SCHEDULE 2

APPLICATION OF PROVISIONS OF PART V TO PATIENTS SUBJECT TO HOSPITAL OR GUARDIANSHIP ORDERS

PART I HOSPITAL ORDER WITHOUT RESTRICTION ORDER (SECTION 60(1)); TRANSFER FROM PRISON WITHOUT RESTRICTION (SECTION 71)

1. Sections 27, 31, 32, 53, 54, 55, 56 and 58 shall apply in relation to the patient without modification.

2. Sections 22, 28, 29, 30, 33, 35, 57 and 59 shall apply in relation to the patient with the modifications specified in paragraphs 3 to 10 of this Part of this Schedule.

3. In section 22—
    (a) subsection (1) shall be omitted; and
    (b) in subsection (2) for the reference to an application for admission there shall be substituted a reference to the order or direction by virtue of which the patient is liable under Part VI of this Act to be detained.

4. In section 28 subsection (4) shall be omitted.

5. In section 29(3) for the words from 'as follows' to the end of the subsection there shall be substituted the words 'as if the order or direction by virtue of which he was liable under Part VI of this Act to be detained before being transferred were an order or direction for his admission or removal to the hospital to which he is transferred.'.

6. In section 30—
    (a) in subsection (1), for the words 'an application for admission' and 'day on which he was so admitted' there shall be substituted the words 'an order or direction by virtue of which he is liable under Part VI of this Act to be detained' and 'date of the relevant order or direction' respectively; and
    (b) in subsection (3), for the words 'this Part' there shall be substituted the words 'Part VI'.

7. In section 33—
    (a) in subsection (1), for the words 'this Part' there shall be substituted the words 'Part VI';
    (b) in subsection (4), for '26, 30 or 34' there shall be substituted '30'; and
    (c) in subsection (5) the words 'by the nearest relative of the patient or' shall be omitted.

8. In section 35(1)—
   (a) the words 'any of sections 26, 30 or 34 of' shall be omitted;
   (b) for the words 'any of the said sections' there shall be substituted the words 'Part V of this Act'; and
   (c) the words from 'whether' to 'both' shall be omitted.

9. In section 57(4) for paragraphs (a) and (b) there shall be substituted the words 'on the date when the patient ceases to be liable to be detained in pursuance of the order or direction by virtue of which he was liable under Part VI of this Act to be detained (otherwise than on being transferred in pursuance of section 29(1)(b) or (c) of this Act.'.

10. In section 59 subsections (1)(b) and (2) shall be omitted.

PART II   HOSPITAL ORDER WITH RESTRICTION ORDER, (SECTION 62) AND ORDERS OR DIRECTIONS HAVING THE LIKE EFFECT (SECTIONS 69, 70 AND 72)

1. Sections 53, 54, 56 and 58 shall apply in relation to the patient without modification.

2. Section 22, 27, 28, 29, 55, 57 and 59 shall apply in relation to the patient with the modifications specified in paragraphs 3 to 9 of this Part of this Schedule.

3. In section 22—
   (a) subsection (1) shall be omitted;
   (b) in subsection (2) for the words 'application under this Part' there shall be substituted the words 'order or direction by virtue of which he is liable under Part VI of this Act to be detained' and paragraph (b) shall be omitted;
   (c) subsections (3) and (4) shall be omitted.

4. In section 27—
   (a) in subsection (1) after the word 'may' there shall be inserted the words 'with the consent of the Secretary of State';
   (b) in subsection (2) the word 'either' and the words from 'or from any specified period' to the end of the subsection shall be omitted; and
   (c) in subsection (5) after the words 'responsible medical officer' and after the words 'that officer' there shall be inserted the words 'or the Secretary of State'.

5. In section 28 subsections (3) and (4) shall be omitted.

6. In section 29—
   (a) in subsection (1) after the word 'may' there shall be inserted the words 'with the consent of the Secretary of State' and paragraphs (b) and (c) shall be omitted;
   (b) in subsection (3) for the words from 'as follows' to the end of the subsection there shall be substituted the words 'as if the order or direction by virtue of which he was liable under Part VI of this Act to be detained before being transferred were an order or direction for his admission or removal to the hospital to which he is transferred.'.

7. In section 55 subsection (3) shall be omitted.

8. In section 57(4) for paragraphs (a) and (b) there shall be substituted the words 'on the date when the patient ceases to be liable to be detained in pursuance of the order or

direction by virtue of which he was liable under Part VI of this Act to be detained (otherwise than on being transferred in pursuance of section 29(1)(b) or (c) of this Act.)'.

9. In section 59, subsections (1)(b) and (2) shall be omitted.

PART III   GUARDIANSHIP ORDER (SECTION 61(2))

1. Sections 43, 44, 46, 48, 53, 55, 56 and 58 shall apply in relation to the patient without modification.

2. Sections 41, 45, 47, 49, 50, 52, 57 and 59 shall apply in relation to the patient with the modifications specified in paragraphs 3 to 10 of this Part of this Schedule.

3. In section 41—
   (a) in subsection (1) for the words 'an application under this Part of this Act' and 'the application' there shall be substituted the words 'a guardianship order' and 'the order' respectively; and
   (b) in subsection (2) for the words from 'Where' to 'shall' and 'named in the application' there shall be substituted the words 'Where a guardianship order has been made in respect of a patient the order shall' and 'named in the order' respectively.

4. In section 45(1) and (3) for the words 'guardianship application' there shall be substituted the words 'guardianship order'.

5. In section 47—
   (a) in subsection (1) for the words 'guardianship application' and 'the day on which he was so received' there shall be substituted the words 'guardianship order' and 'the date of the order' respectively;
   (b) in subsection (3) for the words 'this Part' there shall be substituted the words 'Part VI'.

6. In section 49(1) for the words 'this Part' there shall be substituted the words 'Part VI'.

7. In section 50—
   (a) in subsection (1) for the words 'this Part' there shall be substituted the words 'Part VI';
   (b) in subsection (5) for the words 'sections 47 or 51' there shall be substituted the words 'section 47'; and
   (c) subsection (6) shall be omitted.

8. In section 52(1)—
   (a) for the words 'either of sections 47 or 51' and 'either of the said sections' there shall be substituted the words 'section 47' and 'the said section' respectively; and
   (b) the words from 'whether' to 'both' shall be omitted.

9. In section 57(4) for paragraphs (a) and (b) there shall be substituted the words 'on the date when the patient ceases to be subject to guardianship under this Act'.

10. In section 59(1)—
    (a) in subsection (1) paragraph (a) shall be omitted; and

(b) in subsection (2) for paragraphs (a) and (b) there shall be substituted the words 'to the local authority to whose guardianship he is subject or who approved his guardian.'.

SCHEDULE 3

CONSEQUENTIAL AMENDMENTS

[This Schedule is not reproduced in this work. It makes amendments to various Acts by substituting references to the Mental Health (Scotland) Act 1984 for references to the Mental Health (Scotland) Act 1960.]

SCHEDULE 4

TRANSITIONAL AND SAVINGS PROVISIONS

1. Where, apart from this paragraph, anything done under or in pursuance of, for the purposes of, any enactment which is repealed by this Act (in this Schedule referred to as 'a repealed enactment') would cease to have effect by virtue of that repeal it shall have effect as if it had been done under, or in pursuance of, or for the purposes of, the corresponding provision of this Act.

2. Without prejudice to any express amendment by this Act, where any enactment or document refers either expressly or by implication, to a repealed enactment, the reference shall, except where the context otherwise requires, be construed as, or as including, a reference to the corresponding provision of this Act.

3. Where any period of time specified in a repealed enactment is current at the commencement of this Act, this Act shall have effect as if the corresponding provision of this Act had been in force when that period began to run.

4.—(1) Nothing in this Act shall affect a repealed enactment in its operation in relation to offences committed before the commencement of this Act.

(2) Where an offence, for the continuance of which a penalty was provided, has been committed under a repealed enactment proceedings may, in the same manner as if the offence had been committed under the corresponding provision of this Act, be taken under this Act in respect of the continuance, after the commencement of this Act, of the offence.

5. This Act shall apply in relation to any authority for the detention or guardianship of a person who was liable to be detained or subject to guardianship under the Mental Health (Scotland) Act 1960 immediately before 30th September 1984 as if the provisions of this Act which derive from provisions amended by section 5 of the Mental Health (Amendment) (Scotland) Act 1983 and any amendments in Schedule 2 to that Act which are consequential on those sections were included in this Act in the form which the provisions from which they derive would take if those amendments were disregarded; but this provision shall not apply to any renewal of that authority on or after that date.

6. This Act shall apply to any application made before 30th September 1984 as if the provisions of this Act which derive from provisions amended by sections 8(1) or (2) or (3b) or (3c) or 9 of the Mental Health (Amendment) (Scotland) Act 1983 and any amendments in Schedule 2 to that Act which are consequential on those sections were included in this Act in the form which the provisions from which they derive would take if those amendments were disregarded.

7. Where on 30th September 1984 a person who has not attained the age of 16 years is subject to guardianship by virtue of a guardianship application the authority for his guardianship shall terminate on that day.

8. This Act shall apply to any emergency recommendation or admission following thereon made before 30th September 1984 as if the provisions of this Act which derive from provisions amended by section 12 of the Mental Health (Amendment) (Scotland) Act 1983 and the repeal in Schedule 3 to that Act which is consequential on that section were included in this Act in the form which the provisions from which they derive would take if those amendments were disregarded; but, when the period during which a patient may be detained in pursuance of such an emergency recommendation expires, it shall not be competent for the patient to be further detained immediately thereafter under the said provisions of this Act in the form which they take as so amended.

9. This Act shall apply in relation to any renewal of authority made before 30th September 1984 as if the provisions of this Act which derive from provisions amended by section 16(a) to (d) of the Mental Health (Amendment) (Scotland) Act 1983 and any amendments in Schedule 2 to that Act which are consequential on that section were included in this Act in the form which the provisions from which they derive would take if those amendments were disregarded; and, where an authority has been renewed before that date for a period of 2 years of which less than 16 months has expired on that date, that period shall expire at the end of 18 months from the date on which it began.

10. This Act shall apply in relation to the definition of 'nearest relative' in any proceedings commenced before 30th September 1984 as if the provisions of this Act which derive from provisions amended by section 19 of the Mental Health (Amendment) (Scotland) Act 1983 and any amendments in Schedule 2 to that Act which are consequential on that section were included in this Act in the form which the provisions from which they derive would take if those amendments were disregarded.

11.—(1) Section 98(3) of this Act shall apply to any treatment given to a patient in the period of 6 months beginning with 30th September 1984 if—
   (a) the detention of the patient began before the beginning of that period; and
   (b) that subsection has not been complied with in respect of any treatment previously given to him in that period.

(2) The Secretary of State may by order reduce the length of the period mentioned in sub-paragraph (1) of this paragraph.

12. In the case of a patient who is detained at 30th September 1984 the steps to be taken under section 110 shall be taken as soon as practicable after that date, except where such steps have already been taken.

13. Section 113 of this Act shall not apply in relation to proceedings commenced before 30th September 1984.

SCHEDULE 5

REPEALS

Chapter	Short title	Extent of repeal
1960 c 61	The Mental Health (Scotland) Act 1960.	The whole Act.
1961 (NI) c 15	The Mental Health (Northern Ireland) Act 1961.	In Schedule 5, Part II.
1963 c 39	The Criminal Justice (Scotland) Act 1963.	In Schedule 5, the entry relating to the Mental Health (Scotland) Act 1960.
1967 c 28	The Superannuation (Miscellaneous Provisions) Act 1967.	Section 14.
1968 c 20	The Courts-Martial (Appeals) Act 1968.	In Schedule 4, the entry relating to the Mental Health (Scotland) Act 1960.
1968 c 46	The Health Services and Public Health Act 1968.	Section 75.
1968 c 49	The Social Work (Scotland) Act 1968	In Schedule 8, paragraphs 50 to 59.
1969 c 39	The Age of Majority (Scotland) Act 1969.	In Schedule 1, Part 1, the entry relating to the Mental Health (Scotland) Act 1960.
1969 c 54	The Children and Young Persons Act 1969.	In Schedule 5, paragraphs 42 and 43.
1971 c 77	The Immigration Act 1971.	Section 30.
1972 c 58	The National Health Service (Scotland) Act 1972.	Section 52(1). In Schedule 6, paragraphs 105 to 117.
1974 c 46	The Friendly Societies Act 1974.	In Schedule 9, paragraph 17.
1975 c 21	The Criminal Procedure (Scotland) Act 1975	In Schedule 9, paragraphs 17 to 29.
1976 c 67	The Sexual Offences (Scotland) Act 1976.	In Schedule 1, the entry relating to the Mental Health (Scotland) Act 1960.
1976 c 83	The Health Services Act 1976	Section 19(3), (4)(c).
1978 c 29	The National Health Service (Scotland) Act 1978.	In Schedule 16, paragraphs 12 and 13.
1980 c 5	The Child Care Act 1980.	In Schedule 6, paragraphs 15 and 16.
1980 c 44	The Education (Scotland) Act 1980.	In Schedule 4, paragraphs 2.
1980 c 62	The Criminal Justice (Scotland) Act 1980.	In section 80, subsection (4).
1982 c 51	The Mental Health (Amendment) Act 1982.	In Schedule 3 in Part I, paragraph 31.
1983 c 20	The Mental Health Act 1983.	In Schedule 4, paragraph 16.
1983 c 39	The Mental Health (Amendment) (Scotland) Act 1983.	The whole Act.

Appendix 2

Statutory instruments

Mental Health (Specified Treatments, Guardianship Duties etc) (Scotland) Regulations 1984

(SI 1984 No 1494)

Citation and commencement

1. These regulations may be cited as the Mental Health (Specified Treatments, Guardianship Duties etc) (Scotland) Regulations 1984 and shall come into operation on 30th September 1984.

Interpretation

2. In these regulations, unless the context otherwise requires—
'the Act' means the Mental Health (Scotland) Act 1984;
'guardianship' means the person named as guardian in either a guardianship application under Part V of the Act or a guardianship order made under section 175 or 376 of the Criminal Procedure (Scotland) Act 1975, and which has effect in respect of a patient, and 'guardianship' shall be construed accordingly;
'local authority concerned' means—
  (a) in the case of a patient in respect of whom a guardianship application under Part V of the Act is effective, the local authority to whom that application was addressed;
  (b) in the case of a patient removed to Scotland in pursuance of arrangements under section 81 of the Act or under section 80 of the Mental Health Act 1983 the local authority for the place in Scotland at which he was received into guardianship;
  (c) in any other case the local authority to whose guardianship the patient is subject or who approved his guardian.

Specified forms of medical treatment

3.—(1) A form of medical treatment for mental disorder hereby specified for the purposes of section 97 of the Act (treatment requiring consent and a second opinion) shall be the surgical implantation of hormones for the purpose of reducing male sexual drive.

(2) A form of medical treatment for mental disorder hereby specified for the purposes of section 98 of the Act (treatment requiring consent or a second opinion) shall be electro-convulsive therapy.

Duties of local authority concerned

4. The local authority concerned shall exercise general supervision over every patient subject to guardianship.

5. The local authority concerned shall arrange for every patient who is subject to guardianship to be visited on their behalf from time to time but in any case at intervals of not more than three months.

6.—(1) The local authority concerned shall as soon as practicable notify the Mental Welfare Commission in writing of any permanent change in the place of residence of a guardian or of a patient subject to guardianship.

(2) In the event of the absence of a patient subject to guardianship without leave from the place at which he is required to reside, his return thereto after such absence, his death or the termination of guardianship by discharge or otherwise, the local authority concerned shall as soon as practicable notify the Mental Welfare Commission in writing of that event.

Duties of guardian

7. A guardian, other than one which is the local authority concerned, shall—
   (a) furnish the local authority concerned with all such reports or other information with regard to the patient subject to guardianship as that authority may from time to time require;
   (b) before any permanent change in the place of residence of the guardian or of the patient subject to guardianship takes effect, notify the local authority concerned in writing of the new place of residence;
   (c) notify the local authority concerned in writing of the name and address of the medical practitioner for the time being acting as the general medical practitioner of the patient subject to guardianship;
   (d) in the event of the death of the patient subject to guardianship, as soon as practicable inform the local authority concerned;
   (e) if the patient subject to guardianship is absent without leave of the guardian from the place at which he is required to reside, or if such a patient absent without leave returns or is returned to that place, as soon as practicable inform the local authority concerned of that event.

Revocations

8. The Mental Health (Guardianship) (Scotland) Regulations 1962 and the Mental Health (Guardianship) (Scotland) Amendment Regulations 1975 are hereby revoked.

The Mental Health (Prescribed Forms) (Scotland) Regulations 1984

(SI 1984 No 1495 (S 123))

Citation, commencement and interpretation

1.—(1) These regulations may be cited as the Mental Health (Prescribed Forms) (Scotland) Regulations 1984 and shall come into operation on 30th September 1984.

(2) Unless the context otherwise requires, any reference in these regulations to 'the Act' is a reference to the Mental Health (Scotland) Act 1984, and any reference to a numbered section is a reference to the section bearing that number in the Mental Health (Scotland) Act 1984.

Prescribed forms

2. Any application, recommendation, report or certificate the form of which is required or authorised to be prescribed under the Mental Health (Scotland) Act 1984 shall be in accordance with whichever one of the forms in the Schedule to these regulations is appropriate or in a form to the like effect.

Revocation

3. The Mental Health (Forms) (Scotland) Regulations 1962 are hereby revoked.

FORM 1

Application by nearest relative for admission of patient to hospital

(SECTION 18)

To the Managers of [name and address of hospital].

I [name and address of applicant] hereby apply for the admission of [name and address of patient] in accordance with Part V of the Mental Health (Scotland) Act 1984.

[Either complete (a) and delete (b) and (c), or delete whichever statements do not apply].

(a) To the best of my knowledge and belief I am the patient's nearest relative within the meaning of the Act. I am the patient's [state relationship].

(b) I am a person to whom or I am acting on behalf of a local authority to whom section 54 or 55 of the Act applies.*

(c) I have been authorised by the sheriff under section 56 of the Act to act as the patient's nearest relative. A copy of the sheriff's order is attached to this application. The order is in force.

I last saw the patient on [date].

This application is founded on the accompanying two medical recommendations.

[If neither of the medical practitioners knew the patient before making his recommendation please explain why it was not practicable to obtain a recommendation from a practitioner who did know the patient].

Signed.......................... Date ....

* Authors' note. This refers to children in the care of a local authority or in respect of whom a guardianship or custody order has been made. The authority will generally be treated as the nearest relative.

FORM 2

Application by mental health officer for admission of patient to hospital

(SECTION 18)

To the Managers of [*name and address of hospital*].

I [*name and office address of applicant*] hereby apply for the admission of [*name and address of patient*] in accordance with Part V of the Mental Health (Scotland) Act 1984.

I am an officer of [*name of local authority*] appointed by them to act as a mental health officer for the purposes of the Act.

(If the patient's nearest relative is known, complete either (a) or (b) AND either (c) or (d), as appropriate, and delete (e) and (f).)

(a) To the best of my knowledge and belief [*name and address*] is the patient's nearest relative within the meaning of the Act.

or

(b) I understand that [*name and address*] has been authorised by the sheriff under section 56 of the Act to act as the patient's nearest relative.

AND

(c) I have informed that person of his/her right in accordance with section 21 of the Act to object to this application. The information was sent/given on [*date*].

OR

(d) I have not informed that person of his/her right to object to this application because [*state reasons*].

(If the patient's nearest relative is not known, and no person is authorised to act in that capacity, delete (a) to (d) above and either (e) or (f) as appropriate.)

(e) I have been unable to ascertain who is the patient's nearest relative within the meaning of the Act.

OR

(f) To the best of my knowledge and belief the patient has no nearest relative within the meaning of the Act.

(Complete either (a) or (b))

(a) I last saw the patient on [*date*] and I am satisfied that detention in a hospital is, in all the circumstances of the case, the most appropriate way of providing the care and medical treatment which the patient needs.

OR

(b) I have been requested in accordance with section 19(6) of the Act to make this application. In my opinion the application should not be granted. The grounds on which that opinion is based are [*state grounds on which opinion is based*].

This application is founded on the accompanying two medical recommendations.

[*If neither of the medical practitioners knew the patient before making his recommendation, please explain why it was not practicable to obtain a recommendation from a medical practitioner who did know the patient. Note: this does not apply in the case of an application made under section 19(6)*].

Signed............................ Date ....

FORM 3

Medical recommendation for admission to hospital

(SECTION 18)

I [*full name and professional address of medical practitioner*], a registered medical practitioner, recommend that [*full name and address of patient*] be admitted to hospital in accordance with Part V of the Mental Health (Scotland) Act 1984.

[*delete whichever of (a) (b) or (c) is not applicable*]
   (a) I am the patient's general medical practitioner
   (b) I was otherwise acquainted with the patient before I examined him/her
   (c) I have been approved by [*name*] Health Board under section 20 of the Act as having special experience in the diagnosis or treatment of mental disorder.

I last examined the patient on [*date*].

In my opinion this patient is suffering from mental disorder, being (i) mental illness (ii) mental handicap [*delete (i) or (ii) unless both apply*] and that form of mental disorder is [*delete any sub-paragraph which does not apply*]

   (a) a mental illness of a nature or degree which makes it appropriate for him/her to receive medical treatment in a hospital

   (b) a mental illness which is a persistent one manifested only by abnormally aggressive or seriously irresponsible conduct and which makes it appropriate for him/her to receive in a hospital medical treatment, which is likely to alleviate or prevent a deterioration of his/her condition

   (c) mental handicap comprising severe mental impairment which makes it appropriate for him/her to receive medical treatment in a hospital

   (d) mental handicap comprising mental impairment which makes it appropriate for him/her to receive in a hospital medical treatment, which is likely to alleviate or prevent a deterioration of his/her condition.

This opinion is based on the following grounds:— [*give brief description of salient features of patient's mental state*].

I am of the opinion that it is necessary

[*delete (i) or (ii) unless both apply*]
   (i) for the patient's health or safety
   (ii) for the protection of other persons

that he/she should receive medical treatment in a hospital and it cannot be provided unless he/she is detained under Part V of the Act. The grounds upon which this opinion is based are

[*Indicate whether other methods of care or treatment (eg out-patient treatment or local authority services) are available and, if so, why they are not appropriate, and why informal admission is not appropriate.*]

[*Delete (a) or (b)*]
   (a) I am not related to the patient.
   (b) I am related to the patient, being his/her [*state relationship*].

[*Delete (c) or (d)*]
   (c) I have no pecuniary interest in the admission of the patient to hospital.
   (d) I have a pecuniary interest in the admission of the patient to hospital. The nature and extent of that interest is [*state nature and extent of interest*].

[*Delete (e) or (f)*]
   (e) I am on the staff of the hospital named in the application. The

Prescribed Forms Regulations 1984

                    patient is not to be accommodated in the hospital under section 57 or 58 of the National Health Service (Scotland) Act 1978. The hospital is not a private hospital.

                (f) I am not on the staff of the hospital named in the application.

[*Delete if not applicable*]   (g) I examined the patient in company with [*name of medical practitioner giving the other medical recommendation*]. Neither the patient nor his/her nearest relative objected to a joint examination.

Signed............................ Date ....

FORM 4

Renewal of authority for detention of patient in hospital: report by responsible medical officer

(SECTION 30)

[*Delete as appropriate*]   To the Mental Welfare Commission

To the Managers of

[*name of hospital in which patient is liable to be detained*].

I [*name of responsible medical officer*]

[*Complete (a) or (b)*]

   (a) examined [*name of patient*] on [*date*],

   (b) have obtained the attached report by [*name of medical practitioner*] on the condition of [*name of patient*]

AND

I have consulted [*names and designations*] who appear to me to be principally concerned with the patient's medical treatment.

In my opinion this patient is suffering from mental disorder, being (i) mental illness (ii) mental handicap [*delete (i) or (ii) unless both apply*] and that form of mental disorder is [*delete any sub-paragraph which does not apply*]

   (a) a mental illness of a nature or degree which makes it appropriate for him/her to receive medical treatment in hospital.

   (b) a mental illness which is a persistent one manifested only by abnormally aggressive or seriously irresponsible conduct and which makes it appropriate for him/her to receive in a hospital medical treatment, which is likely to alleviate or prevent a deterioration of his/her condition.

   (c) mental handicap comprising severe mental impairment which makes it appropriate for him/her to receive medical treatment in hospital.

   (d) mental handicap comprising mental impairment which makes it appropriate for him/her to receive in a hospital medical treatment, which is likely to alleviate or prevent a deterioration of his/her condition.

This opinion is based on the following grounds [*give brief description of salient features of patient's mental state*].

I am of the opinion that it is necessary [*delete (i) or (ii) unless both apply*]

   (i) for this patient's health or safety
   (ii) for the protection of other persons

that he/she should receive medical treatment in a hospital and it cannot be provided unless he/she continues to be detained under Part V of the Act. The grounds on which this opinion is based are

[*Indicate whether other methods of care or treatment (eg out-patient treatment or local authority services) are available, and, if so, why they are not appropriate and why informal admission is not appropriate*].

Signed............................   Date ....
     (*Responsible Medical Officer*)

FORM 5

Renewal of authority for detention of patient when restriction direction ceases to have effect: report by the responsible medical officer

(SECTION 74)

[*Delete as appropriate*]   To the Mental Welfare Commission

   To the Managers of

[*name of hospital in which patient is liable to be detained*].

I [*name of responsible medical officer*] have obtained the attached report from [*name of medical practitioner*] on the condition of [*name of patient*] who will cease to be subject to a restriction direction on [*date*].

Taking that report into account, I am of the opinion that it is necessary

[*Delete (a) or (b)*   (a) in the interests of the patient's health or safety;
unless both apply]   (b) for the protection of other persons

that the patient should continue to be liable to be detained in hospital beyond the date on which the restriction order ceases to have effect.

This opinion is based on the following grounds

[*Indicate why other methods of care or treatment, including continued treatment in hospital without liability to detention, are not considered appropriate.*]

Signed.........................   Date ....
   (Responsible Medical Officer)

FORM 6

Medical report on condition of patient when restriction direction ceases to have effect

(SECTION 74)

I [*full name and professional address of medical practitioner*], a registered medical practitioner, examined [*full name of patient*] at [*place of examination*] on [*date*].

In my opinion this patient is suffering from mental disorder being (i) mental illness (ii) mental handicap [*delete (i) or (ii) unless both apply*] and that form of mental disorder is—[*delete any sub-paragraph which does not apply*]

(a) a mental illness of a nature or degree which makes it appropriate for him/her to receive medical treatment in a hospital.

(b) a mental illness which is a persistent one manifested only by abnormally aggressive or seriously irresponsible conduct and which makes it appropriate for him/her to receive in a hospital medical treatment, which is likely to alleviate or prevent a deterioration of his/her condition.

(c) mental handicap comprising severe mental impairment which makes it appropriate for him/her to receive medical treatment in a hospital.

(d) mental handicap comprising mental impairment which makes it appropriate for him/her to receive in a hospital medical treatment, which is likely to alleviate or prevent a deterioration of his/her condition.

This opinion is based on the following grounds [*give brief description of salient features of patient's mental state*].

Signed............................   Date ....

FORM 7

Report by responsible medical officer following admission to hospital of patient removed to Scotland

(SECTION 88)

To the managers of [*name of hospital*].

On [*date*] I [*name of responsible medical officer*] examined [*name of patient*] who was previously a patient in [*name and address of hospital from which patient was removed to Scotland*] and who was admitted to the first above named hospital on [*date*].

In my opinion the patient is suffering from (i) mental illness (ii) mental handicap [*delete (i) or (ii) unless both apply*] of a nature or degree which makes it appropriate that he/she should be liable to be detained in hospital for medical treatment.

Signed.......................... Date ....
    (Responsible Medical Officer)

FORM 8

Certificate of consent to treatment and second opinion

(SECTION 97)
(*Both Parts I and II of this certificate must be completed*)

PART I

I [*full name and professional address*] being a medical practitioner appointed for the purposes of Part X of the Act by the Mental Welfare Commission and we [*full name, address and designation*] being two persons appointed by the Commission for the purposes of section 97(2)(*a*) of the Act, certify that [*name*], a patient who is liable to be detained in [*name of hospital*], is capable of understanding the nature, purpose and likely effects of [*give description of treatment or plan of treatment*] AND has consented to that treatment.

Signed............................ Date ....

Signed............................ Date ....

Signed............................ Date ....

PART II

I [*full name*], being a medical practitioner appointed for the purposes of Part X of the Act, having consulted [*names and designations*] who appear to me to be principally concerned with the medical treatment of the patient named in Part I above, certify that, having regard to the likelihood of the treatment specified in Part I alleviating or preventing a deterioration of the patient's condition, that treatment should be given.

Signed............................ Date ....

FORM 9

Certificate of consent to treatment

(SECTION 98)

I [*full name and professional address*] being

[*Delete either (a)*   (a) the responsible medical officer
or (b)]   (b) a medical practitioner appointed for the purposes of Part X of the Act by the Mental Welfare Commission

certify that [*full name of patient*], a patient who is liable to be detained in [*name of hospital*], is capable of understanding the nature, purpose and likely effects of [*give description of treatment or plan of treatment*] AND has consented to that treatment.

Signed..........................   Date ....

FORM 10

Certificate of second opinion

(SECTION 98)

I [*full name and professional address*] being a medical practitioner appointed for the purpose of Part X of the Act by the Mental Welfare Commission, having consulted [*names and designations*] who appear to me to be principally concerned with the medical treatment of [*name*], a patient who is liable to be detained in [*name of hospital*], certify that the patient—

[*Delete (a) or (b)*]   (a) is not capable of understanding the nature, purposes and likely effects of

(b) being capable of understanding its nature, purpose and likely effects, has not consented to

[*give description of treatment or plan of treatment*] but that, having regard to the likelihood of its alleviating or preventing a deterioration of the patient's condition, that treatment should be given.

Signed............................   Date ....

FORM 11

Guardianship application by nearest relative

(SECTION 37)

(*To be completed by nearest relative*)

To [*name of local authority for area in which patient resides*].

I [*name and address of applicant*] hereby apply for the reception of [*name and address of patient*] into the guardianship of [*name and address of proposed guardian*] in accordance with Part V of the Mental Health (Scotland) Act 1984.

[*Either complete (a) and delete (b) and (c), or delete whichever statements do not apply.*]

  (a) To the best of my knowledge and belief I am the patient's nearest relative within the meaning of the Act. I am the patient's [*state relationship*].

  (b) I am a person/I am acting on behalf of a local authority to whom section 54 or 55 of the Act applies.*

  (c) I have been authorised by the sheriff under section 56 of the Act to act as the patient's nearest relative. A copy of the sheriff's order is attached to this application. The order is in force.

I last saw the patient on [*date*].

[*Complete (i) unless the patient's date of birth is unknown*].

  (i) The patient's date of birth is [*date*].

OR

  (ii) I believe the patient is aged 16 years or over.

This application is founded on the accompanying two medical recommendations and a recommendation by a mental health officer.

[*If neither of the medical practitioners knew the patient before making his recommendation, please explain why it was not practicable to obtain a recommendation from a medical practitioner who did know the patient.*]

Signed............................ Date ....

---

* Authors' note. *This refers to children in the care of the local authority or in respect of whom a guardianship or custody order has been made. The authority will generally be treated as the nearest relative.*

FORM 12

Guardianship application by mental health officer

(SECTION 37)

(To be completed by mental health officer)

To [*name of local authority for area in which patient resides*].

I [*name and address of applicant*] hereby apply for the reception of [*name and address of patient*] into the guardianship of [*name and address of proposed guardian*] in accordance with Part V of the Mental Health (Scotland) Act 1984.

I am an officer of [*name of local authority*] appointed by them to act as a mental health officer for the purposes of the Act.

[*If the patient's nearest relative is known, complete either (a) or (b)* AND *either (c) or (d), as appropriate, and delete (e) and (f).*]

    (a) To the best of my knowledge and belief [*name and address*] is the patient's nearest relative within the meaning of the Act.

OR

    (b) I understand that [*name and address*] has been authorised by the sheriff under section 56 of the Act to act as the patient's nearest relative.

AND

    (c) I have informed that person of his/her right in accordance with section 40 of the Act to object to this application. The information was sent/given on [*date*].

OR

    (d) It has not been practicable for me to inform that person of his/her right to object to this application because [*state reasons*].

[*If the patient's nearest relative is not known, and no person is authorised to act in that capacity, delete (a) to (d) above and either (e) or (f) as appropriate.*]

    (e) I have been unable to ascertain who is the patient's nearest relative within the meaning of the Act.

OR

    (f) To the best of my knowledge and belief the patient has no nearest relative within the meaning of the Act.

I last saw the patient on [*date*].

[*Complete (i) unless the patient's date of birth is unknown.*]

    (i) The patient's date of birth is [*date*].

OR

    (ii) I believe the patient is aged 16 years or over.

This application is founded on the accompanying two medical recommendations and a recommendation by a mental health officer.

[*If neither of the medical practitioners knew the patient before making his recommendation, please explain why it was not practicable to obtain a recommendation from a practitioner who did know the patient.*]

Signed............................. Date ....

FORM 13

Medical recommendation for reception into guardianship

(SECTION 37)

I [*full name and professional address of medical practitioner*], a registered medical practitioner, recommend that [*name and address of patient*] be received into guardianship in accordance with Part V of the Mental Health (Scotland) Act 1984.

[*Delete whichever of (a) (b) or (c) is not applicable*]
    (a) I am the patient's general medical practitioner.
    (b) I was otherwise acquainted with the patient before I examined him/her.
    (c) I have been approved by [*name*] Health Board under section 40 of the Act as having special experience in the diagnosis or treatment of mental disorder.

I last examined the patient on [*date*].

In my opinion the patient is suffering from (i) mental illness (ii) mental handicap [*delete (i) or (ii) unless both apply*] of a nature or degree which warrants his/her reception into guardianship.

This opinion is based on the following grounds

[*give brief description of salient features of patient's mental state*]

[*Delete (a) or (b)*]
    (a) I am not related to the patient.
    (b) I am related to the patient being his/her [*state relationship*].

[*Delete (c) or (d)*]
    (c) I have no pecuniary interest in the reception of the patient into guardianship.
    (d) I have a pecuniary interest in the reception of the patient into guardianship. The nature and extent of that interest is [*state nature and extent of interest*].

[*Delete if not applicable*]
    (e) I examined the patient in company with [*name of medical practitioner giving the other medical recommendation*]. Neither the patient nor his/her nearest relative objected to a joint examination.

Signed............................   Date ....

FORM 14

Recommendation by mental health officer for reception into guardianship

(SECTION 37)

I [*full name and office address of mental health officer*], an officer of [*name of local authority*] appointed by them to act as a mental health officer for the purposes of the Mental Health (Scotland) Act 1984, recommend that [*full name and address of patient*] be received into guardianship in accordance with Part V of the Act.

In my opinion it is necessary in the interests of the welfare of the patient that he/she should be received into guardianship.

This opinion is based on the following grounds:— [*statement of grounds*].

[*Delete (a) or (b)*] (a) I am not related to the patient.
(b) I am related to the patient, being his/her [*state relationship*]

AND

[*Delete (c) or (d)*] (c) I have no pecuniary interest in the reception of the patient into guardianship.
(d) I have a pecuniary interest in the reception of the patient into guardianship. The nature and extent of that interest is [*state nature and extent of interest*].

Signed............................ Date ....

FORM 15

Renewal of authority for guardianship

Report by responsible medical officer

(SECTION 47)

To [names of mental health officer and local authority concerned], I [name and address of responsible medical officer].

Complete (a) or (b)

(a) examined [full name and address of patient] on [date]

(b) have obtained the attached report by [name of medical practitioner] on the condition of [full name and address of patient].

I am of the opinion that the patient is suffering from [insert mental illness and/or mental handicap] of a nature or degree which warrants his/her continuing to be subject to guardianship.

This opinion is based on the following grounds:—

[Give brief description of salient features of patient's mental state.]

Signed.......................... Date ....
    (Responsible Medical Officer)

FORM 16

Renewal of authority for guardianship

Report by mental health officer

(SECTION 47)

[*Delete as appropriate*]

To the Mental Welfare Commission

To [*name of local authority concerned*]

I [*full name and office address of mental health officer*] being an officer of [*name of local authority*] appointed by them to act as a mental health officer for the purposes of the Mental Health (Scotland) Act 1984, having received from [*name of responsible medical officer*] the attached report on [*full name and address of patient*] and having considered that report, am of the opinion that it is necessary in the interests of the welfare of the patient that he/she should continue to be subject to guardianship.

This opinion is based on the following grounds:— [*statement of grounds*].

Signed............................ Date ....

FORM 17

Report by responsible medical officer following reception into guardianship of patient removed to Scotland

(SECTION 88)

To [*name of local authority concerned*].

On [*date*] I [*name of responsible medical officer*] examined [*full name of patient*] who was previously under the guardianship of [*full name and address of former guardian*] and who was received into the guardianship of [*full name and address of guardian in Scotland*] on [*date*].

In my opinion, the patient is suffering from [*insert mental illness and/or mental handicap*] of the nature or degree which warrants his/her continuing to be subject to guardianship.

Signed............................ Date ....
    (Responsible Medical Officer)

Note—This form and the following two forms are not prescribed by legislation but are styles suggested by the authors.

Suggested form to be used by nearest relative for discharge of a patient committed under section 18 of the Act

(SEE PARA 2.7)

To the Managers of [name and address of hospital].

I [name and address of applicant] hereby apply for the discharge of [name and address of patient] in accordance with section 34 of the Mental Health (Scotland) Act 1984. I desire the discharge to take effect on [insert date which is at least 7 days after the date of application].

[Either complete (a) and delete (b) and (c), or delete whichever statements do not apply.]

(a) To the best of my knowledge and belief I am the patient's nearest relative within the meaning of the Act. I am the patient's [state relationship].

(b) I am a person to whom or I am acting on behalf of a local authority to whom section 54 or 55 of the Act applies.*

(c) I have been authorised by the sheriff under section 56 of the Act to act as the patient's nearest relative. A copy of the sheriff's order is attached to this application. The order is in force.

Signed............................   Date ....

---

*Authors' note. This refers to children in the care of local authority or in respect of whom a guardianship or custody order has been made. The authority will generally be treated as the nearest relative.

Suggested form of discharge from guardianship to be used by nearest relative

(SEE PARA 3.1:12)

(To be completed by nearest relative)

To [name of local authority concerned].

I [name and address of applicant] hereby apply for the discharge of [name and address of patient] from the guardianship of [name and address of guardian] in accordance with section 51 of the Mental Health (Scotland) Act 1984. I desire the discharge to take effect on [insert date which is at least 14 days from the date of application].

[Either complete (a) and delete (b) and (c), or delete whichever statements do not apply.]

(a) To the best of my knowledge and belief I am the patient's nearest relative within the meaning of the Act. I am the patient's [state relationship].

(b) I am a person/I am acting on behalf of a local authority to whom section 54 or 55 of the Act applies.★

(c) I have been authorised by the sheriff under section 56 of the Act to act as the patient's nearest relative. A copy of the sheriff's order is attached to this application. The order is in force.

Signed.......................... Date ....

★ *Authors' note. This refers to children in the care of local authority or in respect of whom a guardianship or custody order has been made. The authority will generally be treated as the nearest relative.*

Suggested form of discharge from guardianship to be used by nearest relative when no objections have been raised to application made using form at page 215

(SEE PARA 3.1:12)

(To be completed by nearest relative)

To [*name of local authority concerned*].

Further to my application of [*insert date of application*], I [*name and address of applicant*] hereby discharge [*name and address of patient*] from the guardianship of [*name and address of guardian*] in accordance with section 51 of the Mental Health (Scotland) Act 1984. I desire the discharge to take effect immediately.

Signed ....   Date ....

Appendix 3

Case notes

There is as yet comparatively little reported case law on **the Act**. The summaries of the cases that we have included here are intended only to be a basic guide. Reports of all Scottish cases will be found at the National Library.

Lawyers become familiar with finding case law and reading it. Non-lawyers may find it hard to find the law reports in which it appears. It is worth inquiring at the public library. There are four current Scottish series:

(1) *Session Cases*. This is the official series. It appears some three to four years after the case is decided. A reference to it would take the form, for example, 1987 SC 6. Ie the case is found in the 1987 volume at page 6. If it is a criminal case the reference will have 'JC' in it rather than 'SC'. ('JC' stands for 'Justiciary Cases'). These cases appear immediately before the SC ones in the same volume. If the case is a decision of the House of Lords it will take the form, for example, 1987 SC (HL) 6. These cases will be in the same volume, at the beginning.

(2) *The Scots Law Times*. This is a series that is produced by a commercial law publisher. It comes out weekly and reports cases within months of their being decided. A reference to it would take the form, for example, 1987 SLT 6. (There is no difference if it is a criminal case or House of Lords case.) If the case is from the sheriff court the reference shows that, eg 1987 SLT (Sh Ct) 6.

(3) *The Scottish Civil Law Reports*. This is produced by the Law Society of Scotland. Like the Scots Law Times it includes cases from the sheriff court. References to all cases in it take the form, eg, 1987 SCLR 6. It reports cases within months of their being decided and generally includes a note discussing the law in the case.

(4) *The Scottish Criminal Case Reports*. This is produced on the same basis as the Scottish Civil Law Reports. But it covers criminal rather than civil cases. References to all cases in it take the form, eg, 1987 SCCR 6.

Scots cases are now being reported in an abridged form in The Scotsman (normally on Wednesdays) and The Times. These reports normally appear within days or weeks of the decision. English cases are reported in the Independent and the Guardian as well as The Times. These reports are sometimes too short to go into the sort of detail that a lawyer needs when referring to a case in a court. The full text of what the judges said can be obtained from Lexis (a computerised legal database.)

English cases can be found most easily in the All England Reports, a commercially published series, which comes out every week. References take the form, for example, [1987] 1 All ER 6. The official series is the Weekly Law Reports (WLR). Most cases then appear in the official series that relates to the court where the case started or to the House of Lords if a case goes that far. House of Lords cases have 'AC' (which means appeal cases) in the reference. Eg [1987] AC 56.

Reports of cases in law reports have a roughly standardised form. They start with the names of those involved. Then there are a few lines of catchwords indicating what the case is about. Below this comes a summary of the essential facts and of the point that was decided. There is, then, usually a summary of the lawyers' arguments in court (important only for very detailed study). Then there follows what the judges wrote in their judgments. This is the really important part. The rest is designed to assist the reader.

AB and CB v E 1987 SCLR 419

The brother of a compulsorily detained patient who had been suffering from a mental illness involving schizophrenia for some years, served notice on the managers of the hospital where his sister was a patient, seeking her discharge. As the hospital refused, an appeal was made to the sheriff. At the time the patient was spending three or four days of each week on leave of absence in the community (under s 27). The doctors were changing her treatment from taking medication herself to having injections roughly once a week. This involved increasing the amount of the drug in question. The effect of the change was monitored on the days in the week when she was in hospital. The sheriff had to decide whether the patient was on the facts still someone who was 'liable to be detained' in terms of the Act. He considered that the words 'to be liable to' had been put in s 33(4)(a) to deal with the situation where a patient who was still definitely requiring in-patient treatment from time to time was on leave of absence at the time a sheriff had to consider the matter. A sheriff could not refuse to order that a patient should be discharged just on the basis that it was 'potentially appropriate' for him or her to be detained, eg because it was potentially the case that the patient would not continue to co-operate in taking medication. However, on the facts of this case observation of the effects of the treatment on the patient was a necessary part of the programme of changing her medication to injections. Accordingly she was in a position where it was 'appropriate' (as opposed to merely 'potentially appropriate') for her to be detained. So the sheriff refused the appeal.

A R v Secretary of State for Scotland Unreported case of Sheriff Robin McEwan at Lanark Sheriff Court 29 February 1988

A psychopathic patient had been compulsorily detained for twenty years in conditions of high security, for the majority of the time in the State Hospital. He appealed against a further renewal of the authority on the grounds that the treatment could not cure him. He claimed he was receiving minimal treatment and was merely being held in conditions of high security.

The sheriff found some evidence that the treatment had at least prevented a deterioration of the patient's condition within s 17(1)(a)(i) of the Act. There was also evidence that the patient could be a considerable danger to the public if he was not detained.

The sheriff drew attention to the fact that a sheriff hearing an appeal does not have to consider whether the **statutory grounds for admission** apply (ie in the case whether the treatment would alleviate or prevent a deterioration of the patient's condition). The test to be applied on appeal is whether the patient is suffering from a mental disorder which makes it appropriate for him or her to be liable to be detained in hospital and whether it is necessary for the health or safety of the patient or for the protection of others that he or she should receive such treatment (**the grounds for continued detention**) (s 33(4)).

The sheriff was not strictly obliged, therefore, to be satisfied that the treatment which was being proposed would 'cure' the patient, but rather whether it was appropriate to detain him in hospital. The appeal failed and the patient remained in the State Hospital.

The sheriff noted that there was a tendency for doctors who felt that they were unable to 'cure' psychopathic patients to be unwilling to commit them under the Act and instead leave them to be dealt with by the criminal courts. He believed that this was not necessarily within the spirit of the Act. If, as in the present patient's case, the kind of medical treatment envisaged by the Act, which includes care and training under medical supervision, could prevent a deterioration in the patient's condition, then such a patient should be admitted to hospital under the compulsory procedures.

Re B [1988] AC 199, [1987] 2 All ER 206, HL

A mentally handicapped girl of seventeen was in the care of a local authority. She lived in a local authority residential institution for minors and adults. In the future it was likely that she would be transferred to an adult training centre. She had a moderate degree of mental handicap but very limited intellectual development, suffered from epilepsy and could be subject to extreme changes of mood. She was showing signs of sexual awareness. However, she had no understanding of the link between sexual activity and pregnancy. Evidence was given that she could never make an informed choice herself, that pregnancy would be traumatic to her and that there was at best a 40 per cent. chance of her successfully following a long-term course of contraception. The local authority applied to a judge to allow her to be sterilised. The mother agreed with this. The judge decided that the operation could be carried out. His decision was then appealed by way of the Court of Appeal to the House of Lords. The House of Lords decided unanimously that this decision was correct. The court was exercising 'wardship jurisdiction'. What was at issue was the well-being, welfare or interests of the person in question. On the facts of this case a sterilisation operation was in the judges' opinion clearly desirable. They left open the question as to the legal basis on which a court in England might act if the person had been over eighteen.

B v Forsey 1988 SLT 572, HL

A patient who suffered from hypomania was initially detained compulsorily in a mental hospital on the basis of an emergency recommendation for seventy-two hours. He was then detained under section 26 of **the Act** for a period of up to twenty-eight days. Towards the later part of that period he seemed to be getting better. So it was not thought that the procedure should be set in motion to have him compulsorily detained on a long-term basis by applying to the sheriff. A few days before the end of the twenty-eight days he had a relapse. He was simply detained as if it was an emergency detention. It would not be possible to get a long-term detention approved by the sheriff in the time available. He raised an action using the process known as judicial review. The judge who heard the action said the hospital did have a general legal power to detain him in these circumstances, although the power was not in the Act. He appealed to the Inner House of the Court of Session and to the House of Lords. They disagreed with the judge. The provisions of the Act, with regard to compulsory detention, form a scheme that does not allow hospitals any power to detain mentally disordered people outside the provisions of the Act. Hospitals (and those who work in them) have no powers of detention in the general law. It was particularly clear that Parliament had intended this by changing the provisions that were in the **1960 Act**.

A private individual does have a power to detain 'in a situation of necessity, a person of unsound mind who is a danger to himself or others'. One of the judges, however, stated that even for a private person this power 'is confined to imposing temporary restraint on a lunatic who has run amok and is a manifest danger to himself or to others—a state of affairs as obvious to a layman as to a doctor'. Moreover, the right of a private person to detain in such circumstances is 'confined to the short period of confinement necessary before the lunatic can be handed over to proper authority'.

The judges sympathised with the difficulty the doctors were faced with. It was suggested that Parliament should consider amending the legislation, particularly as it was felt that a similar problem would not arise under the English Mental Health Act.

F v Management Committee and Managers, Ravenscraig Hospital 1989 SLT 49
(Inner House, Court of Session, Second Division)

A patient who had been in the **State Hospital** at Carstairs was transferred to an ordinary hospital for mentally disordered people. Shortly afterwards he assaulted another patient and was transferred back to the State Hospital. He appealed to the sheriff under section 29(4) of the Act. The sheriff heard evidence and refused to overrule the hospital's decision. The patient then appealed to the sheriff principal, who held that it was not possible in law to appeal to him as, in deciding such matters, a sheriff is acting in an administrative capacity and not as a judge in a litigation. The patient then appealed further to the Court of Session. The court agreed with the sheriff principal that it was not possible to appeal such decisions of the sheriff. In particular it noted that the section of the Act which specifically requires the sheriff to give the patient opportunity to be heard in an appeal to him (section 113(1)) would have been an unnecessary provision if such appeals had been to the sheriff acting as a judge in litigation. In a litigation parties must be heard. The court rejected an argument that some appeals to the sheriff under the Act were to him in his judicial capacity.

The Inner House of the Court of Session did not consider whether the sheriff who heard the case had approached the question of transfer to the State Hospital correctly. (The court did not need to consider this as it said it was not possible to appeal.) The sheriff principal did, however, consider this (1987 SLT (Sh Ct) 76 at 80). He thought the sheriff was wrong to approach the matter by making a comparison between the treatment available at the State Hospital and other hospitals taken as a whole. Instead, if transfer to the State Hospital is to happen, there must be evidence from which the sheriff can infer that no other hospital in Scotland is a suitable alternative.

F v West Berkshire Health Authority [1989] 2 All ER 545, [1989] 2 WLR 1025, HL

A thirty-six year old mentally handicapped woman had been a voluntary patient since she was fourteen. Over the years she had made considerable progress, but her verbal capacity was that of a child of two and her general mental capacity of a child of four to five. She had on her own initiative formed a happy sexual relationship with another patient in the hospital. The evidence was that she would not be able to cope with pregnancy or looking after a child, and that 'from a psychiatric point of view it would be disastrous for her' to have a baby. At the same time there would be serious problems in her using ordinary methods of contraception. The doctors and her mother considered it would be right for her to undergo a sterilisation operation and her mother raised a court action for this to be permitted. The Official Solicitor (a lawyer who puts an independent view) and the Mental Health Act Commission (the equivalent of the Mental Welfare Commission for Scotland) took part in the case as well.

The House of Lords held that the question to be considered was whether the operation was in the best interests of the patient. To decide this question a court should consider whether a doctor acting in accordance with with the approach of a responsible body of medical opinion in the field would think it so. One judge (Lord Goff) however, noted that the decision could involve more than a purely medical opinion and there would then be involvement of an inter-disciplinary team in considering it, and also that the court had finally to make the decision. The correct practice was to go to court and get an order (called a 'declaration') stating that it is 'in the existing circumstances in the patient's best interests' and 'can lawfully be performed ... despite her inability to consent'. The order also provided for the matter to come back to court if there was an important change in the circumstances before the operation. The judges considered that operations such as sterilisation, which are not designed to cure or improve some condition, were different from operations that were. These (so long as they are in the best interests of the patient) could go ahead without coming to a court.

R v Mental Health Act Commission, ex p W, (1988) Times 27 May; (1988) Independent 27 May. (This summary has been prepared from the Lexis (computerised legal database) transcript of the judgment)

A twenty-seven year old male patient wished to be treated with a drug called Goserelin. He was a compulsive paedophile. The English equivalent of the Mental Welfare Commission took the view that the treatment was one where under the legislation his consent on its own was not enough. There had to be a second opinion. The people it appointed to give a second opinion refused to certify that the treatment could take place.

Goserelin is a drug originally developed to reduce the male sex hormone, testosterone, to control cancer of the prostate. It reduces male sexual drive. Following scientific evidence the court described the drug as 'a hormone antagonist'. It works by affecting the way the pituitary gland is stimulated to produce a hormone that in turn stimulates the production of testosterone in the testes. The court described it as half turning the lock that opens up the action of the pituitary and then jamming it. The effect is that a hormone that normally opens the lock cannot do so. As Goserlin behaves in this way it is to a scientist quite different from a hormone, even though its chemical structure is similar. Technical scientific words in an Act of Parliament have to be interpreted technically. So this treatment was not 'hormone' treatment as meant in section 57 of the Mental Health Act 1983 and the associated Regulations (the equivalent of section 97 of the Mental Health (Scotland) Act 1984 and reg 3(1) of the Mental Health (Specified Treatments, Guardianship Duties etc) (Scotland) Regulations 1984). As a result the treatment could go ahead without a second opinion. This was held also to be the case because the way the drug is administered is by a syringe with a needle with a larger than normal bore. That is not 'surgical implantation' as meant in the legislation. On both points a contrast was made with another drug, Oestradiol, that is a hormone and is implanted into the skin by a surgical incision or using a trocar and cannula.

The court also considered whether the treatment was for mental disorder. Even, though sexual deviancy is expressly excluded in the legislation from what is covered by sexual disorder, there could be mental disorder that was linked with a sexual problem, treatment for which would be treatment for the mental disorder as well.

Finally the court emphasised that the three people signing the certificate relating to the patient's capacity to understand are dealing with *capacity* to understand the likely effects of the treatment and not possible side effects, however remote. For this to be the case it is not necessary for the patient to understand the precise physiological processes involved in the way the treatment works.

Skinner v Robertson 1980 SLT (Sh Ct) 43

A charge nurse was prosecuted for allegedly having assaulted a number of patients. He was working in a ward containing about twenty-four children and young people. One of the patients was highly excited, screaming and shouting. After trying to calm down the patient, the accused charge nurse had struck him on the face, with his hand, to control his behaviour in an emergency when the patient was attacking a child and pulling his hair. The patient was described by witnesses as being thought to be autistic, hyperactive, aggressive, difficult to control and with 'depraved habits'. He was quite capable of pulling out other children's hair. The accused charge nurse had also thrown water over another patient, aged twenty with a mental age of around seven. Witnesses described her as being similar to the male patient in behaviour, and liable to attack other patients without warning and to try and injure herself. On another occasion the charge nurse had struck a girl patient on the head with one of his knuckles. She was described by witnesses as tending to indulge in repetitive swearing, which affected the behaviour of other children in the ward. Finally, the nurse struck another child patient in this way. On each occasion the intention was to control the patient, not to punish. The sheriff considered that while there might be disagreement about the appropriateness of what the accused nurse did and even though his employers disapproved, he had acted with reasonable care and accordingly because of the terms of section 107 of the 1960 Act (now section 122 of the Act) he was not guilty of assault.

Appendix 4

Helpful addresses

SELF-HELP AND SUPPORT GROUPS

Age Concern Scotland Aims to improve services for older people and campaign on their behalf. There are over 200 local Age Concern groups in Scotland, and the group also provides information, counselling and welfare rights advice. If you want advice or want to be put in touch with your local group, contact them at 54A Fountainbridge, Edinburgh EH3 9PT (031-228 5656).

Alzheimers Scotland Aims to promote better care and to increase public awareness of the disease. It offers advice, counselling, and information to those caring for sufferers and funds research. The Edinburgh branch is at 33 Castle Street, Edinburgh EH2 3DN. For emergency counselling telephone 01-220 6155.

CMH—The Campaign for People with Mental Handicaps A campaigning group working to ensure that people with mental handicaps enjoy the same patterns and conditions of life as everyone else. Write to them at CMH Freepost 27, London W1E 5YZ. (No stamp required).

Manic Depression Fellowship A support system available for all sufferers with manic depression, their families and friends. Contact the Scottish Association for Mental Health (see below) for details of self-help groups in Aberdeen, Dundee, Edinburgh, East Lothian, Glasgow, Inverness, Hamilton and Perth.

Mental Health Foundation Scotland It funds research into the causes of mental handicap and into all forms of mental illness and supports many organisations which provide counselling and support. It can also offer help to carers. Write to it at Freepost, 24 George Square, Glasgow G2 1BR, (No stamp required). (041-221 2092).

National Association for the Welfare of Children in Hospital A voluntary body which campaigns for increased visiting rights for children in hospital, the provision of playleaders etc. They have a telephone helpline on 031-553 6553 or write to them at 15 Smiths Place, Edinburgh EH6 8HT.

National Schizophrenia Fellowship (Scotland) Advice and information for sufferers and their families. Contact them at 40 Shandwick Place, Edinburgh EH2 4RT (031-226 2025).

Nucleus Offers emotional support to parents who have recently learnt that their child has a mental handicap. 18 London Road, Edinburgh EH7 5AT (031-652 1480).

Samaritans Offer confidential support and friendship to the suicidal and the despairing. In the phone book or phone Directory Enquiries (192) for their number.

Scottish Action on Dementia Campaigns for better services for dementia sufferers and their carers in Scotland. All inquiries to Jan Killeen, Co-Ordinator, 33 Castle Street, Edinburgh EH2 3DN (031-220 4886).

Scottish Association for Mental Health An independent voluntary organisation concerned with all aspects of mental illness and mental health in Scotland. Atlantic House, 38 Gardner's Crescent, Edinburgh EH3 8DQ (031-229 9687 or 031-228 5185). They have details of LOCAL MENTAL HEALTH ASSOCIATIONS throughout Scotland.

Scottish Council on Disability A national voluntary organisation for all Scotland's disabled people. It has a comprehensive library and information department. It provides opportunities in the arts for disabled people and campaigns on access and mobility. 5 Shandwick Place, Edinburgh EH2 4RG (031-229 8632).

Scottish Down's Syndrome Association It offers a wide range of information about Down's Syndrome and provides an opportunity to meet other parents. It has many local groups throughout Scotland and produces an excellent informative and entertaining newsletter. Contact it at 54 Shandwick Place, Edinburgh EH2 4RT (031-226 2420).

Scottish Society for Autistic Children The Society runs a school for autistic and non-communicating children, and a residential community for older people. It aims to open further units for the over sixteens as funds become available. Contact them at Room 2, 2nd Floor, 12 Picardy Place, Edinburgh EH1 3JT (031-557 0474).

Scottish Society for the Mentally Handicapped The Society was formed in 1954 to campaign for and provide better care for mentally handicapped people. There are now 79 branches throughout Scotland working to provide social and recreational facilities, day-care, work centres etc. It campaigns at all levels for better care, education and employment for mentally handicapped people. It now has a legal adviser who can assist families and Solicitors with problems which may arise. Contact them at 13 Elmbank Street, Glasgow G2 4QA (041-226 4541).

Scottish Users' Network A network of users and ex-users of mental health services throughout Scotland, which aims to give Scottish users a more effective voice. For details, contact the Co-Secretary, Vincent Donnelly, at the Glasgow Association for Mental Health, 58 Fox Street, Glasgow G1 4AU (041-204 2270).

Sense-in-Scotland Formerly the National Deaf-Blind and Rubella Association. This organisation works on behalf of children and young people who suffered early impairment of both sight and hearing, whatever the cause. Such children can sometimes be diagnosed as mentally handicapped. The organisation can offer advice and assistance on a variety of matters, and inquiries are welcome from anyone. Contact Gillian Morbey or Joyce Wilson at 168 Dumbarton Road, Glasgow G11 6XE (041-334 9666/9675) (24 hour answering service).

Survivors Speak Out A group which urges medical practitioners and others to pay more attention to the opinions of those who have been in psychiatric hospitals. Write to the Secretary, Peter Campbell, 33 Litchfield Road, Cricklewood, London NW2.

We Are Seeking Progress Self-help group for people suffering from phobias. Contact them c/o 10 Silverknowes Bank, Edinburgh EH4 5PB (031-336 3478). Or contact **Action on Phobias (Scotland)**, 2 Welbrae Drive, Strathaven ML10 6JR.

ORGANISATIONS CONCERNED WITH PATIENTS' RIGHTS

Campaign Against Psychiatric Oppression c/o Frank Bangay, 28A Edgar House, Kingsmead Estate, Homerton Road, London E9.

The Campaign for Freedom of Information Campaigns for greater access to 'official' information, such as medical records. 3 Endsleigh Street, London WC1H 0DD (01-278 9686).

Health Service Commissioner for Scotland (Ombudsman) Can investigate complaints about services provided by health boards. For further details of their powers, contact them at Second Floor, 11 Melville Crescent, Edinburgh, EH3 7LU (031-225 7465).

Helpful addresses

Mental Welfare Commission for Scotland (See chapter 6.) 25 Drumsheugh Gardens, Edinburgh EH3 7RB (031-225 7034).

The Patients' Association Unfortunately the Scottish branch of the Patients' Association has ceased to exist, but you can write to them in London at 18 Charing Cross Road, London WC2H 0HR (01-240 0671).

Scottish Council for Civil Liberties Concerned with all aspects of the freedom of the individual, 146 Holland Street, Glasgow G2 4NG (041-332 5960).

ADVICE GIVING AGENCIES

The Law Society of Scotland (See chapter 7.) 26/28 Drumsheugh Gardens, Edinburgh EH3 7YR (031-226 7411).

Scottish Legal Aid Board (See chapter 7.) 44 Drumsheugh Gardens, Edinburgh EH3 7SW (031-226 7061).

Citizens Advice Bureaux See local telephone directory.

WELFARE RIGHTS GROUPS

Many of the groups listed above will be able to give advice on welfare benefits. The organisations listed below specialise in giving welfare rights information.

Child Poverty Action Group Campaigns to reduce poverty in our society. Gives welfare rights organisations (not individuals) comprehensive advice through its Citizens' Rights Office and produces excellent welfare rights books (see booklist.) 1–5 Bath Street, London EC1V 9QA (01-253 3406).

Disability Alliance Produces the excellent, comprehensive Disability Rights Handbook, which is a must for all who are involved with disabled people. 25 Denmark Street, London WC2H 8NJ (01-240 0806).

Disablement Income Group (Scotland) A charity which campaigns for a national disability income for all disabled people. It provides a comprehensive welfare benefits advice service. Contact it at ECAS House, 28–30 Howden Street, Edinburgh EH8 9HW (031-667 0249 or 031-668 3577).

Disablement Information and Advice Line (DIAL) An information and advice service on all aspects of disability. Lammermuir House, Owen Square, Almondvale, Livingston EH4 6PW (LIVINGSTON 414472).

HOUSING ASSOCIATIONS

Ark Housing Association Provides housing for mentally handicapped people in the East of Scotland. 8 Balcarres Street, Edinburgh EH10 5JB (031-447 9027).

Key Housing Association Provides a wide range of accommodation for mentally handicapped people in the West of Scotland. Housing can be offered to people with a wide range of abilities. 1 James Watt Street, Glasgow G2 8NF (041-226 4868).

Penumbra Provides permanent supported housing to people with long-standing mental health problems. It currently has housing throughout the Lothians, but has plants to expand. 13 Queen Street, Edinburgh EH2 1JE (031-226 3676).

Supported Accommodation for People who are or have been suffering from mental illness and for people with a mental handicap For comprehensive lists, contact the Scottish Association for Mental Health and the Scottish Society for the Mentally Handicapped (see above).

Appendix 5

Further reading

This does not aim to be a comprehensive booklist, but instead to list books which the authors found useful and interesting. Suggestions for further reading can be obtained from many of the voluntary organisations listed above and a very useful catalogue/reading list is available from **MIND (The National Association for Mental Health)** at 4th Floor, 24–32 Stephenson Way, London NW1 2HD. (Please enclose a SAE).

Many of the best books are free, or inexpensive, and available from the self-help groups listed above. These will be indicated below.

MENTAL HANDICAP

Information for Parents The **Scottish Down's Syndrome Association** has prepared this extremely helpful and supportive free booklet. It was compiled by parent members of the Association and is intended to help parents in the early days after the birth of their babies and to serve as an introduction to Down's Syndrome.

MENTAL HEALTH

Coping with a Confused Elderly Person at Home One of a series of detailed and very practical free leaflets produced by the **Alzheimer's Disease Society**. It also contains suggestions for further reading.

Dementia in Scotland: Guardianship published by **Scottish Action on Dementia**. They also have a very helpful guide to practical, financial and legal matters; available free to carers.

Depression Jack Dominian. A sensitive and compassionate guide. Fontana paperback.

Depression: The Way Out of Your Prison Dorothy Rowe Published by Routledge. This book combine practical ideas with deep philosophical insights in a very challenging way. See also **Beyond Fear**, a Fontana paperback by the same author.

Talking To Your Doctor by Carol Faulder and published by Virago. Addressed mainly to women.

Talking About . . . A series of very sensible and informative booklets available free from the **Scottish Health Education Group**, Woodburn House, Canaan Lane, Edinburgh EH10 4SG (031-447 8044). The booklets cover Depression, Agoraphobia, Schizophrenia, Anorexia Nervosa and Dementia. They each contain suggestions for further reading. See also **Dementia: A Handbook for Carers** also available free to carers in Scotland.

Improving Residential Life for Disabled People Keith Tully (1986). Published by Churchill Livingstone. An informative self-help handbook.

Talking to a Stranger: A Consumer Guide to Therapy Lindsay Knight. Published by Fontana. Recommended as book of the year by MIND.

Understanding and Helping the Schizophrenic Sylvano Arieti. A Penguin book recommended by the Scottish Association for Mental Health.

RIGHTS GUIDES

Directory of Services for People with a Mental Handicap in Lothian An extremely helpful guide available free from the social work department, Shrubhill House, Leith Walk, Edinburgh EH7 4PD (031-554 4301). Ask your social work department if it has a similar guide.

Disability Rights Handbook This guide is published each year by the **Disability Alliance** and contains essential information on welfare rights, disability benefits, mobility allowances and educational allowances.

National Welfare Benefits Handbook This **Child Poverty Action Group** guide is probably the most widely used guide to supplementary and housing benefits. Available from them each May.

Rights Guide to Non-means-tested Social Security Benefits The essential guide to unemployment, sickness and disability benefits, it also covers industrial injuries and benefits for children. Available from the **Child Poverty Action Group** each May.

Your Rights An inexpensive and helpful rights guide for the elderly, published each April by **Age Concern**.

POLICY ISSUES

Annual Reports of the Mental Welfare Commission for 1984, 1985, 1986 and 1987. For a realistic and unbiased account of the workings of the Act. Available from HMSO.

The Balance of Care for Adults with a Mental Handicap in Scotland by Nikki Baker and James Urquhart (Jan 1987). For the first time ever, a comprehensive study of adults with a mental handicap in Scotland. The study covered almost all the 12,500 mentally handicapped people aged over sixteen. Amongst its conclusions is a suggestion that over 90 per cent. of hospital residents could be accommodated elsewhere, if resources were available. Available from ISD Publications, Trinity Park House, Edinburgh EH5 3SQ.

Community Care: Agenda for Action (the Griffiths Report) 1988 Now apparently accepted by the Government, it cannot be ignored in Scotland although it deals only with England and Wales. Available from HMSO.

Creating Community Mental Health Services in Scotland Edited by Nancy Drucker. A major book, the first of its kind anywhere, showing how a more balanced and imaginative range of mental health services could be, and is being, created in Scotland. Invaluable to anyone involved in planning or offering services. It is published in two volumes. Volume 1 looks at policy issues and volume 2 at community services in practice. Published by the **Scottish Association for Mental Health**, from whom it can be ordered. It can also be consulted in their offices under their 'Open Access to Information' policy.

Disability: Whose Handicap? by Ann Shearer, published by Blackwell. Looks at how society deals with disability.

Mental Health in Focus A report on mental health services for adults in Scotland. Published by the Scottish Home and Health Department and the Scottish Education

Department in 1985, it attempts to set priorities. Available from HMSO. Criticised by H M Drucker in **Lost in the haar: a critique of Mental Health in Focus**, in the Scottish Government Yearbook, 1986. University of Edinburgh.

Mental Hospitals in Focus An examination of the present and future role of mental hospitals in the management of adult mentally ill people in Scotland. Prepared by the Scottish Health Service Planning Council and published in 1989 by HMSO.

Report of the Working Party on Incapax Patients' Funds (1985) Published by the **Scottish Home and Health Department**, this report looks at how the property of people in hospital who are unable to manage their own affairs is managed and makes many practical suggestions for reforms. Available from HMSO.

The Right to be Ordinary Jackie Gulstad (1987). Attacks the Scottish Home and Health Department and local agencies for failing to develop adequate community care services for mentally handicapped and mentally ill people. Published by the **Glasgow Special Housing Group** and available from them at 13 Elmbank Street, Glasgow G2 4DA (041-221 9704).

The Sixth Sense Case studies on the realities of life in the community for people with mental health problems. By Sally Dick on behalf of the **Scottish Mental Health Forum** (an alliance of voluntary organisations active in the mental health field in Scotland). Available from the Scottish Association for Mental Health.

SHARPEN: Scottish Health Authorities' Review of Priorities for the Eighties and Nineties This review, yet to be published, will be available from HMSO. It lists as its priorities: *firstly*, services for old people with dementia, in hospital or in the community, and *secondly*, care in the community, with particular reference to elderly people, people with a mental handicap and mentally ill people. Many workers in these fields wonder when resources will be transferred to these priority areas.

Workshop on the Rights of the Elderly with Mental Disorder Edinburgh 19–20 November 1987. The papers contain much useful information on the background, the law and proposals for reform. To be published by the World Health Organisation.

THE LAW

In The Act A very short guide to the contents of the Mental Health (Scotland) Act published by the **Scottish Association for Mental Health**.

Mental Health (Scotland) Act 1984, Notes on the Act Published by the **Scottish Home and Health Department** and available from them free at Trinity Park House, South Trinity Road, Edinburgh EH5 3SQ.

Scots Law and the Mentally Handicapped by Adrian D Ward, published by the **Scottish Society for the Mentally Handicapped** and available from them by post. An essential guide for anyone involved in the care of a mentally handicapped person. In particular, there are very useful chapters on educational rights and on making financial provision for mentally handicapped children and adults, which we have not been able to cover in this book. A companion volume which looks in more detail at guardianship and the curatory system will be available shortly.

The Law and Vulnerable Elderly People Although this book covers only the situation in England and Wales, not Scotland, the problems it deals with and the proposed solutions are of great relevance to all concerned with the protection of the interests and the management of the property of confused elderly people. Published by **Age Concern** and available from them at 60 Pitcairn Road, Mitcham, Surrey CR4 3LL (01-640 5431).

Further reading

Family Law in Scotland J M Thomson, published by Butterworths/Law Society of Scotland. Although not specifically about mental health it covers much relevant law.

THE LEGISLATION

Below we list the main statutes and statutory instruments (rules made in connection with the statutes) referred to in this book. These may be bought from HMSO or may be consulted in main reference libraries or at the offices of some of the voluntary groups listed elsewhere.

Mental Health (Scotland) Act 1984

Mental Health (State Hospital Management Committee, State Hospital, Carstairs) (Scotland) Order 1984, SI 1984/389

Mental Health (State Hospital Management Committee etc: Membership and Procedure) (Scotland) Regulations 1984, SI 1984/294

Mental Health (Specified Treatments, Guardianship Duties etc) (Scotland) Regulations 1984, SI 1984/1494

Mental Health (Prescribed Forms) (Scotland) Regulations 1984, SI 1984/1495

Mental Health (Prescription of Class of Nurses) (Scotland) Order 1984, SI 1984/1095

Act of Sederunt (Mental Health (Scotland) Act 1984) 1986, SI 1986/545

Housing (Scotland) Act 1987

Social Work (Scotland) Act 1968

Chronically Sick and Disabled Persons Act 1970 (as amended by the Chronically Sick and Disabled Persons (Scotland) Act 1972

Disabled Persons (Services, Consultation and Representation) Act 1986 (Sections 9–12, 14 & 16–18 in effect at 30 September 1988)

National Assistance Act 1948

Criminal Procedure (Scotland) Act 1975 (amended by the Criminal Justice (Scotland) Act, 1980)

SCOTTISH OFFICE CIRCULARS

NHS 1989 (GEN) 23   Powers of Health Boards in relation to property of patients

SW3/1986   Mental health officers: Appointed day.

SW9/1986   Mental health officers: Directions by the Secretary of State.

Scottish Office circulars are available free from the Central Distribution office of the Scottish Office, Room 14, St. Andrew's House, Edinburgh EH1. (Telephone 031-556 8400 ext. 2626 or 2623).

Table of Statutes

	PAGE
Abolition of Domestic Rates Etc (Scotland) Act 1987 (c 47)	
s 16	57
Sch 1A, para 4(1)(b), (c)	58
(2), (3)	58
8	57
(1)	57
9	58
Access to Medical Reports Act 1988 (c 28)	112
Access to Personal Files Act 1987 (c 37)	112
Adoption (Scotland) Act 1978 (c 28)	70
Air Force Act 1955 (c 19)	
s 116	158
Army Act 1955 (c 18)	
s 116	158
Child Care Act 1980 (c 5)	
s 3	127, 150
10	127, 150
Children and Young Persons (Scotland) Act 1937 (c 37)	
s 12	73
(7)	73
Chronically Sick and Disabled Persons Act 1970 (c 44)	4, 59, 63
s 1	59
2	60
17(1)	68
Chronically Sick and Disabled Persons (Scotland) Act 1972 (c 51)	59, 60
County Courts Act 1984 (c 28)	
s 12	164
Courts-Martial (Appeals) Act 1968 (c 20)	
s 16	158
Criminal Justice Act 1982 (c 48)	
s 74(2)	184
75	184
Criminal Justice (Scotland) Act 1980 (c 62)	
s 80(6)	176
Criminal Procedure (Scotland) Act 1975 (c 21)	81, 82, 184
s 4(2)	82
25	82, 94
(3)	82
174	159, 167, 184, 185
(1)	95
(2)	96

	PAGE
Criminal Procedure (Scotland) Act 1975—contd	
s 174(3)	95, 96, 157, 158
(4)	95, 157
(5)	95
174A	97, 160, 185
(1), (4)	97
(6)	97
(b)	97
(9)	97
175	98, 103, 153, 160, 183, 184, 185, 193
(1)	98
(b)	99
(3), (4)	99
(7)	160
176	103, 185
(3)	98
(4)	99
177	172
178	154, 159, 160, 184, 185
(1)	98, 99
(2)	99
(3)	153, 154, 162
180	82
(1)	97, 98
(2)	98
183	160
184	160, 185
(1)	103
(2)(a), (b)	103
(c)	104
(3), (5)	104
186(1), (2), (4)	104
255	159
280	97, 185
330	82, 94
(3)	82
375	184
(2), (4)	95
375A	97, 160, 185
(1), (5)	97
(6)(a)	97
(10)	97
376	98, 103, 153, 160, 183, 184, 185, 193
(1)	98
(b)	99
(4), (5)	95

231

Criminal Procedure (Scotland) Act 1975—contd	
s 376(6), (7)	99
(10)	160
377	103, 185
(3)	98
(4)	99
378	172
379	154, 159, 160, 184, 185
(1)	98, 99
(2)	99
(3)	153, 154, 162
381	82
(1)	97, 98
(a)	97
(2)	98
(4)(a)	82
384	160
385	160, 185
(1)	103
(2)(a), (b)	103
(c)	104
(3), (5)	104
387(1), (2), (4)	104
443	185
462	185
Sch 5, para 4(b)	185
Data Protection Act 1984 (c 35)	
s 21	112
Disabled Persons (Employment) Act 1944 (c 10)	50
Disabled Persons (Employment) Act 1958 (c 33)	50
Disabled Persons (Services, Consultation and Representation) Act 1986 (c 33)	59
s 4	60
9	59
12	58
Divorce (Scotland) Act 1976 (c 39)	
s 1(2)(b), (e)	46
Education (Scotland) Act 1980 (c 44)	
s 1	60, 127
Employment Protection (Consolidation) Act 1978 (c 44)	
Sch 5, para 5	185
Enduring Powers of Attorney Act 1985 (c 29)	48
Family Law (Scotland) Act 1985 (c 37)	46
Friendly Societies Act 1974 (c 46)	
Sch 5	171
Health Services Act 1976 (c 83)	
s 12(1)	128
Housing (Scotland) Act 1987 (c 26)	
s 1(4)	62
19(2)	65
20(1)(b)	65
25(1)(c)	65
29(2)	65

Housing (Scotland) Act 1987—contd	
s 31(2), (3)	65
34	65
38	62
52	65
Immigration Act 1971 (c 77)	159, 161
s 2(1)(b)	167
Industrial Assurance and Friendly Societies Act 1948 (c 39)	
Sch 1	171
Interpretation Act 1978 (c 30)	
s 15–17	185
Sch 1	184
Larceny (Guernsey) Law 1958	
s 43	167
Law Reform (Miscellaneous Provisions) (Scotland) Act 1980 (c 55)	
s 8	50
Law Reform (Miscellaneous Provisions) (Scotland) Act 1985 (c 73)	
s 51	21, 36, 132, 144
Law Reform (Parent and Child) (Scotland) Act 1986 (c 9)	
s 3(1)	78, 79
Local Government Finance Act 1988 (c 41)	
Sch 12	57
para 25	57
Local Government (Scotland) Act 1973 (c 65)	
s 64(4)	126
(5)	185
(bb)	126
210(2)–(9)	183
235	179
Marriage (Scotland) Act 1977 (c 15)	
s 5(4)	46
Mental Health Act 1959 (c 72)	
ss 29, 52, 53	164
Pt VI (ss 81–96)	169
Mental Health Act 1983 (c 20)	3, 73, 127, 167
s 1(2)	3
Pt II (ss 2–34)	163, 164
ss 26–28	164
s 26	164
29	164
30	164
35, 36	82
56	82
57	221
Pt VI (ss 80–92)	168, 169
s 80	185, 193
(2)	157
88	180, 181
139	183
Sch 2	185

Table of Statutes

	PAGE
Mental Health (Amendment) (Scotland) Act 1983 (c 39)	5, 7, 185
s 5	190
7(2)	185
8(1), (2), (3b), (3c), 9	190
12	191
16(a)–(d)	191
19	191
34	97
36(2)	104
Sch 2	190, 191
para 1	185
Sch 3	191
Mental Health (Scotland) Act 1960 (c 61)	5, 7, 32, 185, 190, 219
s 15(2)	185
107	74, 222
Sch 4	185
Mental Health (Scotland) Act 1984 (c 36)	1, 7, 30, 32, 60, 104, 117–192, 193, 194
s 1	122
(2)	2, 3, 19
(3)	3
2	122
(2)	107
3	123
(2)(a)	109
(b), (c)	110
(d)	43, 109
(iii)	108
(e), (f)	109
(3)	101, 105, 108
(5), (6), (8), (9)	109
ss 4–7	125
s 8	126
(1), (2)	60
9	13, 126
10	16, 127
11	127
(1), (2)	61
ss 12–16	6
s 12	127
13, 14	128
ss 15–17	129
s 17(1)	19, 45
(a)	19
(i)	3, 19, 218
(b)	19
(2)	5
18	44, 81, 107, 130, 196, 197, 198, 214
19	130
(2)	21
(3), (4)	17
(5)	21
(a), (b)	17
(6)	17
20	19, 131
(1)(a)	19
(b)	11, 19

	PAGE
Mental Health (Scotland) Act 1984—contd	
s 20(1)(c), (d)	19
(2)(a), (b), (c)	19
21	132
(1)	21
(2)(a)	21
(b)	17
(c)	21
(3), (4)	21
22	132
(1)	23
(2)(a), (b)	23
(4)(a)	24
(b)	24, 45
(c)	24
23	23, 133
(1), (2)	23
24	9, 134
(2)–(6)	9
25	134
(1)	9
(2)	12
(a), (b)	12
(3)	12
(5), (6)	12
26	11, 107, 135, 219
(1)	11
(a), (b)	11
(2)(a)	11
(i), (ii)	11
(b), (c)	11
(3)	11
(4)	11
(a), (b), (c)	11
(5)–(7)	11
27	136, 218
(1)	27
(2), (4)	28
(5)	27, 45
28	137
(1), (3)	28
29	137
(1)	28
(a)–(c)	28
(4)	105, 220
30	138, 200
(1)	23
(2)	27
(b)	25
(3)	24, 45
(4)	25
(6)	26
31	107, 139
32	139
33	140
(3)	108
(a), (b)	27
(4)	26, 45, 218
(a)	218
(6)	27

Mental Health (Scotland) Act 1984—
contd
- s 34 140
  - (1), (a), (b) 27
  - (2), (3) 27
- 35 141
  - (3), (4) 26
- 36 . . . . 33, 141
- 37 . . . . 141, 207, 208, 209, 210
  - (1) 33, 34
  - (2) 34
  - (3)(a) 35
    - (b) 35
      - (ii) 35
- 38 142
  - (1), (3), (4) 36
  - (5)(b) 36
- 39 . . . . 35, 143
- 40 143
  - (1) 36
  - (2)–(4) 37
- 41 144
  - (1) 37
  - (2) 37, 39, 40
    - (b), (c) 45
  - (3) 40
  - (4) 40, 73
- 42 144
- 43 . . . . 39, 145
- 44 145
- 45 145
  - (1) 40, 41
  - (2) 41
- 46 146
  - (1), (2) 41
- 47 . . . . 146, 211, 212
  - (1), (2) 37
  - (3)(a), (b) 38
  - (4), (5) 38
  - (6) 38, 43
- 48–50 147
- 50(2) 43
  - (3) 43, 108
  - (4)–(7) 43
- 51 . . . . 43, 148
  - (1) 43
    - (a)–(c) 43
  - (2) 43
- 52 149
- ss 53–55 16
- s 53 149
  - (3)–(6) 16
- 54 . . . . 16, 150
- 55 . . . . 16, 150
- 56 . . . . 16, 151
  - (1)–(3) 16
- 57 . . . . 16, 151
  - (1)–(4) 16
- 58 152
- 59 152

Mental Health (Scotland) Act 1984—
contd
- s 54(1)(a) 23
  - (b) 40
- Pt VI (ss 60–76) 82
- ss 60, 61 153
- s 62 154
  - (2) 99
- 63 . . . . 102, 154, 157
  - (2) 100
    - (a), (b) 100
- 64 . . . . 99, 100, 155, 157
  - (4)(a), (b) 100
  - (5) 100
- 65 . . . . 102, 155, 157
- 66 . . . . 156, 157
  - (1)–(3) 100
- 67, 68 157
- 69, 70 158
- 70(1) 102
  - (3) 102
- 71 . . . . 102, 159
  - (1) 102
  - (5) 102
- 72 . . . . 102, 159
- 73 159
  - (1)–(3) 102
- 74 . . . . 160, 201, 202
  - (1) 103
  - (2)(c) 103
  - (3)–(6) 102
- 75 161
- 76 162
- 77–89 31
- 77, 78 163
- 79, 80 164
- 81 165
- 82–84 167
- 85–87 168
- 88 . . . . 168, 203, 213
- 89, 90 169
- 90(1) 105
- 91 169
- 92 170
  - (1) 49, 90
    - (b) 49
- 93 . . . . 109, 170
- 94 170
  - (1) 89
  - (2), (3) 90
  - (6) 89
- 95 171
- 96–103 77
- Pt X (ss 96–103) 81
- s 96 . . . . 45, 81, 172
  - (1)(a)–(c) 81
- 97 . . . . 172, 204, 221
  - (1)(a), (b) 83
  - (2) 84
    - (a), (b) 84
  - (3), (4) 84
  - (5)(a), (b) 84

Mental Health (Scotland) Act 1984— *contd*	**Mental Health (Scotland) Act 1984—** *contd*
s 98 . . . . 86, 173, 205, 206	s 126 185
(1)(a), (b) 85	127 185
(3)(a), (b) 85	(1) 94, 99
(4), (5) 85	128 185
99 173	129, 130 186
(1)(a), (b) 84, 85	Sch 1 186
(2) 84, 85	2 187
100 174	3, para 24 94
101 174	28 99
(1) 84	31 94
102 174	Sch 4 190
(1)(a)–(d) 86	5 192
(2) 84, 85	National Assistance Act 1948 (c 29) . . . 4, 30
(3), (4) 86	s 47 30
103 . . . . 75, 86, 174	(4), (6) 30
104 . . . . 76, 175	48 170
105 . . . . 73, 76, 175	49 . . . . 48, 90
(1)(a), (b) 76	National Assistance (Amendment) Act 1951 (c 57)
106 . . . . 4, 75, 175	s 1 30
(1)(c) 76	National Health Service (Scotland) Act 1978 (c 29) 178, 183
(2) 76	s 1 90
(6) 76	7 179
107 . . . . 75, 176	36 90
(1)(a), (b) 76	45 127
(2) 76	ss 57, 58 . . . . 131, 199
108 . . . . 76, 176	77, 78 187
(1)(b) 76	s 79(1) 170
109 . . . . 76, 177	85(1), (2A), (4), (6) 123, 187
110 . . . . 38, 177	85A(1), (3) 123, 187
(1) 26, 67	86 . . . . 123, 187
(a)–(c) 67	108(1) 183
(3), (4) 67	Naval Discipline Act 1957 (c 53)
111 178	s 63 158
112 . . . . 19, 34, 178	Northern Ireland Act 1974 (c 28) 151
113 . . . . 21, 37, 178	Nursing Homes Registration (Scotland) Act 1938 (c 73)
(1) 220	s 10 185
(2) 22	Post Office Act 1953 (c 36) 72, 179
114 . . . . 91, 178	s 87(1) 72
115 178	Prisons (Scotland) Act 1952 (c 61) 159
(1) 72	s 37 161
(a) 72	Representation of the People Act 1983 (c 2)
(b)(i), (ii) 72	s 1(1)(b)(i) 92
(2)–(6), (9) 72	2(1)(b)(i) 92
116 180	7 92
(1) 72	(4) 91
(a), (b) 72	(d)(iv) 92
(2) 72	(6), (9) 92
117 180	19(1) 92
(1), (2), (4) 29	Sexual Offences (Scotland) Act 1976 (c 67)
(7)(b) 29	s 18 176
118 181	Social Work (Scotland) Act 1968 (c 49) 176
(1), (3) 30	s 12 . . . . 59, 62
119 . . . . 6, 74, 181	15(1)(a), (b) 69
120 . . . . 76, 182	
121 . . . . 28, 182	
122 . . . . 22, 183, 222	
(1) 73, 74	
ss 123, 124 183	
s 125 . . . . 19, 75, 183	
(5) 82	

Social Work (Scotland) Act 1968—
 contd
  s 16 80
    (1) 69
    (2)(b), (c) 69
    (5), (7) 70
  17 .... 127, 150

Social Work (Scotland) Act 1968—
 contd
  s 37 69
  59 .... 59, 62
  68 62
Trusts (Scotland) Act 1961 (c 57)
  s 2 50

Table of Orders, Rules and Regulations

	PAGE
Act of Sederunt (Mental Health (Scotland) Act 1984) 1986, SI 1986/545 .... 37, 132, 144, 178	
para 2(2) 21	
4(2) 22	
5(1) 22	
(2) 22	
Act of Sederunt (Rules of Court Amendment No 2) (Judicial Review) 1985, SI 1985/500 22	
Data Protection (Subject Access Modification) (Health) Regulations 1987, SI 1987/1903 112	
Data Protection (Subject Access Modification) (Social Work) Regulations 1987, SI 1987/1904 112	
Mental Health (Hospital, Guardianship and Consent to Treatment) Regulations 1983, SI 1983/893 40	
Mental Health (Northern Ireland Consequential Amendments) Order 1986, SI 1986/596	
art 3(2) 165	
(3)–(5) 165	
(6)–(12) 166	
(13), (14) 168	
(15) 171	
(16), (17) 172	
Mental Health (Northern Ireland) Order 1986, SI 1986/595 .... 165, 166, 167, 168, 171	
art 4 166	
12(1) 165, 166	
13 166	
29 168	
31 168	
arts 42, 43, 45 165	
art 53(5) 166	
97(2) 171	
132 168	
Mental Health (Prescribed Forms) (Scotland) Regulations 1984, SI 1984/1495 .... 130, 139, 142, 147, 152, 161, 169, 172, 173, 195–216	
Form 1 196	

	PAGE
Mental Health (Prescribed Forms) (Scotland) Regulations 1984—*contd*	
Form 2 197	
3 198	
4 200	
5 201	
6 202	
7 203	
8 204	
9 205	
10 206	
11 207	
12 208	
13 209	
14 210	
15 211	
16 212	
17 213	
Mental Health (Prescription of Class of Nurses) (Scotland) Order 1984, SI 1984/1095 .... 12, 135	
Mental Health (Scotland) Act 1984 (Appointed Day) Order 1986, SI 1986/374 127	
Mental Health (Specified Treatments, Guardianship Duties etc) (Scotland) Regulations 1984, SI 1984/1494 .... 145, 152, 173, 193–194	
reg 3(1) 83, 221	
(2) 85	
4 .... 39, 40	
5 41	
6(1) 41	
(2) 41	
7(a)–(e) 40	
National Health Service (General Medical and Pharmaceutical Services) (Scotland) Amendment (No 2) Regulations 1988, SI 1988/1454 58	
Personal Community Charge (Exemption for the Severely Mentally Impaired) (Scotland) Regulations 1989, SI 1989/2234	
regs 3, 4, 6 58	

Personal Community Charge (Exemptions) (Scotland) Regulations 1989, SI 1989/63
   reg 4, Sch 1 58

Social Security (Claims and Payments) Regulations 1987, SI 1987/1968
   reg 33(1), (3) 48

Table of Cases

AB v Mrs M 1987 SCLR 389 ... 80
AB and CB v E 1987 SCLR 419 ... 26, 45, 140, 141, 218
AR v Secretary of State for Scotland (unreported) 29 February 1988 ... 25, 218
Advocate (HM) v Kidd 1961 JC 61 ... 95
Advocate (HM) v Savage 1923 JC 49 ... 97
B, Re [1988] AC 199, [1987] 2 All ER 206, HL ... 80, 219
B v F 1987 SLT 681 ... 11, 22
B v Forsey 1988 SLT 572, HL ... 130, 134, 183, 219
Brennan v HM Advocate 1977 SLT 151 ... 95
Broadfoots Curator Bonis, Noter 1989 SLT 566, 1989 SCLR 317 ... 50
Campbell and Cosans v UK Judgments and Decisions of the European Court of Human Rights, Series A, Vol 48, 25 February 1982 ... 73
F v Management Committee and Managers, Ravenscraig Hospital 1989 SLT 49 ... 22, 105, 138, 220
F v West Berkshire Health Authority [1989] 2 All ER 545, [1989] 2 WLR 1025, HL ... 79, 80, 220
Ferns v Management Committee and Managers of Ravenscraig Hospital 1987 SLT (Sh Ct) 76 ... 105, 220
Fraser v Paterson 1987 SLT 562 ... 47
Gold v Harringey Health Authority [1987] 2 All ER 888 ... 79
Gray v Hawthorn 1961 JC 13 ... 73
McBride v Strathclyde Regional Council (unreported) 4 March 1983 ... 112
Mackenzie v Cluny Hill Hydropathic 1908 SC 200 ... 75
Norman v Smith 1983 SCCR 100 ... 73
Poutney v Griffiths [1976] AC 314, [1975] 2 All ER 881 ... 74
R v Hallstrom, ex parte W [1985] 3 All ER 775 ... 22
R v Hallstrom, ex parte W (No 2) [1986] 2 All ER 306 ... 82
R v Holmes [1979] Criminal Law Review 52 ... 73
R v Hudson [1966] 1 QB 448 ... 76
R v Mental Health Act Commission, ex parte W (1988) Times, 27 May ... 3, 84, 221
R v Oxford Mental Health Tribunal, ex parte Secretary of State for the Home Department [1986] 3 All ER 239 ... 67
Reid v Greater Glasgow Health Board 1976 SLT (Notes) 33 ... 87
Renfrew District Council v McGourlick 1987 SLT 538 ... 22
Retarded Children's Aid Society v Day [1978] 1 WLR 763 ... 73
Sidaway v Board of Governors of the Bethlem Royal Hospital and the Maudsley Hospital [1985] AC 871 ... 79, 80
Sivewright v Sivewright's Trustees 1920 SC (HL) 63 ... 51
Skinner v Robertson 1980 SLT (Sh Ct) 43 ... 74, 183, 221
Smith v M 1983 SCCR 67 (Sh Ct) ... 96
Stewart v Thain 1981 JC 13 ... 73
T v Secretary of State for Scotland 1987 SCLR 65 ... 22, 100, 138
T v T [1988] 1 All ER 613 ... 80
W v L [1974] QB 711 ... 3
Wilson v Chief Constable of Lothian and Borders Police Force 1989 SLT 97, OH ... 75, 88
X, Re (1987) Times, 4 June ... 80

Index

'Abnormally aggressive or seriously irresponsible conduct', 17
Abortion
  mentally handicapped woman, 77, 78–9
Absence
  leave of, 27, 136–7
  without leave, 28, 76, 137, 139
    assisting, 176–7
    guardianship, patient subject to, 145, 147, 194
    meaning, 152, 183
    Northern Ireland, hospitals in, 168
    return of patients, 167–8
    Scotland, hospitals in, 167
Accountant of Court
  oversees curator bonis, 49
Admission
  hospital, to *See* HOSPITAL
  statutory grounds for, 17–19, 24, 24*n*, 44, 98, 101, 218
Adoption
  child, of, 69
Advice and assistance scheme *See* LEGAL ADVICE AND ASSISTANCE
Aftercare services, 60
  local authority provision, 126
Alcohol
  alcohol dependency not sole ground for mental disorder, 2, 122
  loss of mental control, 95
Alien patients
  removal of, 167
Aliment
  children under eighteen, for, 45
All England Reports, 217
Alone and uncared for
  person suffering from mental disorder, 180
Alzheimer's disease
  Alzheimers Disease Society, 223
  community charge exemption, 57
Appeal
  community charge, 57
  compulsory detention, against, 21, 25, 30, 67
  emergency admission, against, 8
  examination, patient of, 141
  guardianship, 148–9
  records, inspection of, 141
  restriction direction, against, 101, 155–6

Appeal—*contd*
  restriction order, against, 94, 99–100, 154–55
  sheriff, to, 141
  short-term detention, against, 10, 11
  transfer from prison to hospital, against, 101
  transfer to State hospital, against, 104
Applicant for admission, 130
Application
  for admission, meaning, 183
  false statement in, 175
Ark Housing Association, 61, 225
Assault
  hospital staff, by, 221
Assistance
  representation, by way of, 116
Attendance allowance, 53–4, 90
Aunt, 149
Autism
  Scottish Society for Autistic Children, 224

Bail
  remand after conviction, 97
Bank accounts
  patients', 47, 87, 87*n*
Brain tissue
  operation to destroy tissue or functioning, 82, 172
Brother, 149

Capital
  disposable, 114
Care
  child taken into, 69, 150
  community, in, 32ff
  services, local authority provision, 6
Carstairs *See* STATE HOSPITAL
Case notes, 217–22
Channel Islands
  patients removed to Scotland, 167
Cheques
  patients', 87
Children
  abandoned, 69
  access to, following divorce, 45
  adoption, refusal of agreement to, 69
  adult psychiatric ward, detained in, 68
  aliment and lump sum payments to, 45
  children's hearing, 69
  consent to treatment, 77

241

Children—*contd*
  custody of, 45, 69
  hospitalised
    parents and guardians' rights and duties, 69
    welfare of, 68
  illegitimate, 13, 149
  legal care, taken into, 69
  local authority care, in, 69, 150
  lost, 69
  nearest relative, child as, 13, 149
  physical punishment of, 72, 73*n*
  relative, child as, 149
  removal from home to place of safety, 69
  social security payments, 55
  voluntarily placed in care, 69

Citizens Advice Bureaux, 225
  legal aid, advice on, 113

Civil law
  insanity, 4

Code of practice
  Secretary of State, preparation by, 6, 181

Community, care in, 5, 32–65
  community charge *See* COMMUNITY CHARGE
  compulsory admission procedure, subject to, 44
  compulsory medical treatment, 43–45
  education, training and aftercare, 58–61
  employment, 50
  financial and property matters, 46–58
  guardianship procedure, 45
  local authority duties, 58–61
  Mental Welfare Commission's responsibility, 106
  poll tax *See* COMMUNITY CHARGE
  power of attorney, 47
  sexual abuse, protection from, 46
  social security benefits, 51–57

Community charge
  Community Charges Registration Officer, 57
  exemption from, 57, 58*n*
    application for, 57
  severe mental impairment, 3, 57, 58*n*

Complaints, 110–112
  Mental Welfare Commission's duty, 110–112

Compulsory admission and detention, 182, 218–19
  absence
    leave of, 27, 136–7
    without leave *See* ABSENCE

Compulsory admission and detention—*contd*
  admission, 22–3, 130–36
    grounds for, 129–30
    statutory grounds for, 17–19, 23, 24, 24*n*, 44, 98, 101
  appeal, 30, 67, 141
    against renewal, 24
    to sheriff, 24, 110
  application, 130–34
    addressing, 19
    errors in, 37
    rectification of, 133–4
    timing, 19
    to sheriff, 15–23
  assessment before trial, 93–4
  case review, 24
  code of practice, 6
  consent to treatment, 76–86, 172–4
  continued, grounds for, 24, 24*n*
  correspondence, 70–72, 178–80
  criminal proceedings, following, 1, 6, 153–62
  discharge, 107–8
    from guardianship on, 43
    hospital managers, by, 26
    Mental Welfare Commission, by, 26, 124
    nearest relative, by, 26–7, 214
    responsible medical officer, by, 26
  duration of authority for, 138–40
  elderly persons living in insanitary conditions, 30
  emergency admission, 3, 7–9, 81
  grave chronic disease, person suffering from, 30
  hospital order, 98
  insanity in bar of trial, cases of, 94–5
  judicial review, 21–2, 25
  'liable to be detained', 218
  medical recommendations, 18, 19
  mental health officer, at request of, 7, 17
  mental impairment, 3, 18
  Mental Welfare Commission visits, 110
  mentally handicapped, 18
  mistakes, rectification of, 23
  nurse, by, 7, 9, 12, 67, 81
  patient must be informed of nature of detention, 67
  persons ordered to be kept in custody during her majesty's pleasure, 158
  place of safety order, 7, 28–30
  protection of patient, 33
  See also GUARDIANSHIP

Index

Compulsory admission and detention—*contd*
psychopathic disorder, 2
relative, at request of, 7
religious persuasion of patient, 178
remand or assessment before trial, 93–4
renewal of authority, 24
appeal against, 25
responsible medical officer, 23
restriction order, 99–100
review of patient's case, 23–5
after first renewal, 24
four to six months, 24
within first month, 23–4
safeguards for patient, 25
search of possessions, 87–8
severe mental impairment, 3
sheriff, application to, 7, 8, 10, 13–23
short-term, 7, 9–11
social work department interview, 23
transfer from prison to hospital, 101–2
transfer into guardianship, 28
transfer to other hospital, 28
transfer within United Kingdom, 31
violent patients, 18
voluntary patients, 67
vote, right to, 91–2
who may apply, 13

Compulsory medical treatment
patients living in the community, 43–5

Computer
medical records held on, 112

Consent to treatment, 76–86, 172–5
certificate of, 204–5
treatment not requiring, 174
withdrawal of, 174
See also VOLUNTARY PATIENT

Contract
insane person cannot make, 4

Conveyance
provisions as to, 182

Convicted offender
England and Wales, removal of patients to and from, 163
guardianship
order, power to make, 103, 153
patient subject to, 147
hospital
detention in, 139–40
order, 153
removal to, 158–9, 160–2
Northern Ireland, removal of patients to or from, 164–6
probation order, 103

Convicted offender—*contd*
restriction direction *See* RESTRICTION DIRECTION
restriction order *See* RESTRICTION ORDER
See also PRISONER

Corporal punishment
children, 72
guardian, not to be used by, 39

Correspondence, patients', 70–72, 178–80
hospital managers' rights, 70
interference with, 71
postal packet
meaning, 179
review of decision to withhold, 180
State hospital patients, 70–1, 178–9
voluntary patients, 70

Court of Session
curator bonis appointed by, 48, 109
divorce cases, 39

Crime
insane person cannot commit, 4

Criminal courts
hospital order, 93, 98, 153
interim, conviction on, 93, 97
mentally disordered people, and, 93–105
restriction order *See* RESTRICTION ORDER

Criminal offence
compulsory detention following proceedings, 93–105
ill-treatment, as, 75
insanity
acquittal by reason of, 93, 96
in bar of trial, 4, 93, 94–5
meaning, 95
legal aid, application for, 115
mental conditions, relevance to conviction, 96
obstruction of persons from carrying out functions within the Act, as, 76
patients absence without leave, in relation to, 76
person involved in care of mentally disturbed, by, 75–6
remand after conviction, 97
remand or assessment before trial, 93–4
sexual offences, 75–6, 175–6
unfitness to plead, 95
wilful neglect, as, 75

Culpable homicide
generally, 4, 96

Curator ad litem
  compulsory detention cases, 20
  court actions, 46
Curator bonis, 48–9
  Accountant of Court oversees, 49
  appointment of, 32, 48–9, 109
  guardian may not act as, 39
  Northern Ireland, reciprocal arrangements, 171
  payment of, 49
  petition for appointment of, 49, 170
  powers, 49
  ward, 48
Custody
  provisions as to, 182
  retaking of patients escaping from, 182–3

Day care centres
  local authority provisions, 59
Dementia, 2
  community charge, exemption, 57
  curator bonis in cases of See CURATOR BONIS
  detention of patients See COMPULSORY ADMISSION AND DETENTION
  guardianship procedure, 32
  Scottish Action on Dementia, 223
Dependants
  invalidity benefit, 53
  social security payments, 53–5
Depressions, 2
Detention
  compulsory See COMPULSORY ADMISSION AND DETENTION
Diminished responsibility
  homicide, 4, 96
  meaning, 4, 96
Discharge
  conditional, 77, 172
    restricted patient, 156
  guardianship, from, 147–8
  hospital managers, by, 26
  Mental Welfare Commission's powers, 26, 107–8, 124
  nearest relative, by, 26–7
    restrictions on, 140–1
  nearest relative, duty to inform of, 178
  prisoners of, restrictions on, 159
  responsible medical officer, by, 26
  State hospital patients, 140
  statutory provisions, 140
District or islands council
  housing responsibilities, 62

Divorce
  children
    access to, 45
    aliment and lump sum payments for, 45
    custody of, 45, 69
  Court of Session cases, 45–6
  curator ad litem, 46
  failure to defend, 46
  initial writ, 46
  legal aid, 46
  lived apart for five years, as grounds for, 45
  mentally disordered person, sought by, 46
  mentally disordered person's spouse, sought by, 45, 46
  patient served with summons, 45
  periodical allowance order, 45
  sheriff court cases, 46
  unreasonable behaviour, as grounds for, 45
  without patient's consent, 45
Doctor
  code of practice, 6
  complaints concerning
    general medical practitioners, 111
    hospital doctors, 111
  emergency admission arranged by, 7, 8, 134
  serious professional misconduct, 111
  short-term detention procedures, 9–11
Document
  false statement in, 175
Down's Syndrome
  Scottish Down's Syndrome Association, 224
Drugs
  compulsory treatment with, 43–5
  drug dependency not sole ground for mental disorder, 2, 122
  high dosage, 109
  long-term administration, 84, 85n
  loss of mental control, 95
  short-term administration, 85
  simultaneous treatment, 109

Education
  educational facilities, local authority help with, 60
  mentally handicapped, for, 60, 61
Elderly persons
  curator bonis, 32
  guardianship procedure, 32
  insanitary conditions, living in, 30
  wrongful detention of, 33

Electro-convulsive therapy (ECT), 84, 109, 193
Emergency admission, 3, 7–9, 134, 172
  alternatives following, 9
  appeal against, 8
  cannot be renewed, 8, 9
  conditions to be met, 7, 8
  discharge, 9
  doctor, arranged by, 7, 8, 134
  length, 8
  mental health officer, consent of, 8, 134
  notification, 8
  patient already in hospital, 8–9, 134–5
  relative, consent of, 8, 134
  treatment for mental disorder, 80
Employment
  dismissal from, 50
  sickness benefit, 52–3
  statutory sick pay, 52
England
  application of Mental Health (Scotland) Act (1984) to, 185
  removal of patients to or from, 163–4
Entry
  Mental Welfare Commission powers, 108
  police powers, 29
  search for and removal of patients, 180–1
European Convention of Human Rights
  physical punishment, 72–3
  restrictions on in-patients' rights, 66
Expenses
  fares to hospital, 55, 56, 91
  local authority help with, 60
  Mental Welfare Commission enquiry, attendance at, 125
  patients' personal, 178
  patients' visitors, 67–8, 91

False statements, 175
Family credit, 55
Fares to hospital, 55, 56, 91
  patients' visitors, 67–8, 91
Father, 149
Females
  mentally handicapped, protection of, 75–6, 175–6
Financial affairs
  bank accounts, personal, 47, 87
  cheques, 87
  curator bonis, 48–9, 88–9
  management of patients', 47–8, 88–9

Financial affairs—*contd*
  money kept in hospital, 87
  negotiorum gestor, 48n
  person capable of managing, 47, 88
  person incapable of managing, 4, 47–8, 88–9
  pocket money, 90
  power of attorney, 47
  social security benefits *See* SOCIAL SECURITY BENEFITS
  therapeutic earnings, 90
  valuables, 88–9
Friends
  visits by, 67–8

General Medical Council
  complaints to, 111
Genetic condition
  community charge, exemptions, 57
Grandchild, 149
Grandparent, 149
Grave chronic disease
  persons suffering from, 4, 30
Guardian
  appointment under Mental Health (Scotland) Act (1984), 32–43
  child in-patient, of, 69
  corporal punishment not to be administered by, 39
  curator bonis, additional appointment of, 39
  death or incapacity, 41, 146
  illness, 41
  powers and duties, 38–40, 194
  prohibited, 39
  residence, change of place of, 194
  resignation, 41
  social work department
    duties towards, 39
    as guardian, 38
  who may be, 142
  See also GUARDIANSHIP
Guardianship, 32–3
  absence of patient without leave, 145, 147, 194
  age limit, 33, 141
  appeals to sheriff, 149
  application, 142–3
    effect of, 144
    errors in, 37
    legal advice, 36
    meaning, 183
    medical recommendations, 34, 35, 142, 209
    mental health officer, by, 142, 208, 210
    nearest relative, by, 34, 142, 207

Guardianship—*contd*
application—*contd*
opposition to, 36
persons able to make, 35–6
private, proceedings may be held in, 36
procedures after admission, 37
rectification, 144–5
sheriff, approval by, 36, 143–4
welfare report, 35
witnesses, 36
authority, duration of, 146–7
care and treatment of patients, 145–6
child under, nearest relative, 150–1
compulsory medical treatment, 45
conditions which must apply, 33
convicted offender, 103, 147, 153
death or incapacity of guardian, 41, 146
discharge from, 41–3, 107, 147–8
compulsory admission to hospital, on, 43
medical officer, by, 44, 147–8
Mental Welfare Commission, by, 42, 147–8
nearest relative, by, 42, 147–8, 215–6
sheriff, by, 42–3, 147–8
social work department, by, 41–2
duration of order, 37–8
duties of guardian, 38–9, 194
grounds for reception into, 141
guardian *See* GUARDIAN
liability for, 141
limited powers, 32
local authority duties, 193–4
local authority as guardian, 142
medical recommendations, 143, 209
rectification, 144
mental health officer recommendations, 210
Mental Welfare Commission visits, 110
mentally handicapped, 32
nature of, 33
nearest relative, applications for appointment of, 13–15
order, 5, 162, 189–90
patient
duty to give information to, 177
reception into, 141–2
procedure, 141–5
regulations as to, 145
religious persuasion of patient, 178
removal of patients
to or from England and Wales, 163

Guardianship—*contd*
removal of patients—*contd*
to or from Northern Ireland, 164–6
to Scotland, 168, 213
renewal of order, 37–8, 211–12
residence, change of place of, 194
social work department
duties and powers, 40
general supervision by, 38, 40*n*
transfer into, 28
from hospital, 137–8
transfer of, 41, 145–6
welfare of patient, necessary to, 141

Health board service committee
complaints to, 111
Health service
meaning, 183
Hearing
patient's opportunity to be heard at, 178
High Court
remand or assessment before trial, 93–4
Holidays
local authority help with, 60
Home
help in, local authority provision, 60
Homeless person, 64–5
'intentionally homeless', 64–5
'priority need', 64
See also HOUSING
Homicide, culpable
diminished responsibility, 4, 96
Hormones
implantation of, 83, 193, 221
Hospital
absence
leave of, 27, 136–7
without leave, 28, 76, 137, 139, 145, 147, 152, 167–8, 176, 183, 194
admission
applicant for, 130
application for, 130–33
compulsory *See* COMPULSORY ADMISSION AND DETENTION
effect of application, 132–3
emergency *See* EMERGENCY ADMISSION
grounds for, 129–30
medical recommendations for, 131–2, 198–9
mental health officer, by, 6, 13, 17, 130–1, 197
nearest relative, by, 130, 196
procedure, 130–6

Hospital—*contd*
  admission—*contd*
    rectification of application and recommendations, 133–4
    sheriff, approval of application by, 132
    voluntary *See* VOLUNTARY PATIENT
    welfare grounds, 33
  bank accounts, personal, 87, 87*n*
  care in, 66–92
  children
    relations with, 69
    visits by parents, 68
    welfare of, 68
  code of practice, 6
  compulsory admission *See* COMPULSORY ADMISSION AND DETENTION
  consent to treatment, 76–86, 172–5
  control of patients' activities, 72–5
    control and punishment distinguished, 72–3
    reasonable control, 73
    seclusion and time out, 74
  criminal court, hospital orders, 1, 93, 98, 153
  criminal offences by people involved in care, 75–6
  detention of patients already in, 134–5
  discharge from, 67, 107, 140, 178
    prisoners, 102, 159
  duration of authority, 138–40
  emergency admission *See* EMERGENCY ADMISSION
  expenses, patients' personal, 178
  freedom to leave, 67
  ill-treatment of patients, 175
  managers *See* HOSPITAL MANAGERS
  meaning, 183
  order, 93, 98, 162
    effect of, 153
    interim, 97
    meaning, 183
    with restriction order, 98
    without restriction order, 98
  patients' correspondence, 70–2, 178–80
  patients' property
    conditions as to, 87–8
    curator bonis, 170
    hospital managers' powers, 170–1
    immediate danger of property being lost or damaged, 89
    management of patients' finances, 88–9
    money, 87
    protection of, 170–2

Hospital—*contd*
  patient's property—*contd*
    searches, 87–8
    valuables, 87–9
  prisoner, removal to, 101–2, 158–9, 187–8
    restrictions on discharge of, 159
  private *See* PRIVATE HOSPITAL
  punishment
    control distinguished, 72–3
    physical, 72, 73*n*
  records, inspection of, 141
  remand or assessment before trial, 93–4
  restriction direction, 101–2
  restrictions on in-patients' rights, 66–72
  'seclusion', 74
  short-term detention *See* SHORT-TERM DETENTION
  special security, 6
  State *See* STATE HOSPITAL
  'time out', 74
  transfer
    from prison, 101–3
    without restriction order, 187–8
    into guardianship, 137
    to other hospital, 137
  visits by relatives and friends, 67–8
  voluntary admission, 5, 87
  welfare of patients, local authorities' duty, 127
Hospital managers, 108
  compulsorily detained patients, 67
  compulsory admission, errors on, 37
  discharge from hospital by, 26
  information, duty to give, 177
  meaning, 183–4
  patients' property, powers in relation to, 170–1
Housing
  adaptations, local authority help with, 60
  advice, 61
  costs, help with, 54
  council waiting list, application to, 63–4
  groups of tenants with support network, 62
  homeless person, 62, 64
  housing
    housing associations, 225
    'intentionally homeless', 64, 65
    local authority duties, 62–65
    local connection, 65
    mentally handicapped, 61

Housing—*contd*
  people with some degree of independence, 63–4
  'priority need', 64
  right of mentally disordered, 61–4
  succeeding tenancy, 63
Housing department, 61, 62
Huntingdon's Chorea, 57

Ill-treatment
  patient, of, 75, 175, 221
  person suffering from mental disorder, of, 180
Illegitimate person
  relatives of, definition, 13, 149
Immigration Act (1971)
  persons detained under, 161–2
Immoral conduct
  not sole ground for mental disorder, 2, 122
Incapacity
  guardian, of, 146
Incapacity to manage affairs
  curator bonis, 4, 48–9
  meaning, 4
  See also FINANCIAL AFFAIRS
Income
  disposable, 114–5
Income support, 54, 91
Independent living fund, 56–7
Industrial tribunal
  unfair dismissal, 50
Inquiries, into cases, 183
Insanitary conditions
  elderly persons living in, 30
Insanity
  acquittal by reason of, 93, 96
  civil law, 4
  criminal law, 4
  legally invalid acts, 4, 91
  meaning, 4, 92
Inspection of premises
  obstruction, 177
Interim hospital order, 97
Interpretation, 183–4
Invalidity allowance, 53
Invalidity benefit, 53, 90
Invalidity pension, 53
Ireland
  Northern *See* NORTHERN IRELAND
Isle of Man
  patients removed to Scotland, 167

Judicial factor
  Northern Ireland, reciprocal arrangements, 171

Judicial review
  compulsory admission and detention, 21, 25
Key Housing Association, 61, 225
Law reports
  English cases, 217
  newspaper, 217
  Scottish, 217
Law Society of Scotland, 225
Leave of absence, 27, 136–7
Legal advice and assistance, 112, 113–14
  assistance by way of representation, 114
  client not qualified for, 115
  disposable capital, 113
  disposable income, 113–14
  divorce cases, 46
Legal aid, 99–100, 113, 115
  applicant's contribution, 115
    failure to pay instalment, 115
  children, disputes over, 69
  citizens advice bureaux, 113
  client not qualified for, 116
  divorce cases, 45–6
  guardianship applications, 35
  nearest relative, application for appointment of, 15
  qualification for, 115
  Scottish Legal Aid Board, 113, 225
  State hospital, appeal against transfer to, 104
Lexis, 217
Liability
  acts in pursuance of Mental Health (Scotland) Act (1984), 183
'Liable to be detained', 218
Litigation
  medical records, production of, 112
Local authority
  after-care services, provision of, 126
  application for admission by, 130–1
  care in the community, duties in relation to, 58–61
  child or young person in care of, 150
  functions, 125–6
  guardian, as, 142
  meaning, 183
  mental health officers, appointment, 126–7
  Mental Welfare Commission, duties in relation to, 125
  patients' property, duties in relation to, 170

Index

Local authority—*contd*
  short term detentions, 136
  supported accommodation, duty to provide, 62
  training and occupation of mentally handicapped, 127
  welfare of hospital patients, duty with regard to, 127
  See also SOCIAL WORK DEPARTMENTS

Manic depression
  Manic Depression Fellowship, 223
Marriage
  divorce *See* DIVORCE
  insane person may not marry, 4, 45
Meals
  local authority help with, 60
Medical commissioners, 106
Medical officer, responsible *See* RESPONSIBLE MEDICAL OFFICER
Medical practitioner
  meaning, 184
  See also DOCTOR
Medical recommendations
  admission, for, 131–2, 198–9
  guardianship, for, 143, 144–5, 209
Medical records
  patients' rights, 112
Medical treatment *See* TREATMENT
Mental disorder
  definition, 2
  generally, 1, 2
  meaning, 122
  psychopathic, 2
Mental handicap
  Campaign for People with Mental Handicaps (CMH), 223
  community charge, 57
  compulsory detention in mental hospital, 18
  educational facilities, provision of, 60–1
  females, protection of, 75–6, 175–6
  guardianship, 32–43
  helpful addresses, 223–5
  local authorities' duty, 125–7
  meaning, 3
  mental disorder, as, 2, 122
  State hospital, 104–5
  training and occupation, 60–1, 127
Mental health officer
  application for admission by, 6, 13, 17, 130–1, 197
  appointment, 126
  code of practice, 6

Mental health officer—*contd*
  emergency admission, consent to, 8, 134
  guardianship
    application by, 142–3, 208
    conditions which must apply, 33
    recommendation for reception into, 210
  meaning, 184
  search and removal of patients, 180–1
  short-term detention, consent to, 10
Mental hospital *See* HOSPITAL
Mental illness
  degenerative disorders, 2
  depressions, 2
  guardianship, 32
  meaning, 2
  mental disorder, as, 2, 122
  paranoia, 2
  physical illness affecting nervous system, 2
  schizophrenia, 2
  State hospital, 104–5
Mental impairment, 3, 18
  definition, 18
  meaning, 122
  severe, 3, 18
    meaning, 122
Mental Welfare Commission, 5–6, 122–3
  Annual Reports, 107
  appeals against detention, 67
  appointment of commissioners, 122
  assistance, application for, 110
  audit of accounts, 123
  body corporate, as, 123
  community visits, 110
  complaints, inquiry into, 108, 110
  constitution, 106, 122
  curator bonis, appointment of, 48–9, 49*n*, 109, 170
  discharge by, 140
    compulsory patients, 107–8
    guardianship, from 41, 147–8
    hospital, from, 24, 107
  enquiries by, 125
    attendance at, 125
    refusal to attend, 125
  examination of patient, 108
  expenditure by, 123
  functions and duties, 2, 107–10, 123–4
    financial, 123
  local authorities' duties, 125
  location, 106
  medical commissioners, 106, 122
  place of safety order by, 6

Mental Welfare Commission—*contd*
  medical records, inspection of, 108
  notification
    change of residence of guardian or person subject to guardianship order, 194
    continued detention, 24
    detention by nurses, 12
    emergency admissions, 8
    guardianship, 37, 144
    leave of absence of patient, 27, 137
    removal of patient to Scotland, 168
    short-term detention, 10, 11, 136
    transfer of patient, 28
  powers of entry and inspection, 108
  private hospitals, inspection of, 6, 128–9
  protection of property, 107–8
  remuneration of commissioners, 122
  report to, on compulsorily detained patient, 23
  resignation from, 122
  restriction directions, powers, 102
  role, 106–7
  seal, 123
  search and removal of patients, 180–1
  Secretary of State's duties, 125
  social security payments, advice on, 109
  staff
    appointment, 125
    payment, 125
  State hospital, responsibility in respect of, 104–5
  treatment for mental disorders, 80, 109–10
  unsatisfactory situation, rectification of, 108
  vacation of office by commissioner, 122
  visits to patients by, 110
Mobility allowance
  payment of, 54
Money *See* FINANCIAL AFFAIRS
Mother, 149
Murder
  diminished responsibility, plea of, 4, 96
  meaning, 96

National Association for the Welfare of Children in Hospital, 68
Neglect
  person suffering from mental disorder, of, 180
Negotiorum gestor, 48*n*
Nephew, 149

Niece, 149
Northern Ireland
  application of Mental Health (Scotland) Act (1984) to, 186
  patients' property, reciprocal arrangements, 171
  removal of patients to or from, 164–5
  return of patients absent without leave, 168
Nurse
  complaints concerning, 111, 221
  compulsory detention by, 7, 9, 12, 67, 81
    alternatives following, 12
    conditions to be met, 12
    notification of, 12
  ill-treatment of patient, by, 221
Nursing home
  definition, 185
  ill-treatment of patients, 175
  patients' welfare, local authorities' duty, 127

Obstruction, 177
  persons carrying out functions under the Act, of, 76
Orders
  Secretary of State's power to make, 183

Paranoia, 2
Parent
  nearest relative, as, 13, 149
Parkinson's disease, 2
Patient
  ill-treatment or wilful neglect, 75, 175, 221
  information to, duty to give, 177
  meaning, 184
  opportunity to be heard, 178
  religious persuasion of, 178
  rights of organisations concerned with, 224–5
Patient's declaration, 91–2
Pension
  collection of, 47
Periodical allowance
  divorce cases, 45
Phobia
  We Are Seeking Progress, 224
Physical illness
  affecting nervous system, 2
  curator bonis, 4–5

Place of safety
  meaning, 29
  order, 28–9
    private premises, power to enter, 28–9
    removal from public places, 29–30, 181
    removal to, 180–1
Plans of treatment, 174
Pocket money, 90
Police
  custody, conveyance and detention of patients, 182
  mentally disordered person in public place, 29–30, 181
  private premises, entry of, 29
Police station
  place of safety, as, 29
Postal packet
  definition, 72*n*
  See also CORRESPONDENCE, PATIENTS'
Power of attorney, 47
Prisoner
  awaiting trial, removal to hospital, 158, 159–60
  detention in hospital, 139–40
  discharge from hospital, 102
  guardianship
    order, 153
    patient subject to, 147
  hospital order, 152–3
  removal
    to or from England and Wales, 163
    to or from Northern Ireland, 164–6
    to hospital, 158–9, 160–2
  restriction direction See RESTRICTION DIRECTION
  restriction order See RESTRICTION ORDER
  transfer
    from prison without restriction order, 187–8
    hospital, to, 101, 102
      appeal against, 101
    State hospital, to, 104
Private hospital, 6, 127–9
  control of, 128–9
  inspection of, 128–9
  maximum patient number, 128
  meaning, 128
  Mental Welfare Commission, inspection by, 128–9
  penalties for offences, 129
  registers and records, 128

Private hospital—*contd*
  registration of, 127–8
    cancellation, 129
    pre-requisites, 128
    renewal, 128
Private premises
  power to enter, 28–9
Probation order, 103
  failure to comply, 103
  treatment specified in, 103
Promiscuity
  not sole ground for mental disorder, 2
Property
  heritable, 170
  managing, 47–8
  moveable, 170
  patients'
    curator bonis, 109, 170
    hospital managers' powers, 170–1
    immediate danger of being lost or damaged, 89
    local authorities' duties, 170
    management of patients' finances, 88–9
    Mental Welfare Commission, protection by, 109
    money See FINANCIAL AFFAIRS
    Northern Ireland, reciprocal arrangements, 171–2
    protection of, 109, 170–1
    searches of, 87–8
    valuables, 87
    what may be kept in hospital, 87–8
  power of attorney, 47, 48
Protection
  mentally handicapped females, of, 75–6, 175–6
  patients, of, 176
Psychiatric report
  remand by court for, 81
Psychopathic disorder, 2
Public place
  mentally disordered person in, 29, 181
Punishment
  control distinguished, 72–3
  physical punishment illegal, 72

Recommendation
  false statement in, 175
Record
  false statement in, 175
Recreational facilities
  local authority help with, 60

Regional or islands council
  curator bonis, application for appointment of, 49, 49n
  housing responsibilities, 62
  nearest relative, as, 14
  notification
    continued detention, of, 24
    short-term detention, of, 10
  property belonging to hospital patient, duty in relation to, 47
Regulations
  Secretary of State's power to make, 183
Relative
  care, child or young person in, 150
  definition, 149–50
  functions of, 149–52
  illegitimate person, of, 149
  nearest
    absence of, 14
    acting, appointment of, 151
      application for, 14–15
    application for admission by, 6, 13–17, 130, 196
    compulsorily detained patients, 67
    consent to short-term detention, 9
    consultation over legal actions, 116
    death of, 16
    definition, 13, 14, 149–51
    discharge by, 26–7, 214, 218
    guardianship
      application for, 34, 142, 207
      child under, 150–1
      discharge from, 42, 147, 215–16
    information to, duty to give, 177
    local authority care, child or young person in, 150
    meaning, 149
    notification
      continued detention, 24
      discharge, of, 178
      emergency admissions, 8, 134
      guardianship applications, 142
      short-term detention, 10, 135
    ordinarily resident abroad, 14
    regional or islands council as, 14
    removal of patients to and from England and Wales, 163–4
    social work department as, 15
    under 18 years of age, 14
    unwilling to act, 14
  person other than, with whom the patient ordinarily resides, 150
  visits by, 67–8, 90–1
Remand
  after conviction, 97
  psychiatric report, for, 81

Report
  false statement in, 175
Residential establishments
  local authority provision, 59
Responsible medical officer
  compulsorily admitted patients, 23
  meaning, 152
  order for discharge from guardianship, 147
  order for discharge from hospital, 26, 107, 140
  remand or assessment before trial, cases of, 94
  renewal of authority for detention of patient, 200
'Responsible person'
  living with patient, 8
Restriction direction, 101–2, 107, 159, 160–2
  appeal against, 155–6
  ceasing effect
    medical report on patient, 202
  conditionally discharged patient, 156
  England and Wales, removal of patients to or from, 163
  expiry, 102
  meaning, 159
  Northern Ireland, removal of patients to and from, 165, 166
  renewal of authority for detention, 201
Restriction order, 94, 98, 107, 154
  appeal against, 99–100, 154–5
  convicted offender, 153–4
  discharge, 99–100
    conditional, 100
    Mental Welfare Commission may recommend, 100
  duration, 99
  England and Wales, removal of patients to or from, 163
  limited, 99
  meaning, 184
  Northern Ireland, removal of patients to or from, 164–5
  Secretary of State's powers, 157
  transfer from prison without, 187–8
Review of treatment, 173–4

Safeguards for patient
  compulsory admission and detention, 25
  short-term detention, 11
Schizophrenia, 2, 218
  National Schizophrenia Fellowship, 223
  treatment by drugs, 43

Scotland
  patient removed from or to, 163-7, 203, 213
Scots Law Times, 217
Scottish Association of Mental Health, 61, 223
Scottish Civil Law Reports, 217
Scottish Criminal Case Reports, 217
Scottish Home and Health Department
  draft code of practice, 6, 80
Scottish Legal Aid Board, 113
Scottish Society for the Mentally Handicapped, 61, 224
Search
  body, 87-8
  material recovered as result of, 88
  patients' possessions, of, 87
  and removal of patients, 180-1
  warrant for, 180-1
'Seclusion', 74
Second opinion
  treatment requiring consent and, 82-3, 172-3, 204, 206
  treatment requiring consent or, 84-5, 173
Secretary of State
  code of practice, 6, 181
  general practitioners, complaints concerning, 111
  guardians' powers and duties, 38
  inquiry ordered by, 183
  Mental Welfare Commission, duties in relation to, 125
  powers, 152, 183
    patients subject to restriction orders, in respect of, 157
    private hospitals, registration and inspection of, 6
  regulations
    guardianship, as to, 145
    power to make, 183
  State hospital, control and management of, 104-5, 169
Session Cases, 217
Severe disablement allowance, 53
Severe mental impairment, 3, 18, 57, 122
  definition, 18
Sexual abuse
  protection from, 46
Sexual deviancy
  not sole ground for mental disorder, 2, 122
  treatment for, 220-1

Sexual offences
  intercourse with mentally handicapped woman, 75, 76n, 175-6
Sheriff
  acting nearest relative, appointment of, 15, 151-2
  appeal to, 141
    community charge appeals, 57
    compulsory admission and detention, against, 25, 110
    discharge, for, 10, 11
    guardianship orders, 149
    restricted patients, 154-5
  application to for compulsory admission, 7, 10, 13-23
    admission of patient to hospital, 22-3
    conditions for admission, 17-19
    duration of order, 15-16
    judicial review, 21
    mental health officer, by, 13, 17
    nearest relative, by, 13-15
    notifications by hospital, 22-3
    preparation of, 15
    rectifying mistakes, 23
    sheriff's role, 19-22
    social work department as nearest relative, 16
    timing of, 19
  approval of applications for admission to hospital, 132
  discharge, order for, 140
    guardianship, from, 42-3, 147-8
  guardianship applications, 34
    approval of, 36, 143-4
    conditions which must apply, 33
    welfare grounds, 33
  patient's opportunity to be heard, 178
Sheriff court
  curator bonis appointed by, 48, 109
  divorce cases, 45
  remand or assessment before trial, 93-4
Short-term detention, 7, 9-11, 135-6
  alternatives following, 10-11
  appeal against, 10, 25
  discharge, 11
  emergency admission, following, 9
  length, 10
  limited application, 10
  may not be renewed, 11
  mental health officer's consent, 10
  nearest relative's consent, 9, 136
  people to be informed, 10
  report on patient's condition, 9
  safeguards for patient, 11
  social work department duties, 10

Sickness benefit, 52–3, 90
Sister, 149
Social fund, 54–6
Social security benefits, 51–6
   attendance allowance, 53–4, 90
   collection of, 47
   curator bonis, 48–9
   disregarded income, 55
   family credit, 55
   fares to hospital, 55, 68
   housing costs, 54–5
   income support, 54, 91
   invalidity benefit, 53, 90
   Mental Welfare Commission advice, 109
   mobility allowance, 54
   national insurance contributions, 52
   personal allowance, 55
   premium payments, 55
   qualification for, 52
   reduction or stopping of benefit, 52
   savings affecting payment, 55
   severe disablement allowance, 53
   sickness benefit, 52–3, 90
   social fund, 54, 56
   special disablement allowance, 90
   statutory sick pay, 52, 90
   welfare rights groups, 225
Social security payments
   invalid care allowance, 56
   people other than the patient, 56
Social work department
   advice, guidance and assistance, provision of, 59
   aftercare services, 60
   day care centre provision, 59
   guardian, as, powers and duties, 38
   guardians' duties towards, 39
   guardians' relationship with, 39, 40*n*
   guardianship procedure, 32, 35
   housing
      duty with regard to, 62
      information on, 61
   information, provision of, 59
   interview of compulsorily detained patient, 23
   nearest relative, as, 15
   persons subject to guardianship orders
      discharge from guardianship, 41
      general supervision, 39, 40*n*
      powers and duties, 40
   practical help, duty to provide, 60
   residential establishments, provision of, 59
   services and facilities, duty to provide, 59–60

Solicitor
   consultation with, 112–15
      advice and assistance scheme, 112, 113–14
      legal aid scheme, 112, 114, 115
      limitation of fees, 115
      making contact, 112–13
      nearest relative, 115
   experienced in mental health law work, 112
Special disablement allowance, 90
Special security
   State hospital, 169
Spouse
   common law, 14
   nearest relative, as, 13–14
   relative, as, 149
   See also DIVORCE; MARRIAGE
Standard scale
   meaning, 184
State benefits
   disablement, mental condition, as, 4
   See also SOCIAL SECURITY BENEFITS
State hospital (Carstairs), 6, 104–5, 106, 169–70
   administrative provisions, 169–70
   discharge, 27
      orders, 141
   insanity in bar of trial, cases of, 94
   management committee, 169, 186–7
      appointment to, 186
      chairman, 186
      constitution, 186
   meaning, 169
   Mental Welfare Commission responsibilties, 104–5
   patients' correspondence, 70–1, 179
   persons ordered to be kept in custody during her majesty's pleasure, 158
   provision of, 169
   renewal of detention order, appeal against, 220
   transfer to, 27
      appeal against, 104, 220
      from other hospital, 104
Statutory grounds for admission, 16–19, 24, 24*n*, 44, 98, 101
Statutory maximum
   meaning, 184
Statutory sick pay (SSP), 52, 90
Sterilisation
   mentally handicapped person, of, 78–9, 219
Suicide
   voluntary patient, of, following discharge, 75*n*, 88*n*

Index 255

Telephone
provision by local authority, 60
Tenancy
succeeding to, 63
Therapeutic earnings, 90
'Time out', 74
Training and occupation
mentally handicapped persons, for, 60–1
Transfer
guardianship
of, 145–6
to, 28
other hospital, to, 28
prisoners to hospital, of, 158–62
within United Kingdom, 31
Transfer direction
meaning, 159
Transfer order
meaning, 158
Travelling costs See EXPENSES
Treatment
children, 77
code of practice, 6
community, in, 5–6, 43–5
compulsory, patients living in community, 43–5
condition other than mental disorder, for, 77–9
consent to, 76–86, 109–10, 172–5
certificate of, 204–5
not required, 85–6, 174
withdrawal of, 174
explanation of, 77–8
freedom to refuse, 76
hazardous, 84
long-term administration of drugs, 84
medical, meaning, 184
mental disorder, for, 76, 80–6
categories, 82–6
compulsorily detained patients, 80, 80–1
voluntary patients, 81
patient unable to understand nature and purpose of, 77, 109
plans of, 174
probation order, specified in, 103
requiring consent and second opinion, 82–3, 109, 172–3, 206
requiring consent or second opinion, 84–5, 109, 173
review of, 173–4
serious deterioration of patient's condition, to prevent, 86
serious suffering, to alleviate, 86
State hospital See STATE HOSPITAL
sterilisation or abortion, 77, 78–9, 219

Treatment—contd
to save patient's life, 86
tutor-dative, 77, 78, 79
urgent, 174
violent behaviour, to prevent, 86, 174
Trust
beneficiary suffering from mental disorder, 50–1
Tutor
Northern Ireland, reciprocal arrangements, 171
Tutor-dative, 77, 78, 79
sterilisation and abortion, in cases of, 78, 79

Uncle, 149
United Kingdom
removal and return of patients within, 163–9
Urgent treatment, 174

Violent behaviour
compulsory admission to mental hospital, 17–18
treatment to prevent, 86
Voluntary organisation
meaning, 184
training and occupation of mentally handicapped, 127
Voluntary patient, 5, 9, 32
compulsory detention of, 67
consent to treatment, 76–7
mental disorder, for, 80–1
correspondence, 70
discharge from hospital, 67
suicide following, 75n, 88n
search of possessions, 87–8, 88n
seclusion, 74
vote, right to, 91–2
Vote
in-patients' right to, 91–2
insane person may not, 4, 91
patient's declaration, 92
voters' roll, 91, 92

Wales
application of Mental Health (Scotland) Act (1984) to, 185
removal of patients to or from, 163–4
'Wardship jurisdiction', 219
Warrant
search and removal of patients, for, 29, 180–1
Weekly Law Reports (WLR), 217
Welfare grounds, 33
Welfare rights groups, 225
Wilful neglect, 75

Will
  beneficiary suffering from mental disorder, 51
  holograph will, 51
  insane person
    cannot cancel valid will, 50
    cannot make will, 50

Will—*contd*
  mental patient, made by, 51
  more than one page, 51
  notarial execution, 51
Women
  mentally handicapped, protection of, 75–6, 175–6